We Jews and Blacks

WILLIS BARNSTONE

We Jews and Blacks

Memoir with Poems

WITH A DIALOGUE AND POEMS BY
YUSEF KOMUNYAKAA

INDIANA UNIVERSITY PRESS
BLOOMINGTON AND INDIANAPOLIS

This book is a publication of

Indiana University Press
601 North Morton Street
Bloomington, IN 47404-3797 USA

http://iupress.indiana.edu

Telephone orders	800-842-6796
Fax orders	812-855-7931
Orders by e-mail	iuporder@indiana.edu

The paper used in this publication meets the minimum requirements of American National Standard for Information Sciences—Permanence of Paper for Printed Library Materials, ANSI Z39.48-1984.

Manufactured in the United States of America

Library of Congress Cataloging-in-Publication Data

Barnstone, Willis, date
  We Jews and Blacks : memoir with poems / Willis Barnstone.
    p. cm.
  ISBN 0-253-34419-0 (cloth : alk. paper)
    1. Barnstone, Willis, date 2. Barnstone, Willis, date—Childhood and youth. 3. Poets, American—20th century—Biography. 4. Translators—United States—Biography. 5. African Americans—Relations with Jews. 6. Jews—United States—Biography. 7. United States—Race relations. 8. Blacks—Relations with Jews. 9. Passing (Identity) I. Title.
  PS3552.A722Z478 2004
  811'.54—dc22
                                    2003022616

1 2 3 4 5 09 08 07 06 05 04

for Howard Barnstone

who lay in sorrow

in his Rothko chapel

God created the world and us and the others. And he commanded us to believe in him and to punish the others. And when necessary to kill the others. But everywhere in the world, God changed appearance and ideas and to many even he has been the infidel. Jews and Blacks understand God's problems of appearance and identity, for they've been uniquely plagued by the same dilemma. But they are lucky too, as God is, for their otherness. Who wants to be all the same? Years ago God was a woman and in the Hebrew Bible he even began as several gods. Genesis 1.1 reads "In the beginning the gods (*elohim*) created heaven and earth."* So God started out as a team. But we Jews and Blacks have often been seen as a strange species, as if no god had remembered to make us, or had done so in an alien land under a wrong name. And with our difference came divine punishment: slavery, demonization, and murder. But that distinction of otherness has also given Jews and Blacks a knowledge of affection and play, and a habit of compassion.

—Pierre Grange, *On God and the Other*

God cooked up birth and billed us with death, leaving us in a global soup bowl filled with every different plant under the sun. And then abandoned us to stew in tasty mystery!

—Velvel Bornstein, *Laughter of the Stoics*

---

*Although *el* is God and *elohim* gods (as in Psalms), in Genesis 1.1 *elohim* is called a "plural of majesty," whose meaning is singular.

Contents

Acknowledgments

I wish to thank Kendra Boileau Stokes, whose enthusiasm and literary cunning added life to these pages. Similarly, I say hello to Susan Fernández for her faith in this experiment, and to Richard Logsdon, Harry Geduld, and David Hertz for their careful reading of the text. I thank Sarah Handler, who saw and helped the text grow; my wonderful family gang, Helle, Aliki, Robert, and Tony, each one a North Star for one in the dark; and those who now live in the dark, Dora, Robert, and Howard, for their light.

There are also all the mythical Jews and Blacks from Noah's kin—Shem, Ham, and Cush; and, in my lifetime, a Portuguese rabbi in Paris; immediate friends in Nubia (mythical descendants of Ham and Cush); and all the people I've met in story, books, nations, and neighborhoods who gave me fragments returned in these pages.

And whoever may see this ink, I hope in your diversity these words about diversity may sound good and sometimes hum a nice tune.

A Chat with the Reader

I'm fascinated by the *other*, by all the exotic features and customs I obsessively and meticulously investigate. I just love him for being so refreshingly *different* from my plain familiar looks and ways, and also want to murder her for being the demon.

—WILHELM SCHEUNENSTEIN, *Confessions of an Ideologue*

The Hell Face of Sacred Distinctions

This memoir is about Jews and Blacks. About identity, denial, bigotry, and the sorrow and humor of it all. If it has value, it applies to women and gays, to race, sex, and gender, among other abstractions, but I go soft on jargon in favor of plain speech and specific occasion. It laments the absurdity of those distinctions in ethnicity, religion, and nation when they seem to justify the destruction of the other. To erase—in the cause of absolutism—those who are different. To send to hell those infidels who do not follow your master and lord.

Jews and Blacks have known their share of hell for belonging imperatively to the other people, and so, as the other two "races" around, we have been pals in days of icy bigotry. From an early age these peoples of otherness are those I knew best, and these pages describe our contention with Christians or Whites whose vast throat and belly we have each inhabited—and not always with delight. The crap throw of birth has stamped everyone with a color and sex and religion and country. That identity is our fascinating singularity and our hell face. As in the past, the hell face of personal and public identities still consumes the world of alien neighbors. But there are signs of growing impatience with the absurdity of sacred distinctions and the malignity of defining heretics. Yet even when we're all one soup, with one name, we'll still squabble about our thickness, ingredients, and flavor.

When I was a child in New York of the late 1930s and early 40s, there was still a special romance of sharing the history of the outsider and a memory of that history that tied Jew and Black together both politically and spiritually. Earlier slavery, epidemics of lynchings and pogroms, and contemporary bigotry provided both peoples with interchangeable metaphors. So the black spiritual sang of Moses leading the Jews out of Egypt where they had for centuries been slaves.

"Go down, Moses, into Egypt land. Tell ole' Pharaoh, 'Let my people go.'"

Now the signs have changed. But the world has not. That same difference from the other that has been the fate of Jews and Blacks continues to feed a timeless dementia inciting all peoples of the world to hatred and to the joys of genocide. Therefore the reenactments of Cain and Abel in Ireland, Rwanda, the Balkans, Tibet, East Timor, the Congo, and the eternal Middle East. When death by anger looks into the mirror, it sees a regression of mirrors copying the same face of anger again and again, reflecting back through time to a scene in the Garden where Eve had to answer to a voice that wished her silent and unknowing. Promethean Eve chose knowledge rather than obedience, and for her diversion she received death. After God passed his death sentence on Eve and Adam for their independence from his will, the practice of killing the other whom we cannot control has persisted everywhere in Judeo-Christian-Islamic neighborhoods. Each ethnicity and religion in the world (Quakers and a few others excepted) shares a history of demonizing and murdering the other. With self-righteous anger and fervid morality, killing exists in family, between families, in the extended family of the nation, and between nations. Romeo and Juliet play out the game of death. Innocents who are really the same person, they must die because others have detected differences in their public family identities.

The gang battles of *West Side Story* are global.

In 1975 I spent much of a year in Buenos Aires. The *dirty war* was raging; families were divided, classes were at each other's throats, and an uncommon number of students, Jews, and journalists were disappearing. Every diversion and division was again a reason to kill. A favored ideology—the ultimate disease of the spirit—was making all adversaries meet in bombings, kidnappings, and dropping drugged, unconscious students from planes into the Río de la Plata. Having been in Greece at the end of its civil war and in China during the Cultural Revolution, I cannot deny that these abominable (*ad hominem*) periods were also gravely fascinating to me as an outsider. War is fun, a great sexual adventure and high-profile sport, the material of arts. Want a thrill? Kill. After the TV blitz of video-game shooting and bombing is over, the aftermath of war is less romantically thrilling for those who survive and remember. But even that memory of war ignites as often as it puts out the old fires. In Buenos Aires the absurdity of the human suffering led the intelligentsia in October 1975 to have a spring celebration called "The Week of Failure," whose ultimate message was *Basta!* (enough). Twenty years later in Madrid in 1997, nearly half the population of the capital city was peacefully in the streets and plazas of the capital city again, chanting *Basta!* in sad revulsion against the latest execution of a young man by ETA, the Basque revolutionary group who kill for their sectarian cause of Basqueness.

More often, however, one's childhood indoctrination in most continents is not to say *Basta!* but to learn more about the centuries of abuse from enemy neighbors. Such knowledge is received as sectarian wisdom. One learns why and when to hate and kill, and it scarcely matters whether the injury was two years ago or two thousand. Methodically, one keeps present every earlier outrage of invasion, massacre, or cultural insult so as to justify killing Muslim or Hindu, Catholic or Protestant, Hutu or Tutsi, Jew or Black.

Hatreds, like mother's milk, nourish the newborn with a poisonous drink never forgotten.

One late dirty war afternoon in Buenos Aires in 1975, as dusk was welcoming the first echoes of bomb blasts, I went to the house of an old Argentine lady, Lila Guerrerol, who was the translator into Spanish of the Russian poet Vladimir Mayakovsky (1893–1930). Lila had lived eleven years in Moscow where she knew the poet. She told me a story that the painter Diego Rivera had related to her about Mayakovsky during the three weeks he spent in Mexico in 1925 before going on to the States. Rivera and his wife, Frida Kahlo, had invited the Russian poet to their hacienda outside Mexico City. There was a wedding. Popular wisdom has it that more people are killed in a Mexican wedding than in a revolution. A matter of disputing families. After the wedding ceremony Mayakovsky was standing on a terraced area above the grass where the guests were drinking and talking and very soon arguing with each other. Now the two families had grouped into opposing camps, screaming obscenities and threats, and it looked like the moment before a shoot-out.

Mayakovsky had no Spanish, but as Rivera's honored guest, he felt compelled to do something. This strong, towering man with a deep voice suddenly made a huge Nijinsky-leap from the terrace down to the lawn, landing between the feuding sides. He raised his arms outward and roared, *"Továrischi!"* (Comrades!). Whether or not his call was specifically understood, the two sides immediately stopped in amazement. They paused before the distraught comrade from Soviet Moscow. The battle was over. Absurd? How good it is for the sometime absurdities of peace when people open their eyes to another way because of a mere gigantic dance leap between warring factions.

Commonality can be a China/America Ping-Pong game or a Greece/Turkey earthquake. Peace, a sometime dream, is as strange and unexpected as war. She is better company at a wedding or in the street than her sister apocalypse.

The Plot

Not long ago, Yusef Komunyakaa and I were having a long supper at the Uptown Café in Bloomington, Indiana. Yusef is shy, withdrawn, and solemn. But his tall gravity is an easy target when I poke fun or something catches his interest. Then he breaks into a substantial laughing smile. We were at each other. I was reminiscing about Jews and Blacks. Yusef insisted that his generation didn't know the tales I was telling him.

"You must write them down," he said.

"Can you give me your side?"

Yusef burned me with his eyes.

Slowly reflecting, he said, "I have poems on Jews, on Solomon, Sheba, and the Red Sea. They were all with me since my childhood in Louisiana. In our church and at home we often talked about the fate of the Jews. They weren't victims. They lasted. And we identified with them as revolutionaries."

"Okay, Yusef. I'll try."

Jews and Blacks of Early Childhood

When you're a kid you're too young to live on memory, so it helps you slog through the snow and sizzle right now, with lots of imagination about who's playing cards on all the icy battleships loafing on the Hudson River. And you learn stuff from everybody. So when I asked the Babe, who was standing in the same elevator, how it felt to swat a ball clear out of Yankee Stadium, he said it's sexy like grabbing the crotch of a Jew girl or a nigger woman. The Babe was a very broad-minded guy.

—PETE STABLER, *Dreams from Hell's Kitchen*

Babe Ruth and author (*left*)

Swans over Manhattan

When I was thirteen, my mother and I moved from windy Riverside Drive to Central Park South and lived in a fancy apartment facing the zoo, the small boating lake, and its swans that occasionally flew up from the waters to soar over Manhattan. Mother, whom I adored, was working on my diction and hand gestures so I would seem like the person she wished me to be: a New Englander like herself (a blond, green-eyed Semite) and not a raw New York Jew. In the late 1930s, *status* was very important. And I really was a New Englander, born in that white clapboard land. But my Maineiac heritage, which even today makes me proud, was ephemeral. Mother returned to her birth city, Auburn, Maine, for a month or so to be near her parents and to have me emerge in her territory.

So I came properly into light in Lewiston, the twin city across the Androscoggin River where the hospital was. It was an event. Not only was I the first member of our family not born in our mother's bed, but apparently, as soon as the nurse in white bent over me, I pissed on her face. It was an awful act of defiance and sin. All these told-to-me things are now in my memory and form part of the lore of a nice waspy beginning. However, many years later in our Vermont farmhouse, I found a home-made recording of me as an eleven-year-old city boy, enthusiastically gabbing about scavenging Coke bottles at the New York World's Fair and hearing Tommy Dorsey live at the Paramount. Despite my mother's worthy efforts, carrying me in her belly back up north for a pedigree birthplace, this little record revealed with loud scratchy proof how miserably, apart from some funny persisting Maine "r's," I had failed to pass the speech test of a Down Easterner of pleasant gentile origin.

No, I came right out of the upper West Side tall-building ghetto of Jews and neighboring Irish where I learned to talk. I grew up on the Drive along Riverside Park, where in late freezing afternoons I slogged up the gully, pulling my sled to the top for another two-guy-on-a-sled wild ride down as far as the railroad tracks by the river. We got hit with iceballs from the toughs, and I yelled back insults like any city boy. The price of my father's office down on Maiden Lane was having to live in this abundant city where I became its son. My adult abandonment of New

York has softened my ethnic East Coast twang, but even today, given a chance to chat with someone from Hell's Kitchen or the Bronx, I unwittingly and happily revert to my childhood voice.

My brother Howard was very keen on saving me from a Semitic semblance. I cannot blame him. Those were different times. He was the family model (though later I was to discover how profoundly tormented he was by his almost lethal denial of being a Jew), and it was my duty to emulate him. I did feel his truths, one being that real white Christians had upturned noses like most of our Irish neighbors on Amsterdam and Columbus avenues. So while my nose was actually quite straight, I often slept on my stomach with the tip of my nose pressed against the pillow with just enough pressure to give it, perhaps I hoped, a permanent upward curl. Sometimes I'd get up in the middle of the night and look at the mirror as sideways as I could twist in order to see if my shaping method was working. I knew it would require patience and many months or even years of training to make my beak truly Irish or Saxon.

Personally, I was also interested in the deeper things, so on my own I acquired a psychology textbook written by a professor from Columbia University. It had a red cloth cover and its title page was austerely impressive. After the author's name were his degrees, and under it his titles, and below all that the name Macmillan, a worthy publisher. This volume had authority and told the truth. The first paragraph began, "The population of America, consisting of whites, Negroes and Jews. . . ." So I learned scientifically that I was not the ordinary New York boy or girl, who almost everyone I knew was, but one of the three racial groups in America whose patterns of emotion and behavior a professor was distinguishing. America seemed bigger, and my place, well, different.

My brother would move me upward into that greater, first group of Whites. And my grandfather, an immigrant tailor from Boston, whom, alas, I never met, initiated this task when, under pressure from one of his sons, my Uncle Will, whom I also never knew, changed his name from Bornstein to Barnstone. So in 1911 eight Jews in New England altered their European identity to become truly pink-white natives. All these preparations on my father's side had happened long before I was born. Now it was up to our own family—Mother, Howard, and me (my sister was married and away)—to keep up the good work of dissimulation.

To be white meant to be Christian. With America's clean English spirit, along with Adolf Hitler's great praise for fairness of skin, most Americans were contentedly of proper background, though there were second-class or borderline Whites, who were Spaniards, Greeks, and Italians, including the pope. But these sub-groups stayed away nationally from political and big business life anyway and were, like the Jews, not found in endangering positions such as in the ranks of college professors or administrators. There was a delicate problem in 1933 when Albert Einstein, deprived of his German citizenship, came to America, to Princeton; but fortunately for the school's reputation and alumni propriety, Princeton solved the matter by establishing, with gifts from Louis Bamberger and Mrs. Felix Fuld, the Institute for Advanced Study. There the German-Jewish refugee, as its first appointee, did his work with excellent facilities, and the university even created a special dining room for him so that Princeton University professors would not be eating with a Jew. What would the alumni think? Princeton's decisive actions of finding a way to squeeze in the tainted scientist, as opposed to the pervasive benign neglect elsewhere, was innovative and courageous for the time, and it advanced American science. The alternative, a regular professorship, would have precipitated scandal and resentment. A man with a name like Einstein on the faculty at Princeton—it was unthinkable. Urbane manners easily prevailed.

About all these high matters I knew nothing in my youth. Only decades later, in a *New Yorker* profile on Albert Einstein by Jeremy Bernstein, were the physicist's initial years in the United States portrayed. The "Einstein" syndrome was not limited to people of high station but pervaded the social structures as trickle-down-bigotry, spraying guilt and poisons at all levels. So I was increasingly aware that if one was a Jew, especially if one looked like a Jew or had a suspicious name, entrance into a "good" American college or university was at best a rare exception.

In Chicago a bright student with a nice Jewish surname applied to the University of Chicago. He was turned down. Two weeks later he sent back the same application signed by a Sanford Brent and was immediately accepted. So was born the name that would later title Chicago's esteemed *Brent's Bookstore.*

Anatole Broyard (1920–90), the Inventor

As for the Negroes, they didn't exist for white universities, colleges, and, as I was soon to discover, even for all-American prep schools. Unlike Jews, Negroes normally couldn't pass unless they were a light-skinned Anatole Broyard, the critic and former daily book reviewer at the *New York Times*. There was ultimately something undeservedly tragic and self-lacerating about his pass from black to white. After a black childhood in a colored neighborhood of the French Quarter in Creole New Orleans and the Bedford-Stuyvesant area of Brooklyn, and an early marriage to a black Puerto Rican with whom he had a child, Broyard jumped color. He followed the path of his father Paul, a master carpenter, who once he had moved to Brooklyn decided, at least professionally, to pass as a White in order to be able to join the carpenter's union and obtain work.

The son, Anatole Paul Broyard, kept his secret professionally and personally till his death. His concerns, his profound embarrassment, his inability to find the right moment to tell his children—his wife knew, though it was not discussed—may today seem anachronistic, pitiful, or ridiculous, but passing was his life, and its boldest and most dangerous enigma.

In his book *Thirteen Ways of Looking at a Black Man*, Henry Lewis Gates said about Broyard that keeping his secret became a lifelong psychological torment, which no shrink could spare him.[1] What he would forget and be free of beset all levels of his spirit. Gates, among others, suggested that his forbidden secret prevented him from writing the great American novel or memoir they so eagerly expected from this charming word magician. He would have to face truths of the self that those genres demanded. He tried, took periods off from work, but was ever blocked. His familiar genius was in the short, aphoristic essay and review, where *le mot juste* was his habit and invention.

We do find essays where he alludes to the quandary of passing but without identifying himself as the black man. In a 1950 *Commentary* article entitled "Portrait of the Inauthentic Negro," he wrote, in despair and disguised self-denigration:

> The inauthentic Negro is not only estranged from whites—he is also estranged from his own group and from himself. Since his companions are a mirror in which he sees himself as ugly, he must

reject them; and since his own self is mainly a tension between an accusation and a denial, he can hardly find it, much less live in it. . . . He is adrift without a role in a world predicated on roles.

Broyard played with his dilemma, of the writer who would not be forced to carry the label of "Negro author." And he was a victim of a malevolent society that wanted him to squeal on himself about a birthright denied, to confess to a sin designed by a sick community. Though he concealed his race—that vague, foolish, arbitrary notion—he was still able to cast his characteristic ironic and literary light on the holy mishmash up to the end. As he lay dying, in an exchange with his wife Sandy (who alone of his white family knew he was once black), he confessed, that is, he clearly alluded to, his Faustian bargain with his body and soul:

> "I think friends are coming, so I think we ought to order some food," he announced, hours before he lapsed into his final coma. "We'll want cheese and crackers, and Faust."
>
> "Faust?" Sandy asked.
>
> Anatole explained, "He's the kind of guy who makes the Faustian bargain, and who can be happy only when the thing is revealed." (Gates, 212)

At his memorial service, a major event attended by literary New York, by his companions at the *Times*, and by a host of loving friends who were to mourn the passing of their best friend for years thereafter, these same friends, including his eulogist Alfred Kazin, were astounded to find that Anatole was black. It was enough for his darker-skinned sister Shirley Broyard-Williams to be there. She had a good life, married to a black ambassador to Ghana, and never broke rank with him. But she did remark wearily, with regard to *what he could not give up*, "The hypocrisy that surrounds this issue is so thick you could chew it" (Gates, 213).

By contrast with Broyard's historical instance in the literary papers, for a modest black man or woman seeking liberation from typecasting and hoping for a better life, there was no national audience to confess to. Relatives of the one who had jumped the race line almost always cooperated by keeping their distance, even if their silence came with sorrow and a snicker. To make the social climb possible, they accepted total rupture of contact, thereby respecting the death of the man or woman of uncertain color and "tainted" blood. The relatives and old friends didn't snitch.

What Was a Jew?

From early on, my brother trained me how to pass and how to overcome the college admissions quota system, which limited candidates not only by religion and race but by "geographical representation" and which had lower admission standards for students who lived west of Atlantic seaboard urban areas, thereby minimizing the admission of blood-tainted Semites who crowded the big, brainy East Coast cities. The disguisement training I absorbed—from family, from reading, and from the air around me—marked out specific diction and facial and body gestures that were to be avoided or concealed at all cost. On the positive side, it proposed the natural assumption of low-keyed Anglo-Saxon poise and of a few essential lies about background, all in the very serious cause of providing ways of entry into the great white world of America.

What was a Jew? How did it feel to be one? As a child I didn't think about it all that much, and until puberty, rarely in negations. There were no educational gates to open, no occasions for denial and masquerade. That innocence was a victory of kinds. Moreover, in the theater of the streets there was a feeling in the New York air of commonality, that we were all together—Jews, Italians, Irish, and Negroes in an interesting salad—and that as long we were in the city, *we* were the people. The notion that other people lived on Park and Madison was true, but it also helped give the rest of us a bit of a romance for our common upward climb into the post-Prohibition era of progress. Other events stirred us, like the Spanish civil war, which even as a kid gave me a strong cause to root for. There were Frank Sinatra (whom I didn't go nuts about then) and the little giant Mayor La Guardia (whose mother was an Italian Sephardic Jew), both of whom showed that Italians could cause an incredible popular storm. As for funny people on the radio, most of them were Jews, and I loved Jack Benny most because he was such a patient creep and a loser. Lena Horne made us sigh when she sang "Stormy Weather," and Marion Anderson pierced us to the bone with her German lieder and Negro spirituals. We all knew of her travails with the Daughters of the American Revolution, who shunned her, and of Eleanor Roosevelt, who gave her a voice at the White House. The Duke got the same putdown. I used to hear him right after Jack Benny on the radio on Friday nights. The Moon Indigo master was supposed to get the

Pulitzer Prize for his compositions, but at the last second the same plantation spirit took over and they turned him down. Two members of the jury resigned. When he got the news, he said, "Fate is being kind to me. Fate doesn't want me to be famous too young." He was 66. On his hundredth birthday, April 29, 1999, he got it, though by then, he was composing and conducting in the sky under the earth. Even as a kid, I knew that when the singing was over, even these black stars, including the Duke or Lena, couldn't stay in the big hotels or get into most snooty restaurants. When they did go to a fancy place to entertain the white folks, they went in and out by the service entrance or the back door.

Dad Grew Up in the Streets

The kind of fighting Dad did in Boston is way different from New York, where almost anyone you street-fight is an enemy—from another group and a different neighborhood. Occasionally there's a professional murder when one outfit from Miami or Havana is trying to muscle into the business of some other hood. Or there's Dutch Schultz, who butchered enemies and mainly friends as often and easily as a businessman changes his shirt. But when he went too far, even Dutch got rubbed out.

Dad grew up in the streets, and to survive on his own in Boston as a kid who left school and home at twelve, of course he had to be a street-fighter. Now he always fights for underdog causes. He wouldn't go near a Hearst yellow rag, by which he means the tabloid *Daily Mirror* or the ugly *Journal-American*, and he tells me that he seriously considers New York City to be like the Balkans: each neighborhood is at each other's throat—envious, infantile, and nationalistic.

He really loses his temper over the Nazi-lovers—Henry Ford, Father Coughlin, the Duke of Windsor, Colonel Lindbergh—who are the scum of the earth. The last two like to take medals from and hobnob with Hitler and his associates at dress-up dinner parties. And the flirtation with fascism of famous English authors gets him sick. He knows all about important modern authors as he does the old master painters in the Frick Gallery.

One afternoon at the Frick he was laughing in front of a beautiful El Greco painting of the Virgin Mary, who he said was really El Greco's own wife, a converted Jew from Toledo. Who was Mary anyway? A gentile?

Those who really hate Jews get together downtown and lie and shoot their mouths off. The big Yorktown-group Bund meetings down at Madison Square Garden, where large, standing, fanatic audiences shout *heil* to Hitler and the Third Reich, have angered a lot of people, not only liberals like Father. Pop doesn't like nationalism either and believes in "one world." Even though he's a businessman, he is solidly behind Norman Thomas, the socialist who runs every four years for president. Of Thomas he says, "There's an honest man. A true idealist."

The year I was born, his own state of Massachusetts electrocuted two young anarchists, Sacco and Vanzetti.

"Sacco and Vanzetti?"

"They were Italian immigrants who were into union work. Two innocent men. Good men. Sacco and Vanzetti," he tells me heatedly. "The murderous state killed them because it hated Italian immigrants and men with their heads in the clouds. And hated them worse when they got mixed up with workers and unions. They were framed and the whole world knew it, yet the governor went ahead anyway and turned on the juice."

Father likes to wear a dark gray coat with a black velvet collar, but he often remembers that he came from a miserable immigrant family. Just a simple addiction to alcohol, which he never had, and he could be down there on Houston Street or even the Bowery with the derelicts, sleeping in a fleabag for a quarter a night. But I can't see Dad as a bum. He keeps his shoes much too clean and shiny for that. He brags about having been sometimes hungry as a child, and he likes it that his father lives with Louise, the black lady, even though he despises everything else about his old man.

"That's the only nice thing I can say about him," he declares bitterly, referring to grandpa Morris, who wasn't even a good tailor in his working days. "He isn't a bigot."

Who was my father's father? What was his face like? Did I look like him? What kind of place did he live in? I never learned when he died. So the unknown figure grew into a lifelong enigma. Sometimes I recreated him, and went to visit him, even before I was born:

Back in 1901

Outdoors, cows and a Vermont barn. Inside
our eighteenth-century summer farmhouse,
I quit standing and oiling wide pine floorboards

and show up back in 1901 in Boston, determined
to know my dad's father, whom I never saw.
On Milk Street, a ghetto named for a London

Milk Street ghetto, I find the lowdown
tenement where the choleric tailor lives
with a black woman, his common law wife.

The building stinks pleasantly of fried liver
and fish aromas sitting like tired old men
on the stairs I climb now like a regular.

Morris Bernstein heard of me from son Robert
but we were a century apart, he in New England,
I off upper Broadway. I knock. It's good

to knock on the unknown, on a nonentity
who may star in the story about the dog
who dreamt heaven in a butcher shop,

which no one yet cares to write about.
Grandfather opens. "Hello, I'm Billy," I say.
"No," he answers. I notice the immigrant English,

a wet shtetl lilt mixed with the Boston *r* that goes
unheard. "No," he insists. "If you are gray
and Robert's boy, then I am dead.

You can't be Billy!" "You're right," I apologize.
"*You* are dead and I am dreaming you."
At once I am ashamed. This is my ancestor,

ghettoized and despised by Poles, who steamered
over the sea from Warsaw to a Boston life
I couldn't guess. "I was kidding, Zeda,

I'm not even born, but I wanted to tell you
I love you." "You love me? You're a numbskull!"
And he kisses me. I think we're doing fine,

yet know I can't get out of these false tenses
and the small shop where his irons,
heating up on a wood stove, are owls looking

at me with contempt. I apologize again. "Sorry,
I've come so late to talk. I never wished to be cruel,
but you were gone when I was a child.

They never told me. So I fashioned your lips,
your Tartar eyes and crooked back,
your wife who isn't home yet. I mean, the maid."

"I don't get you, Billy." He lets go of my hand.
"Stay with me a while. I'm pretty happy."
I sit with him all night. In the morning Zeda gives me

a jacket he made, and presses it with special care.
When did he do it? We were awake together.
I take it. I'm descending slow stairs

smelling of Morris's shop, his owl irons, his glare.
Tonight I'm wearing the meticulously stitched
jacket, though it is tight and I'm a crummy actor.

Languages of the Jews

My parents taught me next to nothing about religion and Judaism,
since they were Reformed, not Orthodox or Conservative. Mother was
straightforward. She kept her kitchen but not her stomach kosher. She
did this for her parents, who lived in Maine, "out of respect and honor,"
she would say, but she didn't share their beliefs or practices. Since we
almost never went to temple, whatever informal knowledge I had about
Jews came from knowing other Jews (and they were almost always as
ignorant as me about the religion, history, and culture) and from Mr.
Segal, a wonderful cantor at a downtown synagogue. Mr. Segal came

three times a week to give me Hebrew lessons. In all I studied the tongue from age seven to fourteen. In that I have since studied and learned several languages, I can say that the methods in those years were abysmal. This is especially sad because as a child one has phonetic and linguistic advantages for acquiring a foreign tongue that after puberty are gone. Children in the right setting are incapable of hearing a language as strange or foreign when thrust into its midst, and they repeat each word perfectly like a native.

The language-learning process is still wide open for children: they haven't learned conflicting deep structures to impede them. Yet Mr. Kissinger, who came a few years too late, could stay another sixty years in America and would really still be speaking German with English words. Had he spent a year as a child in an English-speaking city, he would have lived his life in the United States as a native speaker. As for the pervasive Jewish accent and intonation of most Jews of my time, that colorful and melodic speech (much as I esteem it with nostalgia in its present decline) has proved to be generational and regional. I have observed that one generation in Indiana miraculously cures all telltale signs of European Jewry from one's Hoosier talk.

In Europe the wandering Jew spoke many languages. Even the peasant Jew in the shtetl, amid the multiple ethnicities and speech common in the Pale, was normally multilingual. I spoke English and only English as my native language. It was never my second language. I represented the newly liberated Jew who has lost both the vernacular and the classical language of the Jews. As a descendent of Polish (or perhaps Lithuanian) grandparents, I am referring to the poor acquisition of Hebrew as well as to the loss of Yiddish, not to mention Polish, Lithuanian, and Russian, which were all within the grasp of the more ambitious people of my grandparents' generation. Earlier European Jews (at least the men, since abominable discrimination against women was the rule in Jewish culture) were almost uniformly literate. The notion of "the people of the book" was genuine. In times when few people were literate, the ability to read was important not only for deciphering biblical scripture but just for the distinction of being *able* to read. So Jews read, wrote, and also had a speaking knowledge of the tongues spoken in their adopted country: of Hebrew, the temple language, and of the house language they brought into their diaspora, which in the West was Yiddish, Spanish, or

Portuguese as opposed to the Near East and North Africa, where Jews spoke Arabic or French at home.

The house and secular literary language of North European Ashkenazi is Yiddish, an amalgam of German dialects spoken in the ghettos of Central Europe from at least the year 1100. When Jews were driven out of much of Germany in the fourteenth century, they went mainly East and, like the Spanish Jews expelled at the end of the fifteenth century from Spain who kept Spanish as their native language, these German Jews kept German as their home speech. Neither in their own eyes nor in those of their host countries, however, were these German-speaking Jews perceived as a group of very ancient Germans. By contrast, their Spanish-speaking cousins, the Sephardim, in Holland, Italy, the Balkans, Greece, and Turkey, were always popularly seen as both Jews and Spaniards. These curious distinctions in feelings of national identity in no way diminished the mutual preservation of the pre-diaspora tongue as well as the songs, cuisine, and habits. Greek Jews carried Spanish to Jerusalem, giving modern Hebrew its Sephardic pronunciation. The Greek Jews also carried Greek. The modern word for dance in Greek is *choros* (the *chorus* in ancient drama danced while it spoke). Greek Jews took their round dance to Israel, where it became the national dance called the *hora*.

The sacred language of the Jews, of their prayers and temples, has been Hebrew. But under the Moors in Spain, the Jewish literati also used Hebrew for profane art. Under Muslim rule, especially in Andalusia, the Jews attained the greatest degree of civic freedom and integration into the professions, politics, and culture of the country. There the major poets, Solomon Ibn Gabirol (1021/22–c.1055) and Judah ha-Levi (c.1075–1141) among others, composed their poems, which were largely secular, in Hebrew. Their verse followed the prosody of the rich Arabic poetry flourishing in Andalusia and elsewhere in Spain. The Jewish philosophers stuck to Arabic, the language they heard around them, at a time when the most significant and influential philosophers in Europe were the Arabic philosophers in Spain.

Although with the decline of Rome Aristotle was lost in the West, Arabic scholars introduced Aristotle into Islam in the ninth century, which gave an Aristotelian cast to Islamic philosophy, science, and theology. Aristotle was later reintroduced to the West by Arabs and Jews in Spain who translated him from Arabic into Latin. So it was perfectly natural for the leading Jewish philosopher, Moses Maimonides of Córdoba (1135–1204), to write his major work, *The Guide for the Perplexed*, in Arabic. A glance at the texts might lead one to suppose that he wrote in Hebrew, for he wrote his Arabic in the Hebrew alphabet (Judeo-Arabic), just as diaspora Jews wrote their Spanish, not in Roman, but in Hebrew letters (in Judeo-Spanish or Ladino or simply Old Spanish). By extension Yiddish, which was traditionally transliterated into the Hebrew alphabet, might be properly called Judeo-German or simply Old German.

Spanish Jews

The Jews in New York, like the farmers in Indiana, see themselves as the norm, so my limited knowledge of Jewish society was that some people kept kosher, that everyone's grandparents came from Eastern Europe (unless they were native-German-speaking refugees), and that these old immigrant folks from the East spoke mainly Yiddish. I missed learning it by being third-generation and too far removed from its source. I didn't know there were such things as Spanish Jews. Black Jews from Ethiopia (the Falashim) and from Harlem were common knowledge, but Spanish Jews from Italy, Rhodes, and Turkey?

Then one evening in Mexico City, when I was fifteen, my father (by now divorced) and I went out on a double date with two sisters, Mexican Jews, who were originally Spanish-speaking Sephardim from Constantinople. I sat in the back of the white Buick convertible. Marti Franco was my first real date. A few days later Marti, who was two or three years older than me, gave me a handkerchief with a romantic red guitar in the middle of it, which I lost in the upper berth of a Pullman train going north in Texas. A year later Marti, now my father's wife, was my stepmother, and soon I would have a younger Mexican brother. Later I would marry a Greek (also born in Constantinople) who opened my eyes to a new culture. Now it was the Hispanic world, and, like the Greek world, I'd never leave it.

Poking Mexico, 1943

Father and I were scandalously glad
in Mexico. War tore up Europe yet
here were two guys, he fifty, me a bad
fifteen, on double dates all to forget
our fires back home. Walking a midnight street
(where gold and onyx shone behind the glass)
leading to the great Zócalo, our feet
in brand new leather shoes entered the mass
of *la gran Catedral*. The Indians spoke
to us in Spanish, I interpreted
and Dad was proud. The saints were kind. They stared
from their great Asian eyes. A little poke
and Dad saved me from heaven. Wrongly dead
he takes my hand again. He fled, but cared.

The Spanish Jews from Italy, the Balkans, Greece, Turkey, and some
North African communities spoke Spanish as their home language. The
Italian painter Modigliani from Livorno and the Nobel prize novelist
Canetti from Sophia were Spanish Jews. Elias Canetti (1905–94) learned
Spanish at home before he learned Bulgarian. Then when he was six, his
family moved to Manchester, England, where he spoke English. After
his father's sudden death the family moved to Vienna, where he learned
German, took a doctorate at the University of Vienna in chemistry, and
became a writer. Though he fled to England just before the outbreak of
World War II, he wrote all his novels and memoirs in German, his fourth
language, which he had acquired in the crucial years of linguistic and
literary formation. The wandering Jew had the wandering languages.

My stepmother Marti (Matilde) Franco speaks modern Spanish because she grew up in Mexico where the modern Spanish overcame the
Ladino she learned as a child from her mother, Rebeca, who all her life
spoke medieval Spanish, *Ladino* (Latin), and considered herself a Spaniard.
Even the Spanish dictator Francisco Franco (who carried my stepmother's
name, though he was born in northern Spain and she in Constantinople)
intervened during World War II on many occasions in southeastern Europe
to save the lives of many Spanish Jews of the five-hundred-year diaspora.

One family story about Ladino always thrills me. Marti told me the story of her mother's first encounter with Spanish as a national language. In 1924 when Rebeca and her family reached Vera Cruz, Mexico, and heard the Indians in the maize fields speaking to each other in *castellano* (Spanish), the lady from Constantinople began to scream, *"¡Son de los nuestros! ¡Son de los nuestros!"* (These are our people! These are our people!) She had never before been in a place where the local people spoke her Spanish. A native language unites people soulfully like nothing else. Linguistically, Rebeca was coming home. As for her leaving Turkey itself, I should add that in contrast to the fate of Greeks and Armenians, the Jews were not maltreated in that Muslim country for being Jews. Indeed, they were welcomed after 1492 when the Jews were expelled from Spain, and the Turks even sent ships to Spanish harbors to pick them up.

When I think of Rebeca, I remember a small linguistic detail. In 1947 I was living in an orphanage in Mexico City for Spanish student refugees of the Spanish civil war. I shared a free room on the roof with a Catalan chemistry student in exchange for giving English lessons there. When I'd go to see Rebeca and Marti in their apartment in the slums of that very old historic area behind the Grand Zócalo, I'd usually spend the night, sleeping on a mat on the floor between Marti's brother Sam, a captain in the Mexican army, and the Indian maid. Rebeca would invariably greet me with, "How is my *mancebico* this evening?" *Mancebico* means "young master" and is a diminutive of *mancebo*, a charmingly complimentary mode of address, typically medieval, which was already fading from Spanish speech by the seventeenth century.

Room of the orphans, 1947

After my father's suicide, Marti,
   my Mexican stepmother,

went back to the iron bed with her mother
   Rebeca, a Sephardi

from Constantinople, who normally
   called me *mancebico,*

young man (in medieval Spanish),
   but she was afraid I'd get

her daughter as my father had.
   They rented some rooms behind

the great cathedral, a small hovel
   in the old district. I too

lived that year in Mexico City,
   near her in an orphanage.

If I couldn't make it back by ten
   (I gave evening classes

all over the city to earn some pesos)
   I did an all-nighter,

reading in a lowdown café, or better,
   went to Marti's and slept

on the straw mat on the floor
   between the tiny Indian maid

and her brother Sam, an army captain.
   Often when I was broke

I sold my blood in a clinic, and on
   one Saturday twice—but not

in the same place. Though the nurse
   noticed the fresh pricks

she let me through. Beautiful Marti
   was only two years older than me.

I cared for her a lot and never knew
   that the selling

of my blood was for her a stigma
   that God would not forgive.

For my part, what fun it was to flop
   at her place, on the mat! Besides,

I was tickled to earn my bread giving
   classes and blood to the people.

Being off and on in Mexico from the age of fifteen revealed to me that
Jews in the world, from Boston to Beijing, were not necessarily all from
a generation of assimilating East Europeans living on the eastern seaboard. The nomadic Jew is no less provincial than others in failing to see
beyond neighborhood walls.

Jews and Blacks of Early Adolescence

When Moses looked around, he saw a tidal wave
coming out of Thera, trashing the Minoans in Crete,
thrashing toward the reed marshes of the north coast of
Egypt, making it windy and wet for the Pharaoh and
his Egyptian chariots. Moses had lots of slaves with
him. If he could pass over the Red Sea, he would be able
to get down to some holy writing and give them a book.
With the angel of God before him, he got through
the wilderness and wrote a book predicting milk,
honey in Canaan, and a glorious Solomon who would
take a black bride named Sheba from Ethiopia. Moses
was a dreamer and held to the imagination of the
wandering Jew.

—LEÓN HEBREO (1460–1521), *On Moses, the Dreamer*

At the Red Sea

So, this is the place
    where cries come to us
        like molting seagulls

pecking the air? I never
    thought Crown Heights
        would be so quiet, just

a cantor & a blues singer
    weaving all the old begats
        into Cato, Yankel, Andy,

Michael, James . . . all the others
    transplanted to earthen dams
        & tenements. Sabbath-breakers

& charlatans sow seeds that kill
    fruit. What we forgot
        or never knew is enough

to teach the ant to hate
    sugar. To see injustice,
        don't care where your feet

are planted, you must be
    able to nail your left hand
        to a tree in bloom.

Now, look at Sheba
    in Solomon's hanging garden,
        carved by grace from head

to toe, she was "wounded
    by love of wisdom" hidden
        in a cloud of galbanum

& myrrh. Didn't the King
    trust his heart? Let's hope
        the crystal floor

over that silent stream
    had nothing to do with
        the color of her skin,

but to prove her legs
  weren't like a donkey's.
    We sense what we've done

even if we don't realize why
  we're dismayed or overjoyed
    by how the stones fit

in our hands. The egg
  & sperm we would love
    to deny, they still move

the blood till we can hear
  "I am black but comely,
    ye daughters of Jerusalem."

—Yusef Komunyakaa

Assimilation and Passing under the Shadow of War and Holocaust

In addition to my own language poverty, my childhood knowledge of most aspects of Jews was dismally parochial. It was one I shared with my pals, but at least our city-bound ignorance was largely positive. On the one hand, I knew nothing about Baruch Spinoza (the Spanish philosopher and lens grinder from Amsterdam) or rabbi Yeshua the Messiah from the nation of Yehuda, who was later to be historically deracinated and become famous under his Greek name of Jesus the Christ. On the other, I did learn something about later Palestine, and the pioneer settlements of the Jews. In the 1920s and 30s the idea of a Jewish state was in process, was relatively peaceful, and was characterized by utopian expectations.

It happened that my parents sent me for many summers to Camp Modin in Maine, whose name "Modin" had a Zionist ring to it, where I learned to box and swim across the lake and also to read prayers in the morning. There I also heard a little about Palestine. To repeat the spontaneous simile of Mohammed, a Moroccan friend, in describing intuitions about his cuisine, "You step on the grapes with your feet and feel their sweetness." In reality, however, I think my parents sent me to Modin, not to imagine the sweetness of that Asian homeland of milk and honey, but simply because they had heard that Modin was a good camp for Jews. In those days a Jewish child, unless he or she faked it, couldn't get into a gentile summer camp. Summer camps were for a child the equivalent of country clubs for their parents with respect to "restricted" terrains. In Eliah Kazan's film *Gentleman's Agreement* (1947), Gregory Peck is a newspaperman posing as a Jew to test whether an exclusive hotel was "restricted." He asks the manager about their policy, and is thrown out *senza complimenti*.

Since my parents never spoke about Palestine or a homeland for Jews, I think of my encounter with Jewish pioneering as accidental. A far-off Palestinian homeland and the distant murder of Jews became increasingly taboo subjects as the war years were penciling the greater concerns of a planet at war. Then, and even during the holocaustal war, only Charlie Chaplin, who was not a Jew, took on the subject of Hitler and the plight of the Jews. Hollywood was mum, although a large portion of its studio owners, producers, and screen writers were Jews. And there were many Jewish actors who could pass, under altered names, including Kirk Douglas and Cary Grant (who are Sephardim), Lauren Bacall, and Julius Garfinkle, who became famous as a tough-guy hero with a sweetheart under the name of John Garfield.

To pass, meaning to have an acceptable commercial movie name, did not necessarily mean passing or denying in everyday life. In Kazan's *Gentleman's Agreement*, Garfield played the role of a Jewish U.S. Army captain returning home after the war to anti-Semitic insult. By contrast, the famous Austrian director-actor Erich Von Stroheim (1885–1957), who played the roles of German army officers, including field marshal Rommel, felt the need to disguise his background completely. By his account, he was Hans Erich Marie Stroheim von Nordenaal, son of an aristocrat, an officer in the royal guard. His birth-certificate name was Erich Oswald Stroheim, and he was the son of a Jewish hatmaker. To disguise one's background was not more unusual or sorrowful for Jews than for a contemporary Japanese of Korean blood to conceal ethnicity, since today a normal Japanese marriage requires, among its papers, a legal background check to confirm that there is no Korean blood in the veins of the prospective spouse.

The Jews were furiously assimilating, as were other exotic and less exotic peoples in America. It was unwise to make a wave. Earlier, because of anti-German sentiments during the first World War, large numbers of non-Jewish Germans anglicized their names to avoid ethnic stereotyping. During the second World War the quintessential singing trio in wartime America was "The Andrews Sisters," three fair-haired figures out of America's heartland who entertained and inspired the troops with rip-roaring patriotic songs. These dynamic singers, of Armenian background, also changed name and appearance to pass and be graced by broad American acceptance.

Wartime American Jews were, after all, not running for their lives as were their European cousins. There was no urgency of survival, and with Hollywood taking the lead, the correct role was to join the broader American war effort. Loath to single themselves out as outsiders or to identify in any prominent way with victim Jews in the jaws of central

Europe, Jews, with admirable exceptions, held their peace, saying little. There were no shouts, no demonstrations. While Cuba and the Dominican Republic and even the Dutch island of Carousal took in large numbers of Jewish refugees, our borders were virtually closed. The American visa applications, which were as long as books and were intended to exclude, were a vote for death. So the Jews were trapped in Europe. They hid until picked up and exterminated. The facts of the camps and the gas chambers were common knowledge, broadcast constantly over the BBC.

Although the Allies had complete air domination during the last years of the war, the railroads to the death camps were never destroyed, nor were the gas chambers selectively bombed. The pragmatic grounds for not wiping out the chambers or the tracks were that if the Germans were so stupid as to waste trains to transport Jews, Slavs, and Gypsies to their deaths rather than fill them with munitions and soldiers for the front, then let it be, for thereby the German forces were weakened. If the people stuffed in cattle cars has been British or American prisoners of war or civilians on their way to gas chambers, the tracks and chambers would have been gone in days as were the missile launching sites in Denmark when the V2 bombs began to rain down on London. The sites were hidden under stone cliffs, fiercely protected with everything the Germans had, but Allied dive bombers immediately threaded under the rocks and destroyed them, a feat incomparably more difficult than bombing wide-open tracks and the identified buildings containing the gas chambers. When I visited Auschwitz after its liberation and examined the banally sordid execution rooms, I was astonished that this death city survived intact while the rest of Europe was being bombed away.

The Camp near Kraków

Over the gate the sign ARBEIT MACHT FREI.
I guess my village outside Vilna, which
was razed, came here in cattle cars to die.
Today it's raining on the Kraków church,
its peaceful domes, and on the camp which is
a gray museum. I see the children's skulls,
the shaven heads of Jews and Gypsies, Poles,

photos of eyes like prehistoric flies
stuck on the walls outside the shower room
in which the rain prepared the bodies for
the ovens and the sky where bodies bloom.
ARBEIT MACHT FREI. Auschwitz is mute, the war
already fugitive. The rains evoke
a Slav, black-hatted Jews, tattoos and smoke.

To save Jews, Slavs, Gypsies, homosexuals, and underground anti-Nazis from extermination was not on any Allied official's priority list.

In light of these crimes against humanity, was the Jews' own discreet silence in America and England a form of stoicism, evasion, wisdom, cowardice, or madness? Was discretion obtuseness, or did it reflect a conviction that any other course was unfeasible? Whatever the truth of the times, and those were other times, silence prevailed.

Silence about the slaughter was linked with similar reticence about addressing the creation of a Jewish refuge to which the hunted might flee. Gone were cheery prewar days when a new Israel of farmers was a private and innocent dream. Now, when the need for a place of refuge was overwhelming, the war changed the scene and the rules.

In the United States, Jews could enter the army, become enlisted men and officers, and die among the Whites. Blacks were not afforded that privilege. Segregation persisted in the army until the Korean Conflict when Truman ordered integration. Blacks could fight white Germans on the front, but they had to know their place, which was, as always, a real or equivalent back door to army powers, even if that place happened to be the front lines.

In summary, with America at war, sectarian concerns diminished.

Jews found equality in the war effort. To shout about their massacre in Europe or suggest a refuge for those who might escape would send assimilation back to square one and imperil the appearance of equality. Jews would be seen as strident, their patriotism divided and suspect. In killing Jews, Adolf Hitler all but insured the later creation of a homeland. The boatloads of wartime refugees heading for Palestine, intercepted and sent back to their deaths by both the Axis and the English sea forces, insured a great postwar migration of survivors to a half-promised land.

Yehuda Maccabee and Hellenization
of the Jews

Modin was a summer camp in the early 1930s, when Zionist dreams were easy, cheap, and uncontroversial. Zionists wanted a homeland for the Jews. The camp was named for the legendary birthplace of Yehuda Maccabee of Modin, the Jewish general who in 164 B.C.E. defeated the army of the Syrian ruler Antiochos IV, a hellenizing Seleucid monarch.

The rebellion by Yehuda of Modin and his brothers was prompted by Antiochus IV's decrees in 167, which called for the eradication of Judaism: "All Jewish customs and ceremonies were forbidden, including Sabbath and festival observance and circumcision. All Torah scrolls were to be seized and burned. All sacrifices and offering to God at the Jerusalem Temple were abolished."[1] Those who disobeyed the decrees were to be executed. The Temple became a place of worship for the Greek God Zeus Olympus, and its altar was desecrated by sacrificing the pig on it. Antiochus IV was determined to destroy the monotheistic faith of Israel. Had second-century Yehuda Maccabee not rebelled against the Seleucid's decrees, Judaism would indeed have disappeared. And without Judaism there could have been no charismatic itinerant rabbi Yeshua ben Yosef, whose Greek scriptural name was *Iesous Christos*—Jesus the Christ—or more properly, Yeshua the Mashiah. Without the parent religion Judaism, its scriptures, and Christian (Messianic) Jews, there could have been no daughter religions of Christianity or Islam.

With the victory by the Maccabees over the Greeks, the Temple was restored in Jerusalem. Hence the candles firing bright at Hanukkah. Eventually, the Maccabeans, or Hasmoneans, became themselves thoroughly hellenized, and their monarchs represented the mirror opposite of the Essenes or Zealots who went to the Dead Sea sands to escape the spiritual dangers of Greece and Rome. The legend of the Maccabean place of origin took on its own reality in late 1995 when road makers were digging out a foundation for a highway to Jerusalem and uncovered a cave with ossuary urns of the royal family of the Maccabeans, including perhaps the remains of the Maccabean general, under a stretch of land with the traditional name of Modin. On one of the urns, in Roman and Hebrew letters, was HAS, pointing to a Hasmonean origin. The uncovering almost caused the Hasids to riot for disturbing the place of the dead. A few weeks later, however, Modin (my dear camp in Maine) lost its ancient glow when, in a brief notice, the archeologists announced that the attribution to the Hasmoneans was false.

Yeshua ben Yosef (Joshua Josephson in American) seems to have been a Pharisee opposed to Roman occupation who was crucified by the Romans as a Jewish seditionist, or some say (less persuasively) an Essene or Zealot. Recently, contemporary theologians speak of him as a Galilean peasant or an itinerant Cynic philosopher. Whoever Jesus was, he favored traditional Jewish biblical beliefs over the Hellenic thought and practices that by the first century had also been adopted by the Hasmonean hierarchy as well as by a large segment of the Jewish populace. Greek names were common. Hellenic culture was almost as dominant in Jerusalem as in Alexandria where a Jew such as the neoplatonist Philo Judaeus (?20 B.C.E.–50 C.E.?) was Greek in training, language, and philosophy. Jesus's followers, the sect of the Christian Jews, eventually adopted the essential neoplatonist ideas of eternity and the immortality of the soul. Later, the traditional Jews of Jerusalem were also platonized by Greek philosophy and by the increasingly platonized Christians, and the Jews accepted Greek and Christian ideas of the transmigration of the soul from earth to a heavenly or hellish incarnation. Such transcendental concepts had little or no basis in Torah (the Hebrew Bible) or in Greek scriptures (the New Covenant). But Jews and Christians went along with the dominant ontology of the Greeks and changed, as peoples and scriptures of all religions do, toward the spirit of the age.

In practice, first-century Israel, like the extended Hellenic world, was replete with mystery religions competing for dominance. I think it would have been more fun, and certainly less spiritually painful, if the followers of the tradition of Hermes Trismegistos (a fine pagan mystical gnostic), or even better, of Plotinos or Hypatia, had won out. I say followers, since the ahistorical personages of Hermes, like Yeshua and his messianic followers, and Laoze and his Daoists, all have similar mythic brilliance and elaborate uncertainty. If someone other than Judeo-Christians had triumphed, the sculptures and literary texts might not have been trashed by the iconoclasts' hammer and flame, and women might have had a fairer shake, since women have never been able to throw off the monstrous burden of being co-evilly typed with Eve for committing the original sin of choosing knowledge over obedience. It's good to remember that for the gnostics, Eve was, like Prometheus, a hero for her defiance of the Demiurge (Yahweh) and her extraordinary acceptance of death for the sake of gnosis.

Gnosticism and Other Heresies

The reader by now must know that I have been thoroughly brain-washed by the gnostics (who were Jews, Christians, pagans, Muslims, and French Cathars), not by the Jews who were still awaiting the messiah. My obsession with the gnostics is especially with their early development during the first, second, and third centuries, when they and their contemporaries were filling the ancient world with wonderful speculation in Jerusalem, Antioch, and Alexandria. So I have been a student of a possible spiritual way that failed and essentially disappeared in the Far East and the West after the fifteenth century.[2] But I still like the hints of their truth and defiance in later literatures and philosophies and in attempts by a Bruno, Spinoza, Milton, Blake, Melville, and Borges to lead us pleasantly astray. Jorge Luis Borges summed up the rather arbitrary way spiritual history has gone or might have gone in his comment that had the gnostics prevailed, "Had Alexandria triumphed and not Rome, the extravagant and muddled stories that I have summarized here would be coherent, majestic, and perfectly ordinary" ("A Defense of Basilides the False").

The last major gnostic heretics to be extinguished were the Neomanichaean Cathars in Languedoc southern France. To eliminate this pacifist sect of the inner light of gnosis (and bring southern France politically under northern hegemony), in 1208 Pope Innocent III launched the Albigensien crusade. As a legal instrument to complete the job of rooting out gnostic centers, Pope Gregory IX in 1233 gave the task of finding heretic differences to the Dominicans friars. So was born the medieval Inquisition, which later spread to northern Italy and Germany. (The Spanish Inquisition established by Fernando and Isabela in Spain in 1478, with its notorious autos-da-fé, was independent of the medieval

Inquisition and was finally abolished in 1834.) The Dominican inquis-
itors labored through southern France in the thirteenth and fourteenth
centuries to extinguish virtually all discoverable remnants of the alien
religion. In Toulouse, Albi, and Narbonne the Dominican friars set up
their Inquisition, arresting great numbers of heretics whom they examined and burned. After a hundred years of war and executions, there was,
almost everywhere in southern France, a drop in population of perhaps
more than half. Our detailed historical knowledge of these events we also
owe to the Inquisition, which in their archives, especially in Toulouse,
kept records of their activities and preserved the documents of heresy,
their splendid Cathar scriptures, such as *The Gospel of the Secret Supper*. So
after fifteen centuries the heretical gnostics lost to the ever-changing
Christian orthodoxy in power, and, as we see by way of Borges's memory,
those ancient classical gnostic spiritual leaders of Alexandria took on
names like Basilides the False.

The larger question of the plight of those who are different is their
demonization by those who, by virtue of being in power, carry the title of
the orthodox. The ones who are perceived to challenge orthodoxy—as
long as they are losing—are the heretics. However, should, by revolution
or conversion, the heretic gain ascendance, it is not unlikely that a new
orthodoxy of intolerance and revenge will replace earlier abuse of power.
History provides no sanctuary for the weak. The twentieth-century
Teutonic holocaust in Europe, even with its technological efficiency, was
perfectly in keeping with world historical patterns, where the other, the
different, the ethnic or religious enemy—whether Sumerian under Babylon, Canaanite under Jew, Manichaean under Zoroastrian, Christian
under Roman, gnostic under Christian, Protestant under Catholic, Catholic under Protestant, Albanian under Serb, or Serb under Albanian
—must be assembled and killed.

A Summer Camp in Maine with the
Scent of Palestine

So the game between the empowered and the disenfranchised describes survival on earth. Every solitary choice of a larger identification
brings in a possible battle between orthodoxy and dissent. Even the

mention of the word *Modin*, with its representation of liberal versus orthodox biblical Judaism, suggests the deep spiritual choices that a contemporary, whether a person of faith or a lost secular like me, must confront while passing through the light and mists of this world. Having said this, I return to ordinary early times, to Camp Modin in Maine, and to what those choices meant for this preadolescent.

Summer camp gave me my first glimpse of an active, worldly view of Judaism that pertained to America, Europe, and Palestine. This glimpse included, of course, Theodor Herzl (1860–1904), the founder of the Zionist movement. The Hungarian-born Austrian went to Paris in 1894 as a correspondent for the *Frei Presse* to report the Dreyfus affair. Captain Alfred Dreyfus, a French general staff officer, was on trial, accused of treason, of spying for the Germans, and was sentenced to solitary confinement for life on Devil's Island, a prison off the coast of French Guiana. The charges were trumped up, the real spy being Major Ferdinand Esterhazy, a French officer in debt, who passed on secrets to the German Embassy in Paris. But when the facts came out in a retrial, Esterhazy was still acquitted within minutes by the military. These trials split France. Eventually, the supreme court exonerated Dreyfus, promoted the reinstated captain to major, and decorated him with the Légion d'Honneur, but not until after twelve years in solitary. Esterhazy had fled to England.

The Dreyfus Affair brought out heroes like Émile Zola and Anatole France who denounced the judicial farce, but it also fanned winds of fierce antisemitism. At this moment the Jews in Eastern Europe were being slaughtered in the infamous pogroms. These assaults were vicious, interminable, and intolerable. Herzl and others, despairing about justice and freedom from persecution, now even in Western Europe, concluded that secular Jews must constitute a state in another continent. In 1903, after rejecting the British offer of a homeland in Uganda, the World Zionist Congress in Vienna selected Palestine as the biblical land of return.

So at Camp Modin, Palestine was the rage. The future poet Yehuda Amichai and his family had already left Berlin to settle on a farm in Palestine. Indeed, there was so much dreamy hope and speculation in the 1920s and 30s about a happier, safer life in the blossoming desert that even Franz Kafka, in 1923, the year before his short life ended, began to study Hebrew again and cooked up plans to go to Jerusalem with his

Zionist girlfriend to open a restaurant in which she would be the chef
and he the waiter. The wild notion of waiting to be served by Franz Kafka,
a waiter, evokes Kafka's story "The Great Wall of China" in which the
messenger sets out from the Great Wall to Peking and, after agonizing
years of journeying, still never reaches the capital city. Nonetheless, I
contend that to be served by Franz Kafka, even if the food never came,
would be the dessert of one's life.

In our camp of dreams in Maine, at morning service I heard biblical
stories told as radio adventure tales and also heard about utopian agri-
cultural communities, the kibbutzim, in the new and old homeland of
people whom the gentiles curiously called the "Hebrews." The strictly
religious part was not oppressive. I didn't mind standing up in a group to
chant Hebrew prayers that I didn't much understand, and my spirits rose
as we came to an ending with a cordial *amein*. More, I was terribly moved
when I saw the riding counselor grieve as he said Kaddish for his dead
father, as I would also be saying in a few years. But I had already taken a
dislike to God, alive or dead. I thought him an old bully and escape artist
when, in a modern fix, he should have been there. I would have stood with
the rabbis in Auschwitz who put God on trial for his absence and found
him guilty of negligence. But here was a place to think all those things
over. During those before-breakfast prayers in the big hall by the lake, I
had a chance to formulate what I suppose can be called, in a formal sense,
spirit.

After the summers, all the Zionist Jewish stuff was largely forgotten.
However, I did have one religious friend, only one, Sammy Propp. Here's
what I remember, as a kid, of Sammy, who was deep into Hebrew and all
those customs and rites I knew nothing about. Sammy was the real thing,
a faithful pal, and we had many good and dangerous adventures together.

Sammy Propp of the Black Shoes

I don't know whether Sammy Propp is smart, wise, or dumb
like Jerry, who goes to school though something's wrong. But
Sammy knows things. He knows Hebrew. And not just to read

the sounds out loud. He has a big smile like a half-opened book, and his black hair is short like a brush lying bristles-up on the dresser. And what feet! His black shoes don't end. You could slice them up thin, tie the pieces together, and make a swinging cord bridge from here to the North Star. They stick out under chairs, on rugs. In the street he seems to be plodding the tar on black snowshoes. We play punchball, and Sammy comes along when we sled the gully. He's got giant feet, but since he's a hopeless klutz in sports, he is usually the extra.

"Wanna go skating?" Alfred asks him, as we're coming out of school. "Gotta study. How 'bout tomorrow? You know, fellows, I'm working on Midrash."

"What the hell's the Midrash?" Eliot pops in. I don't know what it is either, but Eliot's the guy who thinks he knows everything, and here Sammy's got him duped. Alfred brags that Sammy knows other languages. Whenever I go to his apartment, I wait in the hall with benches and books and ten grandparents who keep their hats on and don't see us. The furniture is black. Alfred says our pal with the shoes is religious, but he's so nice it is hard to believe. On Saturday morning when we don't have school and take off for the river, Sammy can't come with us. He's got a big hat on in a room with old men. I hear he has to do that all day until sundown. Sundays we often hike somewhere together. He smiles, and I guess he's smart, maybe a brain, but I don't understand him. For his age—I think he's my age, eleven— he seems like an old man of forty.

We're friends. Though Sammy's different, he's serious and a good man you can trust. All you have to do is to see him smile and you know what's inside. When he breaks into a basso laughter, he opens his thick lips wide—he already has some scrabbly mustache hairs under the nose—and behind the open teeth is another dark world, a mysterious place far below. And he's never conceited.

"Billy, give me a lift," he asks me. I'm on my two-wheeler. It's got fat tires and easily supports us both.

"Hop on, Sammy."

We're off on a crazy trip. Sammy wants to get some firecrackers, and Chinatown is the only place in the city where any day of the year you can find a store or a pushcart with fireworks. We head down Columbus, under the El. Every time a train passes, it thunders overhead in your hair and then is gone in a quick groan, disappearing totally like a ship that has left forever. Men in undershirts in the tenements have their eyes glued to the passing trains. Maybe it's carrying them someplace. They're often smoking slow cigars. We stick to the West Side until the garment district, where the streets get too jammed with dresses and coats hanging up on carts with roller skate wheels that are rolled all over the curb and sidewalk by young fellows with Mediterranean mustaches.

We go east as far as we can. Mulberry Street, not far from Chinktown. We're in a poor Jewish neighborhood—Jews I never saw before, wearing yarmulkes in the middle of the day, men with curly sideburns and everyone wearing much too much baggy clothing. The common word you hear for Jews is "kikes," depending on who's talking. Chinks, wops, kikes, niggers, they're all about the same word. When some wise guy at a newsstand or barbershop or a huddle of laughing thugs gives out a compliment like "slimy chiseling kike," I hear it because I'm a dirty-blond kid named Barnstone. These Jews we see with their pushcarts and small shops, I'd call them colorful immigrants carrying around a hell of a lot of grimy Bibles in their hands.

I ask Sammy about the funny-looking Jews. He says they're "decent," but his parents call them "the superstitious Hasid." Sammy explains things better than I know, like an older teacher. "Grandfather says 'We're orthodox and we're also scholars.' If you ask me, Bill, it's because these people are poor," he says, almost whispering. And he gives me his big crazy smile with those eyes popping out like black marbles. "My parents see them as low-class Jews and are ashamed, since my folks are really proudest of being Germans—German culture, people, who knows? even German race. The whole schmeer. We happen to live on the upper West Side and have better clothes and nicer manners. My parents came right from Germany when they were very young, but they had some money and manners and never passed through Orchard or Mulberry Street. The Lower East Side is not in their memory."

"You mean your folks are snobs."

"Yeah, snobs."

Sammy has a mind for you. "The Lower East Side is not in their memory." I can't believe it. Somehow, he looks inside and always comes up with the right word and makes those sharp bookish distinctions. I wish I could talk like that. A ton of information in just a few words. In fact, I'm surprised he likes to bang around with me, since he does most of the explaining. But when you see him walking out of his house on a Saturday morning with a striped silk shawl on his shoulders and wearing a loose yarmulke, you'd think he had nothing at all in his bean.

I'm pretty clever, I think, but am not too sure of myself, especially in public. There are a lot things I don't know and think everyone else must. Only with close friends like Sammy or my friend Eliot the Turd am I really myself. And if that's the real me, who is the other fellow I am when I'm alone in the room or roaming about Manhattan? Call me a weather vane. A kid with many faces.

Now with Sammy, it's good. I don't worry who I am. Even though he's puzzling, I feel completely natural with him. Pretty soon we're on Canal and going into Chinatown. Many restaurants with huge vertical block signs in Chinese letters. The characters intrigue me, and I get the nutty idea that a painter was copying winter trees when an emperor or another big-shot official decided it would be a good way to write their language down with odd chopped-up tree branches.

About six Chinese kids look at us, and one yells, "Get a horse!"

"Go fly a kite," Sammy yells back.

"Go fly a friggin' kite!" I shout.

Just then a large black Packard drives slowly by, passing us on the right, brushing up against us. His running-board cracks me in the ankle, I swerve to the left—it's a one-way street—I try to straighten out the wheel, stay up, but we crash and Sammy flies off, hitting his arm against the curb. The car doesn't stop. I tear my knickers from skidding on the pavement, but Sammy has a bruise on his arm, which is bleeding a little, and his wrist is broken.

Sammy gets up.

"You okay?"

He sticks his arm out, and part of it hangs down.

"Let's get the crackers, at least," he tells me.

"I'll pay for them. I'm sorry."

"Wasn't your fault."

"Does it hurt?"

"Sure."

"Let's start pumping. It's going to be a long trip?"

"Lucky it's my left arm," he says.

Sam hops on the back fender, holding his wrist in his lap.

It's a slow trip back, and Sammy doesn't complain a bit. We do run into a store to pick up a bundle of firecrackers. Then we head right for Dr. Labaar's brownstone office, which Dad says was the correct thing to do. Dad isn't sore at me at all, but Sammy's father is hopping. I don't know what language he's cursing me in.

And Sammy? He tells the story a hundred times, every time someone asks about his cast. I never see him so happy as when he's being the hero, cast and all, saying we told the Chinese kids to go fly a fucking kite, though we didn't really use the word. Surprised that Sam, so meticulous about words, would change a crucial syllable. Yet if we had said "go fly a fucking kite," maybe we'd have gotten into a fight and by then the car would have already gone by and we wouldn't have spilled. As Sherlock Holmes says, to avoid injury, my dear man, you must use a powerful curse. Can't blame Sam for exaggerating, which unlike my other pals he almost never does. He's trying to make me feel good. Strange funny bastard.

We bother the neighbors for weeks with all those fireworks.

Until Alfred said it, I never saw how short Sammy is! There's so much to his mind you never think of his height. I usually notice his black shoes, since none of the fellows wear black shoes and his are round like black balloons. As I said, you could lay a pontoon bridge with them to Alaska. But Sammy holds the world up with a few words. And I bet they're in Hebrew. If the old patriarchs from Genesis talked to him or bawled him out or asked him to do something awful, he'd give it right back to them in their own tongue. So Sammy could talk to old fogies who were paddling around about 3,000 years ago. Normally, when we're in the street, coming home from school, he walks with enormous steps in baggy temple trousers, always talking to me, smiling, and asking things. But his head is also elsewhere. I have the strange inkling that if he ever finds the answers or the really right words, or maybe the one single word containing all things and all knowledge in the universe, it will be the end of our world.

Black People

After my parents split in the late 1930s and my mother and I left the Upper West Side to live in swanky Central Park South next to the swans, I never saw Sammy again. I recall him with enormous affection. Also, curiously, I never became friends again with a religious Jew. I've known Jews who believe in God, like the poet Yehuda Amichai or the thinker Hillel Barzel, but I've never known an "observer," the word used for those who follow the religion and its demands closely. If I did know an observant Jew, I don't think it would matter any more than it did with Sammy. I've never been a bigot for or against any religion or spiritual group. And as I said, I'm fascinated by the gnostics. I would not be insulted even by their belief that our transient imprisonment on this alien earth is a dark error in our journey back up to the mother-father principle of light.

Fifty-ninth Street opposite the park was indeed a beautiful and disturbing street. A half block to the east was the Saint Moritz Hotel, then the Plaza, and on Fifth up a block was the Hotel Pierre, the most expensive hotel in the area, where my father used to live when he was losing a fortune and needed to convince himself that all was not lost. To the west was the Hampshire House, the Essex House, and the truly bigoted and racist New York Athletic Club, which even in those days, despite the membership of the poet Wallace Stevens, was a cabal of largely elderly businessmen as portly athletes, which no Jew or Black could aspire to join.

But this was New York and bigger than the silliness of exclusion and shallow stereotyping of peoples. Exclusion existed only inside buildings. Outside was a cosmopolitan diversity of people and places and even precious nature. The swans were public and free as was the zoo, and this area had so many seasons of intense beauty. Just a walk or jog a quarter mile into the green led you to places you could sit, day or evening, and gaze back at the various skylines surrounding this amazingly cultivated hunk of nature in the middle of Manhattan. My dad often took me rowing in the lake, and we enjoyed bright Impressionist afternoons, lolling and being near the blond sun and the people in other rowboats. I also sailed my own tiny balsa-wood boats, stubby vehicles carrying lighted candles to propel them puffing around in brave circles. And some days I had an expensive black sailboat I got for my birthday, a pirate ship about thirty inches in length that never sailed quite right. It tipped, it raced away on its own, or it wouldn't budge, endowing it with forces of indeterminacy that might have made a mathematician or physicist ponder with glee.

To be a Jew in New York was normal. Guided by the spirit of the times and my family, I would soon become a non-Jew outside New York, which was a mission of many Jews of my age. To be a Black was something else. Segregation was still the law in the South in 1954 when I was a draftee in Camp Gordon, Georgia. As for New York Blacks, there was the public image of entertainers and sportsmen and a few female singers, but that was remote from our personal contact. Those national figures were Marion Anderson and Paul Robeson at the top, and then there was the Cotton Club in Harlem, Count Basie, the Duke, and Louis Armstrong. These were the jazz and swing years, the big white swing bands and the jazz clubs up in Harlem that white people visited, but no white musician could play in those terrific groups. After hours the musicians would jam together privately, whites and blacks, learning from each other, having fun. Benny Goodman had a great jazz quartet, two Whites and two Blacks recording unseen in a studio, that was a national sensation; but these musicians, Jews and Blacks, couldn't be seen together on stage in any white hotel, theater, or club. No one risked ostracism and career by jumping the ghetto line until Goodman finally broke it all wide open.

Only Benny, son of poor Jewish immigrants and now America's most popular musician, could get away with it when he integrated his touring band with the best musicians in the country.

I loved Louis Armstrong. How can I not? He could make any kid or grownup feel wonderful. Among the great black jazz musicians, it was Satchmo who most consciously, in memoir and public statement, identified with the outsider status and the art of the Jews—the latter with a hilarious twist. When Louis introduced the song "Heebie Jeebies," he did his own wacky, rocking interpretation of it, a body-shaking and improvised mumbling of meaningless syllables to a melody, which was called "scat. When asked about scatting, he told a friend, Phoebe Jacobs, who recalled, "One day I heard Louis talking with Cab Calloway, the bandleader, about scatting, and Louis said he got it from the Jews 'rockin,' he meant davening'—that is, praying and swaying. But Louis never talked about this in public, because he feared people would assume he was making fun of Jews praying, which wasn't his intention at all. So he kept it to himself."[3]

Satchmo, grandson of a slave, father of jazz, was dirt poor, living on a dirt floor with his young mother, a prostitute, whom he worshiped always. As a child he was befriended by the Karnoffsky family, Jewish immigrants from Lithuania, who were, in his words, "poor as Job's turkey." The sons Morris and Alex were young junk peddlers, who sold old clothes and coal buckets in the red-light district. And they took the young boy with them on their two small horse-drawn wagons. From dawn to dusk he would blow a ten-cent tin horn, with great imagination. They helped him buy a b-flat cornet for five dollars, cleaned and oiled it for him, and he blew it all through his later honky-tonk days in New Orleans. But most important, they took him in as one of the family. He ate much of the time with them (he was crazy about Jewish food), and they loved and encouraged his amazing musicality. He learned to sing a Russian lullaby with them while the mother put a baby boy to sleep. So he passed his days blowing his tin horn and later his cornet on the junk wagon. "When I reached the age of eleven, I began to realize it was the Jewish family who instilled in me singing from the heart."[4] Later, he wrote, "If it wasn't for the nice Jewish people, we would have starved many a time," and as a result, "I will love the Jewish people all of my life."[5]

Louis Armstrong (Louis Armstrong House and Archives)

Louis was an extravagant example of that identity of situation and moment between two dissenting peoples of the heart, Jews and Blacks, and in every way, all his life, this was his experience.

For me the hero man was Joe Louis. Heavyweight boxing champion of the world, Joe Louis was down there in our street-talk. I remember walking with my pals on 89th between West End and Broadway and talking about nothing but Joe. It was 1938, and the Brown Bomber was about to fight Max Schmeling, the German paratrooper who had defeated Louis two years earlier in a 12-round match. Now everyone in America was hoping that the Bomber would kill or at least knock out Max Schmeling, Hitler's favorite. All of us stayed up for the late radio broadcast to hear Joe blast the German superman into the hospital before the first round was half over. The next day everyone, white and black, was crossing his fingers, hoping the German wouldn't recover. Joe Louis united the country.

But as for young black friends, I didn't have any. There were no colored kids in school. I knew well only one black person, and knew her very well, since Leah was our maid and I spent more time with her than with my mother.

Leah Scott

Camp gave me all kinds of sports, including swimming and softball, that we never play in the street or the park, and something about religion. I like some of the stories but I also fight it all. Religion has a lot of scare in it, some truth, but that's also a scare; and it's the same kind of heart-felt nostalgia for peoples, for nations, that Dad can't stand. Killing or even simply hating for God—even for your own one, who is boss of your superior religion—is a bunch of bull. I'm sorry for people who are scared. I'm not that way.

It's good to be back in the city. I always have good friends. But when I leave them for early supper, I'm in the kitchen with Leah, in a gray uniform, who is cooking or still scrubbing. Leah lets me sit on her back while she washes the kitchen floor. I stay up there five or ten minutes at a time—and I'm really too big to play horse and rider games, but we started it years ago.

After Lucy left, Leah came. I was seven or eight, and she stayed about four years. It was empty after Luce went away, since she was my nurse and we were engaged. Leah's the maid for the house, not for me. Yet there's no one like Leah. She's very quiet, but her brain is going like a sewing machine. She's not too young, has a nice figure and a special sweet smell of herbs about her. I don't know what it is, but I like it. When she finishes her work late in the afternoon before supper, she takes out one of the library books she brings with her, a novel or a "classic" as she calls it, and sits beside the broom closet and reads away. Though she has beautiful Jamaican English, British English, since Leah's the silent type (English reserve), she can spend three hours in the kitchen and you never hear a peep out of her. It's different on nights she sleeps over when my parents are away. Then my brother goes to their room to stay in their double bed. She's in my brother's sack, and around midnight I wake up hearing a racket. Over and over again in her sleep, Leah is screaming, "Get down, Satan! Get down, Satan!"

I never heard her yell before.

"Get your filthy fingers off me, Satan!" She's screeching almost like a soprano.

I never saw Leah scared when she was awake. Nor talk about God or filthy-fingered Satan. I was astounded by her hidden side and by Satan who came out of an utterly strange world. But who am I to talk about how someone sleeps? Though I'm streetwise and mostly unafraid of any neighborhood any place in the city, for years I think a robber, a big masked thug or someone, is under the bed. Not an ordinary thief but a horror film guy who could be a murderer. I really am not suspicious of gangsters and would like to talk with a New York professional Mafia hit man or juicer, but I dread that sinister monster waiting under the bed. To show how ridiculous it is, it's enough for me to cover my head with the drawn-up sheet or blankets to keep him away. And suppose he really were there. Would blankets stop him? If I can't see him, he's gone. What a dumb way of facing things, but my body hasn't figured that out. And what a boring way for a tough guy to be wasting his time!

If the light is on, the murderer doesn't come to life. He's vanished like the terror. As soon as the light goes out, I'm petrified again. I don't think about it. I just dive into the sack, sometimes going headfirst under the covers, through the cold sheets to the foot of the bed, circle around like a swimmer doing a flip turn, and come back grabbing the overhead sheet to stretch it out so I won't have to stick my exposed head out in the darkened air. When Leah's in the room, even in the darkness, the man is gone.

"Now stop squirming and fussing around, Billy, and go to sleep," she orders me in her deep melodious voice.

"Leah, have you read any poems by William Wordsworth? You've read everything, haven't you? And you know everything by heart. Dad says you're such a brain—if you weren't a poor colored lady you'd be a professor."

"I said hush," she says.

She frowns but I guess she's very pleased. I admire her English so much that I want her to recite some of the things we're reading in class. She has big white perfect teeth and a large mouth, which I'm sure helps her speak better.

"Come on, Leah, just one poem!"

"If you'll stop being an impossible child and go to sleep at a reasonable hour, I'll tell you a few lines."

"You got my word."

Leah raises her head, gives me a serious smile, and recites:

> A slumber did my spirit seal;
>   I had no human fears;
> She seemed a thing that could not feel
>   The touch of earthly years.
> No motion has she now, no force;
>   She neither hears nor sees;
> Rolled round in earth's diurnal course,
>   With rocks, and stones, and trees.

I don't understand some of the words. "In earth's diurnal course, With rocks, and stones, and trees." I have an uplifting feeling of a dead girl merging with the whole world. It's just a feeling.

"Is that about sleep or death?" I ask her. "Would you be willing to tell me what it means?"

"It's about life and death and nature, and many things I can't explain."

I never saw this woman so dreamy. Then she snaps back into her reserve.

"Hey, Leah, you're a ham. Did I tell you that Alfred can recite Scottish ballads? Long ones, and say them real fast."

"He can do that because Alfred's a very smart boy who listens to his mother."

"That's not fair. *I* listen too."

"But you don't listen to Leah."

"Why do you always hurt my feelings?"

"Because I don't care for you much, Billy Barnstone."

"That's exactly how I feel about you, only double, and I hope you drop dead."

Leah comes over to the bed, gives me a kiss with her large mouth, and I'm off to sleep.

Leah was the only black woman at Mother's funeral. By then she was gray, but her face hadn't changed a bit under her proper black hat, which didn't have the small white flower she usually wore in it, and she wept as much as any of us. I overheard someone say Mother had to get *schwarze* maids so Father would keep his hands off them. There was a big fuss a while back about a good-looking Hungarian. She was a looker with green eyes and good legs, which I found out Hungarian women are supposed to have. Mother let her go. Leah is not only dignified, educated, and smart, but profound, everyday profound. She's a good woman, and I love her a lot. When she doesn't stay over, I am lonely, which is the real me.

My window faces Jersey, a dark place except for a few yellow or blue neon signs and the Bridge. Jersey's lonely too. I watch the shore for hours. The Crisco sign gives an eternal message of CRISCO, but each 60 seconds it flashes off to give the time. I wait hours and weeks for signs to change their words, hoping for at least one word to change everything I know. I could wait like a man sitting on a black horse in a garden of gigantic flowers. Years would be easy to wait. Some nights I stare all night, don't go near the bed, until Leah comes in at 6:30 in the early morning. She has the milk and the subway paper.

Leah reads the *New York Tribune*. She's already done her first work for the day, ironing and sweeping the kitchen floor. No one else is up, and she's sitting in the corner, next to the wall incinerator, reading the paper. This morning I notice that if I look at Leah's thick glasses while I'm lying on the floor, at a certain angle, with the light flashing on her through the kitchen window, I can almost read the headlines mirrored backward on the lenses. After this scientific observation, I gulp breakfast, squeeze her just once, a very tight hug, ask her not to be so vicious with me, and go out hunting for friends.

My Unseen Black Grand-Stepmother

My father knew a lot more about black people than I did. In fact, he was brought up by a black stepmother, at least part of the time. He was born in Boston, and his mother died soon after his birth.

Gas Lamp, 1893

In brownstone Boston down on old Milk Street,
up two gray flights, near the gas lamp, the tailor
waits glumly for the midwife. August heat
has worn the woman out. Amid the squalor
she looks around the bed, clutching a cape
she brought from London as a child. It's dawn
and dirty. The dark tailor wants to escape
to his cramped shop. The woman's sheets are drawn
below her waist. She isn't hollering now.
Her eyes are dark and still; blood on her thumbs.
Her name is Sarah. No. I'm guessing. How,
untold, am I to know? Hot day has worn
into the room. The midwife finally comes.
Grandmother bleeds to death. My father's born.

Eventually, his father lived with a black woman. I never heard any details, but one day, long after grandfather's death, I asked my sister why no one ever took me to meet my grandfather. After all, Boston wasn't that far away from the city. "He was no good" was the answer. In fact, my father did leave home and school at twelve, and it wasn't for love of his father. But I told my sister that our grandfather lived with a black woman, and that was far ahead of his time.

But she countered (and not because she was a bigot), "Billy, you think it was so great that Morris lived with a black woman, but the truth is that no one else would put up with him."

Grandfather

Born over there, in mist, not even God
or Germans have a record of the house
or village outside Vilna. Here, the old
poor tyrant snips a cloth, stitches a blouse
or shirt, and finds a black woman to live
with when his wife is dead. His smart son sells
papers in Boston subways, won't forgive
the tyrant fool for whipping him. The smells
of steam and cooking mix with yellow cheeses
when suddenly the wrathful tailor seizes
a belt and flogs his son for rotten grades!
Last drama. Twelve years old, my father leaves
his home and school for good. The tailor fades
from all of us forever, stitching sleeves.

As for my Dad, who was a proud Jewish liberal, he was part of the political romance in those days between "Jews and Negroes," who saw their common histories of slavery and discrimination as a bond. I never heard him say one negative word about black people. In fact, he was always upset by the treatment of black people in America. He seldom spoke about the problems Jews might have had in those days, except a rare comment on "the places you couldn't get into" if they *spotted* you.

Othello

My father is singing in the bathroom of the master bedroom. The green bed, a Chinese rug alongside, the small hall, really a dressing room, and then my father shaving and singing. It's operetta or a love song from the same *Chocolate Soldier* Sigmund

Romberg era. That mellow tenor is proud; he is romantic about his deep semi-trained warble. He's Caruso in love as his voice wavers from the north end of the apartment.

We go to all the operettas by Hungarians and Austrians that come to town. The theaters are formal—it's not Chico Marx at the 10,000-seat Roxy—and I see a lot of red rugs, red-cushioned seats, and women in uniforms who smile knowingly and who have thin flashlights to guide us properly through the crowded darkness to our seats. Dad always tips at least two quarters. The atmosphere is at once humming and hushed as we wait for the orchestra to start. Once the lead tenor begins to hop around in stage clothes and screech and shout, Dad, very discreetly, is singing under his breath.

My voice is awful, though I too like to sing. The shower and my room, when no one's in the house, are the only safe places I belt out songs, off-key, always hearing in my head the other aspiring voice down the hall. His voice hums in me. I really care to do things right and would sing songs in tune if I could. But it would not be beautiful like his song.

On this Sunday morning Dad comes into my room and takes my hand. I'm by the window, where, if I'm not reading, I often sit to look at the Drive and the Hudson River. He's very strange today. Up to something. I see a hidden twinkle. I wonder if he has another operetta up his sleeve.

"Billy."

"What's up Dad?" I'm sitting on a chair near the window, reading *Green Mansions* by a man named Hudson, who's got me loony over Rima, the girl of the South American jungle. It's Sunday, almost noon, and father has his gray pin-stripe on, his overcoat on his arm, ready to go out. What's he doing all dressed up at loafing time?

"Since everyone knows you've turned into a reading monkey," he tells me, "Blondie and I think we have to do something about it."

"What you going to do?" He's giving me malarkey. "Get a leash for me? How about some bananas? This monkey's starving."

"We'll have a good talk, and then I'll take you to some place civilized in order to turn you back into a recognizable two-legged human being."

"You mean we're going to a game? Is it the Yanks?"

"Worse than that."

"What's worse than the Yanks?"

"Shakespeare."

"Boy, he stinks. At least *Julius Caesar* does." We've just finished reading it with Miss Howard. Brutus gave me the creeps.

"Have you heard of *Othello*, you dumb-ox? He doesn't stink."

"Sorry, Dad. Don't know who he is yet. Is Othello some kind of butler?"

"You're stabbing in the dark," he says deadpan. "Othello means *little* Otto, and a little Otto might be a little butler. But Shakespeare didn't write a great drama about little Otto the butler."

"Then is he a fancy Englishman, with a title, walking around his country estate?"

"You're getting hot," he laughs.

"Come on, Pop. Spill it."

"Othello is a noble Moor in the service of the Venetian state."

Dad has this way of sounding stuffy when he wants to be funny. "Like that Englishman after all," I say. "Yeah, I remember. He's a colored man, who is supposed to be noble like Leah."

"This afternoon *Othello* will be performed by Paul Robeson," Dad explains. I'm waiting for the lecture and the big words. But he sits me down on the bed and gives it to me straight.

"Robeson is someone I personally admire. Wait until you hear him. This colored gentleman is everything. He is the son of a runaway slave who became a minister. A four-letter athlete at Rutgers, a Columbia University lawyer, the best bass singer around today—his specialty being "Ol' Man River"—and the only black man playing Othello they allow to walk out on a white stage."

"What a character!" I'm thinking quick. "Listen, Ol' Man River," I tell my Dad. "I got a hunch. Why don't we call up Leah, and ask her to come along? You know how smart she is. With all the books she reads, I bet she knows *Othello* by heart."

Dad pauses a moment, with his serious face on, and I almost fall over when he picks up the phone.

"No emergency, Leah, and please don't worry," he's insisting. "It's just that Willis asked if you might be free to meet us downtown, outside the theater at two-thirty, for the matinee of *Othello*? I'm sorry to call you at the last moment and on a Sunday," he says correctly.

We're on 47th off Broadway outside a plush theater, and Leah, dressed to kill in a white suit, is waiting for us at the glass doors. She's not wearing her glasses. The theatergoers are standing and chatting around the ticket booth, looking as if they're already sipping a cocktail. I bet they guess our maid, Miss Leah Scott, is a well-known actress.

The man at the box-office, who may be the manager, asks Dad who Leah is. He asks him very politely.

"Is your friend, the lady, a celebrity from England?"

We smell a rat and already Father's turning colors. I whisper in his ear, "Cool your engines, Dad."

Leah takes my hand.

"Is it your custom to inquire into the background of the guests of our nation?" Father says, very stern. He's giving it to him as he knows how. His voice is pure ice. I thought he was going to make Leah into Paul Robeson's English cousin, but he stopped at just the right place. If Eliot were with us, I know the Turd. Even though he's only ten, he'd put his two cents in and tell the jerk something like "Shut up, shithole," and they wouldn't let any of us in.

"Sorry, Mister. Just curious." And the man smartly hands us three tickets for the orchestra.

Inside, before the curtain goes up, we take our good seats in the spitbox, close to the stage, Dad and I on either side of Leah, who's in seventh heaven. And I'm up there too. I've seen a lot of professional football and baseball games but never a Broadway play. I don't know what it's going to be like. It's surprising how once you're in a classy joint you begin to feel and act different. Suddenly I love Shakespeare, and the play hasn't even started.

Since Dad tipped me off about all the things Paul Robeson is, when the Moor first comes on stage it takes a while before I can forget he's also a football player and a singer. "What do you think, Pop," I whisper again in his ear, very loud, leaning across Leah's lap.

"Leah and I think you're full of good ideas."

"Lay off. You make me sick."

I get very embarrassed when Dad makes me happy like that, and anything can come out of my mouth. I have trouble taking compliments or gifts. If someone offers me a toothpick, I might crack up. The people behind are shushing us.

Iago is a hypocrite. Desdemona is as beautiful as her name. But I'm with Othello. Although I miss a lot of words, I want to get up on stage and tell Othello not to be such a dope. They're always hitting him also for being colored. Iago acts like his closest friend, but even on his wedding night he calls the Moor a black ram. He tells Desdemona's own father,

> Even now, now, very now, an old black ram
> Is tupping your white ewe.

I'm getting nervous. Othello convinces me it's stupid to be jealous. It's making him into a madman, and yet he's a good man and a great man. "Cold, cold, my girl!" After sticking the dagger in Desdemona, the Moor falls apart. "Blow me about in winds! roast me in sulphur! Wash me in steep-down gulfs of liquid fire! O Desdemona! Desdemona! dead! Oh! Oh! Oh!"

I wish he had thought of it before he did it.

When he talks about being a base Indian throwing a pearl away, Leah squeezes my hand so hard she's breaking it. Her face is full of tears. Since she'd put on her glasses, she has to take them off and wipe them to see. "Drop tears as fast as the Arabian trees

Paul Robeson as Othello, London, 1930 (Paul Robeson, Jr.)

their medicinal gum." These speeches are the greatest words I've ever heard. They also beat a Mayor La Guardia talk or any book I've read.

> Set you down this;
> And say besides, that in Aleppo once,
> Where a malignant and a turban'd Turk
> Beat a Venetian and traduced the state,
> I took by the throat the circumcised dog,
>   [*stabs himself*]
> And smote him, thus.

And he dies upon a kiss.

When Othello falls on his sword, Dad trembles. He tells me, hiding the tremble, "*Othello* is personally my favorite play by Shakespeare."

We don't walk out of the theater. We are washed away. Leah hasn't said more than a dozen words since we came in, and she's the only one with a real English accent. She's got more rights than anyone to talk, especially since she's a bookworm. Dad takes me aside. He's upset. He tells me confidentially that he wants to go to a nice restaurant nearby to relax, to talk over the play with me and Leah, but he says they wouldn't let us in a nice place with her. He likes colored people, since his stepmother is one, and hates all these rules.

We decide to take a taxi, all three of us. We don't even discuss the drama in the cab. It's a long interesting silence. The play is going on in our minds, at least a good part of it. When we reach our building, Dad won't let Leah get out to walk to the subway and take a train the rest of the way up to Lennox Avenue. He slips the cabby an extra few bucks and gives him instructions.

We hop out, standing there in the windy cold, our breath steaming, as the driver puts his money away. I'm huddled next to Dad. Rocking on my shoes. Leah has rolled down the window. She looks very pretty. She is stately in her white suit.

"Thank you, Mr. Barnstone," Leah says. "I had a very wonderful afternoon." Then she looks at me, beckons me to her, and
through the window gives me one of her smackers on the lips.

"We thank you, Leah, for your company," Father says warmly,
in his minister's voice. "Both of us do, sincerely."

And Leah speeds away up to Harlem in the yellow cab.

Reading the Bible in Hebrew

The closest I got to a good childhood reading-knowledge of biblical
Hebrew was during the years immediately before and after my bar
mitzvah (at age thirteen). After years of private tutoring lessons, reading
Hebrew with Mr. Segal, whom I liked immensely, I hadn't learned much.
I was a bad pupil and needed a more formal discipline. I forgot as quickly
as I learned and couldn't do much more than sound out the black Hebrew
characters. My vocabulary was pitiful. But then I was sent to an enlightened school, the Jewish Center on 86th Street near Central Park West,
where we read biblical texts three nights a week. We began with resonant
Genesis, with its formulaic speech, which is easy because of the repetition.
We followed Joseph into Egypt and observed the dreamers and the
dreams. Miss Fischer was excellent, spirited, and so were we. It was
thrilling to understand the text in its original Hebrew and to do so
together in a group. In retrospect I still see our classroom brimming with
an intellectual eagerness—from students and teacher—the first of this
kind I was to experience in an academic setting. It was a conspiracy of fun,
discovery, and knowledge. I didn't experience the same fervor until one
year at Columbia when I took a graduate seminar in close-reading of
Dylan Thomas and Joyce, and among the smart students a nun and a
rabbi kept us in stitches with their endless whimsy and scholarship.

But even the Hebrew from these years didn't stick. Later, as a professor, I followed a few semesters of classical Hebrew at Indiana University, but until this course about all I really retained from childhood was a
few hundred words and a deep intimacy with the Hebrew alphabet, that
backward-written, fattish, and rather beautiful set of letters. Those exotic
shapes have always seemed natural to me. Even after decades of reading

modern and ancient Greek, the Greek alphabet, which I love, is pleasantly alien. I didn't start soon enough.

The specific goal of private lessons and Hebrew School was to get me
through the obstacle of the bar mitzvah, which effectively assured that
every young Jewish male was literate. In my lifetime, the bar mitzvah has
taken on a wacky side. Bar mitzvah jokes are to a boy what JAP (Jewish
American Princess) jokes are to a young woman. But my experience with
the actual event was very dark and humorless.

Bar Mitzvah

We read out loud. It's for my grandparents, who are dead, I'm
doing this, my folks tell me. In another class they teach me to
chant according to the notations on the biblical passages. The
entire Bible becomes a song. Shir Hashirim (The Song of Songs),
is the best, the book for lovers and heretical mystics. I'm thirteen
and must lead a congregation. The shawl is a kind of large cape
with fine stripes like an expensive silk shirt musicians wear. And
it's mysterious, maybe because it is also a flag of faith I don't have
at all.

My voice is small but disagreeable. They train me until my
baritone-soprano of adolescence is less out of control. Of course
I always like to sing by myself, loud, however bad. They train me
to sing in the big holy room for the congregation at the school.
There is a purpose in all this singing.

The showdown Saturday morning has come. The family is
retrenching economically—their words—so on this Saturday
they don't take me to the elaborate synagogue at the 86th Jewish
Center but to a modest, tiny-room temple. It's a hidden sanctuary behind a butcher shop on upper Broadway. Since it's a
kosher butcher, the meat-cutting and selling activity is on hold
for the day because of *shabbat*. We cross the sawdust floor, where
all the big knives and choppers are also celebrating a day of rest,
hanging with no meat-cutting and slapping for the day.

We enter a bare anteroom passageway and then go into the

small run-down hall with a few strangers, none of them young, and no friends or relatives, except for Mom and Dad who, for my benefit, show up together. I go to the altar and chant. My training saves me, but I'm doing it for no one. It never occurs to me that God is listening in and checking out the performance. The melody is haunting, despite my voice. I get through yet am deeply melancholy. This religious joint may have a lot of character, it may be a good period piece for a film or novel, yet I see no beauty in the sordid holy room behind the butcher shop. The griminess has nothing to do with it, I think—maybe I'm wrong, since if the ceremony took place somewhere in the Near East, as it once did, it would have to be old and run-down to be authentic. God knows why it's so depressing. I swim in these guilty thoughts.

In this sacred passage to adulthood I fail.

Did the lamb chop holy room have any later resonance? I don't know. I still don't fathom my alienation from its world, a world which has nothing—or is it everything?—to do with Franz Kafka's late obsessions with the Kabbalah. Once I will enter an old synagogue in Paris, and twice Santa María la Blanca, the synagogue in Toledo of the Spanish Jews, where Saint Teresa's Jewish parents worshiped until 1492. But except for Toledo, after the sawdust place with all its fascination of old world lingerings and those spacey strangers in their devout shawls, except for one afternoon in Paris at a special ceremony, I never again, at least not yet, enter a live Jewish temple of worship. The God of Israel has survived millennia of diaspora. He can survive, even benefit from my absence, my diaspora.

After the bar mitzvah, I strictly avoid the temple, but I go on another year and a half studying biblical Hebrew, and the class gets better and better, now more advanced, reading Job, Isaiah, Ecclesiastes, and the Psalms:

> If I take the wings of the morning and dwell in the
> uttermost parts of the sea.

> Even there shall thy hand lead me, and thy right hand
>   shall hold me.
> If I say, Surely the darkness shall cover me, even the night
>   shall be light around me.
> Yes, the darkness hideth not from thee; but the night
>   shineth as the day.

These lines in Hebrew are the first profound poetry I read. How can you get any deeper—unless you stumbled out through some medieval cobbled ghetto of Córdoba with *The Guide for the Perplexed* in your hand?

I wish I could have gone on with those bright kids and Miss Fischer. It was what the city offered, and I was lucky to have some of it. The prep school and private colleges offered other things. Anyway, by now, my brother thinks, I have enough of New York, of being a Jew, albeit from Maine, and it's time to think seriously of college—and how to get into a good one. He's thinking far ahead and about what will look good in the future. He's already been to Amherst and is now at Yale. So it's time to be a Quaker. College Admissions will like that. There are no quotas for Quakers. The Friends are a good idealistic group, and they themselves accept everybody (except Negroes), including Japanese during a war with Japan.

Othello's Rose

This is pure velvet,
    darned with strands
        of maiden hair,

the hem & sleeves
    frayed a bit. Years
        ago, when an admirer

sent it with an embossed
    certificate of authenticity,
        I wonder if she knew

she snared me in colors
    bright as Joseph's coat.
        All these towns along

the eastern seaboard
    & through the midwest,
        this damn robe's kept me

moving as if bloodhounds
    dogged my trail. Sweetheart,
        I must add your perfume

to that concoction
    stealing my senses. After
        each curtain call you sit

in my lap, hugging
    roses to your breasts,
        in the arms of Ira Aldridge

at the Theatre Royal
    in a gold-leafed room,
        riding the fantasy wheel

to its true mark.
    The African Roscius.
        Into my left sleeve

I tucked a woman's lace
    handkerchief & a letter
        from Sir Edmund Kean.

Born on Green Street,
    New York City, I arrived
        in Liverpool as the yesman

of James Wallack. After
    Shylock & Lear, it was still
        hard to keep my head

when Queen Adelaide
    awarded me the Verdienst
        Gold Medal. Forget

what Théophile Gautier
    said in St. Petersburg.
        As we travel from Boise

to Spokane, I hurt
    for Tolstoy's wit
        & Shevchenko's metaphors,

I hunger for the old days
    in Europe when they wanted
        to drag Iago off stage

& thrash him good. Now
    they only come to flesh
        out fears, & I can't help

but desire to wield a dagger
    that doesn't have a spring
        buried in a rhinestone handle.

—Yusef Komunyakaa

Early Jewish Corruption and Bayard Rustin, the Black Nightingale

There is a time to fight, there is a time to run away; and, to bring a poor clump of dirt into Eden, there is a time to sing like a black nightingale.

—PIERRE GRANGE, *Singing for Bread*

Early Corruption

My first encounter with deception and corruption occurred when I applied for admission to George School, one of the most enlightened schools in the country. There were a few Jews there, and it was probably not necessary to lie on one's application blank, but we didn't know this or couldn't be sure. In having not only a few Jews as students but a Japanese teacher, George School was truly unique. As for Blacks, not yet. In 1942, nowhere in the United States were Blacks admitted to a private school.

Corruption of the spirit is complex and diverse. It begins when one is forced to make a choice in an evil situation.

In the *Politics*, Aristotle's first moral generalization is that in a good state a good man (man or woman) is a good citizen. This is straightforward, easy for the man and citizen, for there is no immediate temptation to subvert. However, in a bad state, a bad man is a good citizen while a good man is a bad citizen. The bad state yields to state corruption and a subsequent exoneration of compromised behavior as a matter of survival and sometimes of virtue, as in contemporary totalitarian states where dissidence by a "bad" citizen is a courageous and risky act. Sometimes state corruption may soften evil, as in Italy during the war, when Italian corruption provided a measure of freedom compared to Nazi draconian order. In a very bad state, where there seem to be no right public or personal ways, the significance of one's actions is questionable and morally blurry. I know mine were.

The age of my youth was one of stifling discrimination against Jews—urbane, smug, academic, business, and social—and of absolute legal segregation of Blacks in the South, with a fate only a little better in the North. By comparison, pre-Hitler Germany and Austria—despite a deeply anti-Semitic tradition seen in all quarters (including Wagner's vituperatively jealous letters about the French-German Jewish composer Jacques Offenbach, born *Jakob Eberscht*) and persisting into the 1930s—were better places for Jews. In Berlin and Vienna, Jews flourished in the arts and sciences and were prominent in the universities as teachers and students. This widespread integration of the Jew had no counterpart at that time in America. France was uneven, yet Léon Blum (1870–1950), a Jew, served as her prime minister before and after World War II. In the

United States it was considered a major breakthrough even as late as 1960 when John Kennedy, a Catholic, was elected president. Now the Catholics have made it, and the pervasive climate of urbane antisemitism has faded, though other ethnic madnesses have replaced it. The Black remains down under, and each improvement in the life of African Americans is matched by a fearful step backward.

In the bad old days of my childhood, one's response to the politics of exclusion was tricky and always painful. A common response was to dissemble.

My brother knew this when his applications to Ivy League schools were denied the first year. The next year he lied about "religious affiliation" and was accepted at Amherst and later at Yale. I was not quite fourteen and had no experience in these contests with admissions committees. Every application asked for religious preference. The required photograph spotted Blacks or other people of color. In response to the fearful blank about religion, my brother counseled me not to put down "Jewish." Mother said I should listen to my brother, who knew what was right. For applications to the "good" schools, at all levels, to enter "Jewish" would almost certainly mean rejection. There were exceptions— Leonard Bernstein was taken by Harvard—but they were very few. After so many decades I am not sure what I wrote in the blank, but I know it wasn't "Jewish." As I remember, Howard came up with an untrue and evasive "Ethical Culture," referring to a group that seemed like a religion but that, like the Quakers and Unitarians, stressed earthly behavior over transcendental happenings. Upper-middle-class professionals met on Sundays in the elegant Ethical Culture building near Central Park and fed their spirit on good sermons. God and his priests were absent. Many of the members were Jews disenchanted with traditional religious resources.

I suppose I was very uncomfortable. Whatever I felt at thirteen and fourteen, an age of denial had begun. It lasted a long time in one way or another. It was more serious than my mother's desire for me to retain the speech and appearance of a New Englander. (That didn't work.) But on paper I could disguise myself. Yet was it necessary? America was not evil Germany or occupied Europe where denial and concealment were obligatory to save your life. In the French film *Au revoir les enfants,* the boys are disguised as Catholics in a Catholic school until they are ratted on and then taken away to the death camps. A friend of mine, a French Jew, spent the first years of the war in a French convent, dressed as a nun and hidden by the nuns among them. She was seventeen when she was ratted on, and somehow, in part because of the strength of her youth, she survived two years in Auschwitz.

By comparison, the penalties of religion and race in America were minor. Denial and dissembling was a social and practical matter. It opened doors. But it took its toll on the denier, no matter what the justification and rationalization. The public shame of being a Jew was real (the shame of being a Black was immeasurably worse) and penetrated one's psyche. Rejection of that stupidity by way of ethnic pride, historical information, and spiritual enlightenment did not lighten the public reality. Hatred and degradation were common and transparent. If Jews are hated, be quiet. I was quiet and I lied. But in the end to respond to bigotry by cloaking one's religion, people, or whatever you want to call being a Jew exacted a soul price worse than any practical benefit from such disguisement.

Today, to my surprise, I can speak of concealment almost objectively, without horror or grave guilt. I am almost detached. Yet the catharsis I feel, even the need to lay it out in a memoir as a past record and a warning, suggests how deep the wounds once were, no matter who inflicted them—society, my family, or myself. Ironically, a Black, or a Jew with a Jewish name, had a distinct advantage over a Jew who could pass: there were no lurking temptations of concealment.

Yeshua ben Yosef Passing as Jesus Christ

The major corruption of historical identity is found in the New Covenant (New Testament). There the Jews began to conceal their background, or at least as they are presented in the Gospels. Yeshua ben Yosef, his family, and his followers try to pass. They speak demotic Greek, not even a Semitic language. This presentation is not theirs, however. There is no way that Yeshua, "King of the Jews," or John the Baptist (Yohanan the Dipper), who followed the Jewish rite of immersing, or Miryam or Yosef could have conceived of themselves as other than Jews. The stage of the Gospels is as inconceivable as if we were given Plato's dialogues with scenes of an historical Sokrates debating in Hebrew with the rabbis of the Second Temple.

Yet had Jesus not been able to conceal his Jewishness and pass as a Christian (as a follower of himself, the Jewish messiah), he would have been ripped off the cross in every church in the Third Reich and perhaps in all churches until he had denounced and sought pardon for his life and death as a Jew.

How did Jesus get himself into such a pickle?

He didn't. Others put him there.[1]

Over a period of a century after Jesus's death, the Jews who saw rabbi Yeshua as their messiah passed from being Christian Jews (*Christian* meaning "messianic," or Jews for whom the messiah had come) to being Jewish Christians, and ultimately to being Christians who in separation and extreme rivalry with traditional Jews saw their own or adopted ancestors as the children of Satan. Then, nourished by an evolving New Testament (scriptures originally gathered for, by, and about Jews), the leading messianics, who would in the next century be called Christians (the Greek translation of *messianics*), demonized their coreligionist Jews. And thereafter, antisemitism prospered all over the world.[2]

What is the historical basis for understanding the Jews in the period before the destruction of the Second Temple? Josephus (Yosef ben Mattias) is the main Jewish historian of the early Roman period, but he says little about Jesus, and even those few sentences are now known to have been added in the eighth century. Essentially, the life of Jesus has no significant source outside the Gospels. The principal record of all the Jews of antiquity appears in the Bible, its Old Testament and New Testament, which presents events in a commingling of history and faith. The books of the New Testament (New Covenant), surviving only in Greek like the Apocrypha in the Septuagint, were finally established by Bishop Athanasius of Alexandria in 367 c.e. and canonized by the pope in 401.

The Greek scriptures lack a Hebrew or Aramaic source. Only Paul wrote originally in Greek, and his seven authentic letters are by the one identifiable author in the scriptures—the other authorial names in the New Testament (and Old Testament) are pseudepigraphic. Jews are the main figures in both Old and New Testaments. In Torah (the Hebrew Bible), where there are disputes among Jews, these are presented as intra-family squabbles. In the New Testament, however, differences among sects are presented anachronistically as combats between Yeshua and his followers, against the faithless, evil Jews. But the Romans who executed Yeshua as a seditionist come through favorably. Even the centurion who commanded the execution squad (Richard Burton in the film) is the first to recognize, as he and his soldiers stare at the corpse in awe, that Jesus is God, is good, is innocent, and has risen.

Yeshua ben Yosef at the Stake

When they spike him and raise the T-cross,
he screams. Then flies buzz around the rabbi's
nose and none of his friends dare speak out.
All those hours of pain weaken him
with the insufferable iron in his ankles, hands.
He shouts to God, "Why don't you come?"
The soldiers laugh. "Let Yahweh save you,
Jew!" Pilatus is bored. He's crucified so many
of them. Miryam of Magdela alone
is brave enough to climb the knoll and sponge
his mouth. She kisses his dripping wounds.
Seconds left. It's Friday and the Seder. He'd be
with friends. Yeshua dies. The temple curtain tears.
Yeshua ben Yosef is tossed into the regular
garbage pit outside Yerushalayim, into the fire
of Gehenna, a black grave or a pearl
in heaven. The true story and man are dead.
The burning rabbi cannot open his eyes.

The achievement of concealing Yeshua's Jewishness occurred initially after the Roman destruction of Jerusalem in 70 c.e. and the expulsion of its traditional Jewish sects and Christian Jews. By the early second century an emerging Christianity began to separate itself from its Jewish core, though it retained the Old Testament as its sole scripture and it flourished in the synagogues, where it vied with other Jewish sects for mastery. Paul's letters were to congregations in Corinth, Rome, Antioch, Thessaloniki, and other cities of Hellenistic Judaism, and in them he debated with James, who represented a more traditional form of Judaism based in Jerusalem. Paul said in Romans that physical circumcision (reflecting the Abrahamic convent) was not necessary and could be replaced by a new circumcision in the heart, that is, by a new covenant of the spirit. Whereas Paul was in the trenches, proselytizing and mixing Judaism and neoplatonic cosmology to form the foundations of Christianity, the main representation of the life of Jesus is in the Gospels, where Yeshua the Messiah, his family, including his mother Miryam, and his students (disciples) are deracinated and effectively cease being Jews.[3]

The gospels as we have them are altered and amended with orphan endings to reflect views of a later Roman church that must invent a Pesach plot in order to exonerate Rome for executing a nationalist Jewish rebel. On the first night of Pesach in an absolutely implausible scene, Matthew (Levi) has the Jews out in the streets implausibly screaming their own everlasting blood curse: "His blood be on us and our children forever" (Matt. 27:24).

How have the gospels Christianized Jesus? He is not seen as a Jew. He vilifies the Jews and pronounces their eternal damnation. Except for his cry in Aramaic from the cross, he doesn't speak his own language. While occasionally he carries the epithet "rabbi Jesus" (elsewhere it has been edited out), in the some thirty instances where Yeshua is addressed as rabbi, this title in Latin translation and in other languages disappears. *Rabbi* becomes "master," "teacher," or "Lord Jesus." Even in Richmond Lattimore's wonderful New Testament (1962), accomplished as his last major work, the distinguished classical scholar follows the deplorable tradition of rendering each instance of *rabbi* as master, teacher, or Lord.

The gospels are beautiful and painful for a Jew to read. In the name of Yeshua ben Yosef, the most famous Jew in history, as Borges calls him, the Jew will be burned in Spain, will be massacred in a thousand places, and will wander as the eternal exile. In John's (Yohanan's) mysterious, esthetically wondrous, and deeply metaphysical gospel, it is not pleasant to hear Jesus fulminating against the Jews: "Ye are of your father the devil, the lusts of your father ye will do. He was a murderer from the beginning and abode not in the truth, because there is no truth in him" (John 8:44).

The question of Jews passing as Christians is very old.

My minor experience with dissembling is a tiny symptom of grandiose historical denial, yet it reflects a dominant spirit in the air and its wide practice of concealing the cursed assignation of the Jew, of the source of a Jewish sect that must now reject its mother and father. In the instance of the developing Christian sect, the original players had no part in the denial. The crucified rabbi did not, would not, could not have dreamed of being anything but the itinerant, charismatic rabbi. Similarly, the early Jewish followers of Jesus, including the apostles and evangelists, made no effort to disguise themselves. They were another rebellious sect, like the Essenes and Zealots, to name a few. But later denial was achieved in great part by redacting and shaping the Greek scriptures in such a way as to make Yeshua appear as a strange, alien God born in their midst.

The nineteenth-century French historian Ernest Renan asserted that Jesus wasn't a Jew at all but an Aryan Galilean, a notion the German Protestant church under the Third Reich enthusiastically adopted. This notion of an Aryan Christ, a Messiah who wasn't even a Jew, provided the perfect cover.[4] This deracination was necessary and inevitable if the new sect of Messianic Jews was to achieve independence from traditional Jewry. In their anxiety they simply had to kill the father. The cover-up persisted for two millennia; even today it is seldom understood, and when so, very poorly, by Jew and gentile alike.

As someone who has stumbled into Bible studies, I should laugh, and I do sometimes, at texts, at jumbled identities, at me, at the world stumbling along with understandings and misunderstandings, at ideas of love and ideas of hatred, so many derived from the sacred. There is language of extraordinary beauty; there are aphorisms of a popular nature that taste of the universal sages of Asia; but the Bible also gives us sectarian anger, self-pity (which is worse), and revenge. I cannot wish it to be destroyed. But I wish it had not lived in our experience as it has.

So Long, Sammy

I want to go to Music and Arts High School, take the test but I flunk. I also take the exam for Peter Stuyvesant, a science school, and this one I pass. So I'll be a scientist, not an artist. We've also moved from Riverside Drive to midtown, to Central Park South, and now I go to school by subway, shooting downtown and changing at 14th for the Canarsy line. I'm good at chemistry, trig, and Latin, not much good at English. By now I'm into diving, and once after a meet with some other school, they write up the match in the Stuyvesant school paper, doing a number on my name. A pal, who only knows me as Bill, comes up to me in the hall and says, pretty excited, "Say, you hear about the new guy who won the diving event, Billy Barnstoni, an Italian kid?"

"Yeah, I know who he is."

Now that we're midtown, where no kids hang out around the buildings, I'm on a hello basis with some guys at Stuyvesant and am in awe of old Mr. Cohen, my art teacher, who has me draw with colored pencils, and likes freedom, "freedom with a pencil," he says. And there are the fellows I've deserted from uptown. Sammy and his ten grandfathers have moved to Los Angeles. It's hard to imagine all that black furniture, the striped shawls, prayer books, and black hats in the West among the cowboys, orange trees, and European actors and writers. When Sammy left, he looked a hundred years old; he was carrying a slide-rule and had decided to become an engineer. But he had that other side, the smile, which was still so huge, especially the last day when it had canyons and canyons inside it, and no end in sight.

At Stuyvesant I hear my first stories about sex. In Latin class I share a seat with a boy who stinks of garlic and piss. Besides, he's got lots of pimples on an unshaven face. He can't be more than fifteen or sixteen (I'm almost fourteen) but his slick sandy hair already looks thin. He doesn't take off his leather jacket in class, which makes it even more crowded. When he talks to me about two girls he screwed last night behind a car in a Brooklyn parking lot, I almost pass out. I'm breathless.

"Two? What do you mean two? How can you screw two girls at the same time? How many cocks do you have?"

"You dope," he tells me. "We were two guys and stuck 'em one at a time. Then we switched."

But Stuyvesant doesn't last long. One good year of cramming for science and I'm off to prep school. It's time to make me over.

Off to the Quakers

The Jewish thing was on hold at George School. Completely. There were a few Jews in the school and me. Two of them were Stephen Sondheim and George Segal (a class behind me), whom I have no memory of knowing then. I never spoke to the Jews as coreligionists. No one did that in New York either. I didn't feel bad. I just didn't think about it. I never mentioned to anyone that I was a Jew, no one asked, and I don't think anyone told me what they were either, except for those who were Quakers. I was quickly becoming a Quaker too, at least by conviction and pleasure, since Quakers were for peace, thought, and light, and were of the earth, not a site in the sky.

Bayard Rustin, the Black Nightingale Singing His People into the Heart of the Makers of the Underground Railroad

The Quakers have no religious texts—or if they do, they don't use them. They are ethical but also have no old or new poets—except for the beautiful Shaker songs. (The Shaker clan of the Quakers have quietly almost died out since they were not for making love). Quakers have no songs of the Shulamite and her lover, who spent the night as a bouquet of myrrh lying between her breasts, or of the deer who grazed among the mountain lilies; they have no poet Judah Halevi from Tudela, who confesses that

Bayard Rustin

his heart is in the East, who affirms in the early twelfth century that in Spain, at the edge of the West, he cannot taste what he eats, that he must leave good things of Spain to see the glorious dust of a ruined shrine in Zion.

But Quakers have the light, the inner light, and outer good works.

From New York I leave behind stickball and streets, roller skates, elevators, the Polo Grounds Giants and the last of the mob, Babe Ruth, and instruction in reading the Shulamite and Judah Halevi. I change my life, accent, beliefs, sport coat, manners; and I come upon the "inner light" of the quaking Friends. Waiting there for students are the ways to interior brightness, explained and ready to be personally discovered in a school in the woods and rolling fields of Bucks County, Pennsyl-

vania. George School is only twenty-five miles north of Philadelphia, the first city of the Quakers and of their earliest governor, William Penn.

My first irreversible contagion of dirty jokes, pranks, women,
social conscience, civil rights, and meditation I pick up at this
Friends boarding school. Ethical flavor is equal to the constant
smell of breakfast cakes in the large dining hall, which lingers in
the hallway where we students hang out and even creeps into the
administrative offices off the corridor, including the forbidding
one of the Pope (our headmaster), an unknown den for most of
us. That other flavor—the ethical one—shapes me with its
omnipresent taste of guilt and deeds for peace.

One morning Bayard Rustin is the speaker at assembly. We
learn from him about Blacks and private schools. They don't jive.
There are no Blacks at private schools. Students and teachers
insist that the dialogue continue, so for three days we meet in the
assembly hall in classrooms; everybody is meeting everybody,
including the Pope, all with the intention of tearing down the
walls of bigotry that have denied entry to black students. We are
driven by Rustin's speech and his song. His almost countertenor
voice, the voice of the invisible nightingale, is behind his words.
And on stage when he doesn't talk, he actually sings. It's more
than we can take. The school is in turmoil, classes suspend regular
programs to discuss integration. We have to act, and we do.

With Bayard Rustin, the early black activist, speaking and
singing, we slip en masse into a dramatic group dream of the
Underground Railroad when Quakers secreted the slaves North.
Before and especially during the Civil War, the Quakers were
abolitionists, even in the South, and did something about it,
risking their own lives by working closely with black people for
their freedom.

Now the former slaves have an outrageous agenda: they want
to study at a Quaker school, but our good school board won't let
Paul Robeson's son or any Black in—until Rustin sings. We hear
that Paul Robeson's romance with the Soviet Union came when
even George School, a liberal place near his hometown in New

Jersey, wouldn't let his son Paul study there. So, we were told, he put him in a high school in Moscow. And Paul Robeson never came home to America.

Bayard Rustin has come to change our ways. He talks and sings spirituals for three days about the grief of the Blacks and their exile in our country. Our institution is transformed—its students, faculty, and staff. We go to class, but there is only one burning mission in everybody's mind. Break the color barrier. Let Blacks study. Rustin, the singing man of spirit (who many years later will die of AIDS after a long life of major activist missions) has opened eyes, and the George School Overseers Board caves. We become the first private school in the United States to become integrated. It is 1943.

It is time.

A few months later, Rustin, who was brought up as a Quaker and who worked frequently for the American Friends Service Committee, refused to register for the draft. He also declined alternative service in camps set up by Quakers and other religious pacifists and so served three years in the federal penitentiary as his form of protest against war. Later he was to persuade Martin Luther King to remove the arms from his house—the house was loaded with "protective" weapons in case any of the many of the threats against him were carried out. Rustin's message of non-violence, formulated in India as a result of his friendship with Gandhi, was to become a touchstone of King's philosophy and entire peace movement. Rustin organized the huge 1963 March on Washington for Jobs and Freedom where King gave his "I Have a Dream" speech. He succeeded in having chain gangs abolished in North Carolina, worked on behalf of the Viet-namese "boat people" and Cambodians refugees in Thailand, and was an active member of the Holocaust Memorial Council. He was everywhere, singing, organizing. Before he died, he had received more than a dozen honorary doctorates from distinguished universities.

A few days earlier a soprano, Elizabeth Schwartzkopf, sang strong and perfectly, but when Bayard Rustin, standing on stage in the assembly, elegantly pure and alone, sings his freedom songs, sliding ecstatically up into countertenor range, every soul is with him in feeling and conviction, and we know the inner light.

In the dorm my farmer roommates keep bushels of apples under their bunks, seeding them among us circumspectly, as if measuring rainfall. Big Jack has an iron plate in his skull (showing on a third of his forehead) from a tractor crash. When we measure our dicks in the dark, he claims his is eight inches. It is raining. Pails of water fall regularly on anyone entering the rigged door to our room. We also manufacture balloon bombs by slipping the mouth of a condom over a faucet head, forcing water into the rubber, and filling it until it wobbles from its own weight, ready to explode. Then at night we drop the water bombs out the window on late students walking underneath, usually fellows, not girls, and also on the old night watchman, Bucket-balls, as he plods around with his cane and tilting lantern. They call him Bucketballs because of the big baggy thing bouncing under his pants as he goes the rounds. But I'm doubtful. I'd be surprised if what's swinging back and forth is really his balls.

After lights out, boys sneak from room to room in the dark-ness. Timothy, a senior about to leave for Harvard in classics, asks me to lie down in his bunk bed, then takes my hand and puts it on his penis, holding my fingers on his rod, pumping it up and down, trying to get me to jerk him off. He's talking to me rapidly about Socrates and Aristophanes, and he comes immediately. It all happened so quickly. Then he offers to whack me off. I refuse and get out of the bed. Truth is, I had never heard anything at all about homosexuality, but after falling into his lights-out trap, the way I see it, I'm annoyed at Timothy.

Later on I find out there is a whole thing about and against homos. "If you can't get a woman, get a Harvard man," is the singsong saying. Timothy goes on to Harvard. At George School there are snickers, but no big deal. It's not a cause.

Though both my roommates are virgins, they talk low from

bunk to bunk for hours in the dark, telling the most elaborately obscene jokes about laying women, about a truck driver who loses his boot inside an eager whore in the back room of a truck stop and climbs inside to get it but finds just an old man, holding a lantern, looking for his horse and wagon. Jeffrey's going nutty about Betsy West's breasts and her red hair. I want to play kneesie with Betty Ross at supper but am hesitant. I need another year around women.

Women are my other planet. They're out there, warm, closer to the sun, in an orbit I can look at from far; maybe they're on Venus or Mercury, but there's no way of taking a spaceship and spending a few good hours with them. The girls' dorms are off limits. Only Norman and Rosie, kids of Philadelphia Quaker officials, go off to meet in the woods to smoke and take their clothes off together. They got caught once, but they still keep on going.

I have written notes to girls, hand-carried late at night. I've watched them as they walk and gossip. As they giggle at me. No, but I'm still an outsider. I've followed them but failed to say hello. I wait for them to rescue me. We've just read "Prufrock" in English class, and while my arms and hair are not getting thin, and I'm certainly not sprawling on a pin, wriggling on the wall, and no eternal Footman holds my coat and snickers, some of the girls snicker, and when they do, I think they must be right. Will I ever learn about women or mermaids singing or that race apart? I see them as beautiful flesh with light inside and out of reach.

If there are races at all, they are a wonderful one, endlessly desirable and harboring unceasing mystery of the near-familiar but remote, and one day I want to marry into it—if they'll let an outsider in to share their light.

The other element I cannot know is that elusive illumination the Quaker thinkers talk about. The flooding of light inside all of us that shows all, changes all, and gives us words (though maybe inexact and distant ones) to describe the experience. In fact, the

Quakers say that the words, which are at best metaphors, may not work at all, since in the end, light is light and words are words.

So while light may give words, light is not words. In that critical connection and separation, I think, is all the creation and despair of knowledge.

Despite all my anti-religion, all my anti-God fuss against a false, deified bully, the Quakers trigger in me a lifelong obsession with difference that will later lead me from the ladders of Philo the Jew to Jacob Boehme's gleaming tin vessel, from John of the Cross's darknesses and sonorous silence of love to Jorge Luis Borges's otherness, who glances though algebras and labyrinths but never finds light, truth, or any false and constricting absolute.

In such moments of George School's "inner light" sessions, one is supposed to be elsewhere, and it may be so intense and different that it is not only hard to describe but even hard to recall, as if one were coming out of dream or oblivion. Yet it is the essential Quaker experience. They say it is a universal one—from shamans in central Asia to early mystics in the West. The Friends' school starts me off with a good ignorance of women and love, and slowly I learn about meditation—although I never stand up to receive a Quaker luminescence and begin to talk. For while I now look at darkness and see that there is a universe of darkness under and behind my eyes, a knowledge of that inner light is not mine.

It has not illumined me.

Summer gone, winter here, and again in Pennsylvania at George School, where they teach all kinds of love but not of the lips, and certainly not of the groins, nor of the crotch of a tree under which a demented aunt might sit and muse about loves in her youth. The Quakers are for the spirit and for people. We're told not to hate or kill, even if Nazis wipe us out. And love comes from that inner light, and when it comes, you stand up to share and speak about it publicly with friends. Although we are thinking about it all the time, no one speaks publicly about love between two bodies in a bed. The Quakers—today at least—are not Puritans fixed on bodily rejection and heavenly selection. They're just more interested in other human matters.

The last love, good for life, I don't know is mine. It is the poem. The disease, the obsession, the failure, the solitude. I do not know it yet. No poem is written or even conceived. Yet its presence, slyly, has begun to enter my ear, if not my off-key humming tongue. A summer later, during an all-night walk in moonlighted green fields of northern Vermont, my closest friend, Jaime Salinas, a Spaniard, tells me, exasperated, arguing, *"En tu caso,* Willis, *es distinto, porque tú eres poeta"* (In your case, Willis, it's different, since you're a poet). I argue back, telling him I've never written a poem in my life. Or thought about it. But it's lurking. In a few years, nearby in northern Maine in Hawthorne's old freezing dorm room, it, the poem, the lifelong sickness of solitude, with no apparent warning will wake me in the dark out of my sleep. Then, while the half-moon is still high on the coldest night of the year, I reach for a scrap of paper and a pencil.

George School and poetry. First, Robert Peter Tristram Coffin from Brunswick, Maine, introduced as the New England Yeats, sings his ballads as a cappella liturgy, transforming the auditorium into a dreamy chapel. He was not very good. Then Robert Frost from Ripton, Vermont, comes to chant birches. I liked Frost then and always. While the old man vainly intones his simple deep verses, while his New England nights and mornings come alive with death, madness, haunted wives, hired hands, and an old man sleeping alone in a winter farmhouse, in my ear I hear another song. It is that ethereal gentleman from last year, who sang his verses in a high tenor voice. He sang of the new Jerusalem for all peoples. He recalled the melodies that emerged even from the slave ships, the chains, and the auction blocks. And he turned suffering and death and slavery into notes of compassionate beauty. The song transcended its literal meaning and became, compellingly, a song, a mission, an alto note of faith. I hear the activist, this magnetic Black who single-handedly informed the conscience of a Quaker boarding school and caused the first African Americans to be admitted to the private domain of white preppy instruction, whose example would soon spread across the nation. I hear the handsome, enigmatic Mr. Bayard Rustin on stage in the assembly hall, singing poems like an angel, like a black nightingale.

More Deadly Application Blanks

I have learned to live without regret. I really have, though in the past I was an awful regretter. I can't say why or how I came upon the strength or luck or whatever it was to cast regret to the winds. Perhaps because I became convinced that mistakes always help, like choosing jobs and women, typos, or miscounting lines of a sonnet. Mistake and accident always lead to something better if one has the eyes to see. The mistake I made at George School was to leave it. The war was raging, and I expected to be drafted, and so, like others, I "accelerated." That meant by taking extra courses and going to summer school, I could go to college a year earlier. I was already a year ahead when I got to George School, since I came from the New York school system which allowed you to "skip" if you did okay in the classes. I'd heard that if one could get some college in before being drafted, it would be better.

But by leaving George School early and entering college early, at age sixteen, I lost the chance to read Virgil in third-year Latin, to learn to be a bit more natural with women, and to go to a school I really wanted to go to. As it was, I entered all-male Bowdoin incredibly immature, and I was still seventeen when the war ended, which canceled the purpose of accelerating. (I was drafted nine years later, for the Korean Conflict—when the army sent me to France.) But during this period of looking around at schools, I didn't have my brother to advise me with the applications. He was a young officer in the navy.

I've never been good about applications and deadlines. Later I did well in obtaining fellowships, but I wonder if I would have under today's stricter rules. I filled out an application to Amherst but never put it into the envelope. I really wanted to go to Swarthmore, a Quaker co-ed college, but I never asked for an application. Don't ask me why. The one school I applied to was Yale, and they turned me down. For the religious blank, I wrote "Quaker." I didn't have my brother and mother prodding me. I did it on my own. I think they turned me down because my application, the smudgy work of a fifteen-year-old, wasn't very good, not because they suspected that Barnstone was Bernstein or even its variation, Bornstein. Even today, many people either hear Bernstein (meaning "amber" in German or literally "burning stone) when I say Barnstone, and my pals in the know often kid me for having a phony name. I love the name Barnstone, as I do Willis (one lacking will). A "barn stone" is a thing in nature. And I've lived most of my adult life in a rebuilt barn, which my brother designed.

Since my father was a jeweler, importing Swiss watches, he imported, at my sister's suggestion, a watch with our own mark on it: Pierre Grange (meaning Stone Barn). They were beautiful watches that he designed, with Corbusier-like shapes, and in the last years I always quote Pierre Grange in scholarly and creative books. He's very kind to me and lets me say what I would not feel as comfortable saying myself. He also has a mind of his own and gets inspired to say aphoristic words and quotable paragraphs I'd never come upon or dream up. For my book *The Poetics of Translation: History, Theory & Practice* (Yale, 1995), he was unduly generous. I cited him epigraphically and in many tight spots. Conforming with proper acknowledgments, in the bibliography I had his diverse books and essays all translated from the French by a Pole living in France, Velvel Bornstein. If my grandparents had stayed on in eastern Poland until the village of Haradok was bulldozed by the Nazis and the people taken away, or if I had ventured to live with my parents in Warsaw itself, I would have carried the good name of Velvel Bornstein. Soon after the war I went to Warsaw and was taken to the ghetto by a friend, Bronislaw Zielinski. He had been in the Polish resistance, was captured by the Germans and tortured by them; later he was tortured by the postwar government as a Catholic opponent.

Velvel Bornstein in the Warsaw Ghetto

I am a starving child. Outside
　　The gate the garbage stands
In cans. My father said to hide,
Not let the Germans get their hands

On me, but I can't stand it, so
　　I slip outside the gate
At sundown. I am like a crow
Pecking away at crumbs. It's late

And I try to sneak back, but a
　　Nice soldier grabs my arm
And picks me up. I'm miles away
From fear. It feels so far from harm

To have a healthy tall man hold
　　Me in his arms. He takes
Me to the center of the road
And talks to me. Carefree, he shakes

Hands with a buddy, grabs me tight
　　Again, and tighter. Then
He starts to hug me and I'm light
And happy, yet my oxygen

Begins to fade. I realize
　　He's choking me. I bite
His wrist. I kick. His giant size
Subdues me and I lose the fight.

I'm dead. He carts me to a man-
　　hole, lays me on the ground,
Opens it up, shoves all he can
Till I am drifting underground

In the black sewer under the square.
　　Bronislaw Zielinski sees
Me drown. Years later exactly where
I died, Bron tells my agonies

To an American in War-
   saw, who has come to be
My witness. That Jew and visitor
Is writing this. He could be me.

There were surely many joyous and fated Velvel Bornsteins in the prewar Pale, perhaps in my own unknown and disappeared family in the village of Harodok. But was there a real Pierre Grange? "Grange" is rare in France; "La Grange" plentiful, like "Miller." My dear friend Professor Pierre Citron recently wrote, informing me that he had found just two authors in the *Bibliotheque Nationale* in Paris with the names Pierre Grange. Their books were quite marvelous: *The History of Toads* and *The History of Conjugal Syphilis of the Nerves*. It's nice to be related to serious historians. As for my Polish friend, who looked exactly like a youngish Gregory Peck, a few months ago I read in the *Times* that Bronislaw Zielinski, the noted translator of Melville's *Moby Dick* and Hemingway's novels, had died. My dear Warsaw companion left. One day in those early postwar years, as we were walking through the ghetto—already elegantly rebuilt and no longer a site for Jews—Bron told me he had experienced and seen too much raw cruelty: "I am a ruined species. The option of forgiving or forgetting is not an option. We cannot forget. My generation must die."

Bronislaw was a prince. Indeed, sitting in his small place, still with very old, elegant furniture around him of another era, he confessed his long aristocratic ancestry, which he proudly contrasted with the upstart Russian nobility. As to forgetting, I must believe he did. At least enough so as to have had a whole existence, free of dark constancies.

Jews and Blacks in College, and Freedom in Europe

Human life began in Africa and the jungle is filled with dancing black guys and big-eyed sculptures, and the Jews are people of the Book who go nuts at klesma weddings. Niggers and kikes can't be all that bad. So if one of them wants in, let the fraternities open their doors wide. We need some fun.

—PEDRO GRANERO, *College as Lunacy*

Bowdoin College: The Jewish and Black Ghetto in Old Longfellow Hall

In addition to college, I had to apply to another prep school that had a summer semester, where I could finish up. I applied to Philips Academy at Exeter.

They took me, the young Quaker.

At Bowdoin the horror of being a Jew flowered. I helped it, of course. The heart of the sorrowful matter was there in every aspect. As always, it was worse for Blacks. Bowdoin had just one black student, Matt Branch. Happily, he fooled them all. He was better than a quiet hurricane. It didn't require one-hundred-fifty-mile-an-hour gale winds. It required his decency. And again, for the first time in private college history, at least as far as the ignominious fraternities go, he even became one of them, taking his chapter out of their national organization, which was the price for initiating a Black into an all-white national fraternity. My case was more complex, since I was working on several levels at once: a continuing denial, idealism, and very soon, activist outrage.

When I came to Bowdoin College in the autumn of 1944, I was wearing a tweed sports jacket and smoking a pipe; my body was good and well-trained—I would win my letter on the swimming team as a diver and come in fifth in the New England College Championships. My head was filled with endless idealism, but it had no self-righteous anger in it. My one-world eyes weren't cranky, just curious and adventurous. The Quakers, my months of working in Indian villages with the Society of Friends, and the light of the Friends had burned me. To come back to Maine, to the cold north, the beautiful north, and to be at the real level of learning in a good college, was all that a sixteen-year-old could ask for. My roommate, Nathan Whitman, an upperclassman, was an art historian and an intellectual model. I didn't like the lack of women. But that's how almost all the good Ivy League schools were. No women except in their own women's schools. And Maine fall was lovely. Very soon, however, I found that college was a big step down, not only from the ideals but from the decency of all the high schools I had been to.

I liked my professors and the classes. I had friends and wasn't lonely.

But I was not prepared for the overt, officialized bigotry that controlled the campus. The vets had not yet come back from the war. That was two years away and would indeed turn things upside down. They had fought in a war, and most of them wouldn't put up with the nonsense of big-man-on-campus politics, religious exclusionism, and fraternity domination. Bowdoin, to its glory, was the first college in America to bring the fraternity to its knees. But that took many years. Eventually, it abolished them altogether.

My first week at Bowdoin was registration, followed by "rush week," when fraternities courted all the incoming freshman class except for the Jews and Matt Branch, who was black. Since the frats had access to the files and could see my religious denomination as "Quaker," I was rushed. I hardly knew what was going on, which was part of the scene, but before I knew it I had pledged ATO. The first year we were all in the dorms. Twenty-two students in the school had not been pledged. Of these, twenty were Jewish, one was Black, and one was a short nonconformist tumbler who, with the slightest urging would do rolls, back flips, and cartwheels from one side of the room to the other and who, as my brothers said, did not look like fraternity material.

At George School there were so many new things going on that my silence on Judaism was minor, at least to me. But at Bowdoin, with the flagrant bias against Jews and Blacks, and the college, which permitted the fraternities to go happily on in their ways, the issues were increasingly becoming major. No one suffered from my prep school silence, and I don't think many people would have been too interested anyway. These matters were usually relegated to silence. At Bowdoin, however, there was suffering, because there was a group of students who were excluded from the social life of the campus. I should have been among them, but my concealment kept me nominally with the frat rats. I did take some measures. Rather than eat or live at my fraternity in their near-campus, I ate and lived with the Jews, who were herded together in one side of Hawthorne Hall, where I also lived. I never moved into the frat house, though I was a dues-paying member. So one part of me refused to move into the fraternity in order to stand in solidarity with the Jews (or do penance for my lie), while another part would not openly identify with the Jews. An abomination of the spirit. If I say I had been conditioned by my family and society to deny, it would be true and a cheap way to go. Well, it *was* a cheap way to go, but the superficial wounds of bigotry I experienced were deep enough to be habit, so in those bad days I stuck to evasion and false acceptance. I never felt good.

(Later I was to discover that passing was widespread, even by Jews who had been hounded out of Europe, though had I had this knowledge, I doubt that I could have rationalized it into better feelings. Nor can I today change judgment, though I am now at peace—somewhat.)

Because there were not enough students to justify keeping the Moulton Union dining room open, those of us who didn't eat at fraternities were given a rebate on the package room-and-board fees, and we trudged downtown to the greasy spoons for our meals both in the nice seasons and in winter in the dark snow in order to get back for an eight o'clock class. It was sordid.

I ate with the Jews, but I was not one of them. Actually, the question of who was and wasn't a Jew didn't come up (it was a bad subject), and we scarcely even spoke about the exclusion of the Jews. Everyone knew that fraternities didn't take Jews and Blacks. It was a fact, and that was it. I do remember that there was some prophetic talk that maybe the vets wouldn't stand for it. However, we did talk about Matt Branch, because he caused a sensation. Since Matt was a great athlete, a track star and college quarterback, on the Dean's List, and premed, he was as good as a White, and Sigma Nu fraternity, after the first semester, pledged him. He accepted. The Sigma Nu chapter was expelled from the national fraternity, had to invent a new Greek letter acronym, went "local," and that was it. It never went back on its decision, despite financial threats from Bowdoin Sigma Nu alumni and pressure from the nationals. So Bowdoin was the first school in the country to have a Black in a white fraternity, just as George School was the first prep school to admit a Black.

How did I feel about this? Most of the time I was thinking about calculus or the swimming team or my date at Wellesley. But when I did think about being a disguised Jew, I felt miserable. It was heavy. And I seemed paralyzed, caught in my own traps. And in the winter, Bowdoin was isolated and gloomy. In contrast to George School and Exeter, here the students were largely conformist, anti-intellectual, gentleman-Cgrade, good fellows. "Finks" or "grinds" were the epithets screamed at us as we walked near the Moulton Union by James Longley, president of the student body, the BMOC, and future governor of Maine. A terrible and superficial type. My own "shirking from origins" stayed with me all through college as this sonnet reveals. By then I was living in Hawthorne Hall:

Bowdoin, 1948

Hawthorne once had this yellowed room. We share
the morning gloom of alcoholics or
nocturnal masturbators, north and nowhere,
too isolated for a date or whore.
Were you a grind like me? A dreamer slob
and weird? I sleep, the window open to
the black Maine snow, hearing my roommate throb
and scream, an epileptic getting through
another siege. He's a philosopher;
I'm lost. But he was born a bastard, he
says bitterly; my origins I shirk
from. Worst (or best?) I doubt there is a me
concocting words in terrifying blur
within. Dream, Hawthorne. Words no longer work.

To be in the cauldron of bigotry, and specifically of antisemitism, at Bowdoin College carried a huge, bitter irony, for this was Longfellow's school, and Longfellow composed the most compassionate and comprehending poem about Jews to have been written by a major English-language poet in the nineteenth century. Henry Wadsworth Longfellow and his classmate Nathaniel Hawthorne graduated from Bowdoin College in 1825. Longfellow was later a professor at Bowdoin and Harvard. Here we have, not the sentimental Longfellow of long romantic narrations, but an unusually socially committed poet of conscience, and our first superb and major translator of European poetry, including Dante's *Commedia*. An amazing literary document, "The Jewish Cemetery at Newport" is a meditation on the Spanish and Portuguese Jews buried in the graveyard of that Rhode Island seaport town. The poet severely chastised his fellow Christians for persecuting the people of the "Hebrew book." He understood the depth of the hatred and hurt that the Jews suffered in the

European ghettos and Judenstrassen, which drove them to America and ultimately to this graveyard. Longfellow would have burned with indignation at those Bowdoin institutions and its people who added to the millennia of abuse as they created ghettos in his own college. (And he would not have been happy with me for abandoning my identity):

> How came they here? What burst of Christian hate,
>   What persecution, merciless and blind,
> Drove o'er the sea—that desert desolate—
>   These Ishmaels and Hagars of mankind?
>
> They lived in narrow streets and lane obscure,
>   Ghetto and Judenstrass, in mirk and mire;
> Taught in the school of patience to endure
>   The life of anguish and the death of fire.
>
> All their lives long, with the unleavened bread
>   And bitter herbs of exile and its fears,
> The wasting famine of the heart they fed,
>   And slaked its thirst with marah of their tears.
>
> Anathema maranatha! Was the cry
>   That rang from town to town, from street to street:
> At every gate the accursed Mordecai
>   Was mocked and jeered, and spurned by Christian feet,
>
> Pride and humiliation hand in hand
>   Walked with them through the world where'er they went;
> Trampled and beaten were they as the sand,
>   And yet unshaken as the continent.

Before Longfellow we have divergent views of the Jews by the metaphysical poets John Donne (1573–1631) and George Herbert (1593–1633). Each speaks of "usurpation," but with opposite intent. In later life Donne was the dean of St. Paul's Cathedral in London. His last magnificent work was his nineteen "Holy Sonnets," including "XI," in which he depicts "you Jewes" not only as vile but as killers of "an inglorious Man," Jesus (who by a miracle of disguise was not to be perceived as a Jewe). More, he recalls Jacob in a way to make him fulfill the stereotype of the tricky, money-minded Semite. But in his penitence, Donne asserts that he, John Donne, is even worse than the Jewes, since he crucifies Jesus daily:

Spit in my face you Jewes, and pierce my side,
Buffet, and scoffe, scoure, and crucifie mee,
For I have sinn'd, and sinn'd, and only hee,
Who could do no inquitie, hath dyed:
But by my death can not be satisfied
My sinnes, which passe the Jewes impiety:
They kill'd once an inglorious man, but I
Crucifie him daily, being now glorified.
Oh let mee then, his strange love still admire:
Kings pardon, but he bore our punishment.
And *Jacob* came cloth'd in vile harsh attire
But to supplant, and with gainfull intent:
God cloth'd himselfe in vile mans flesh, that so
Hee might be weake enough to so suffer woe.

George Herbert graduated from Cambridge and became a country deacon. Like Longfellow's radically sympathetic "Jewish Cemetery at Newport," which speaks of the people, referring to Newport's Spanish Jews, who came here with "a burst of Christian hate" that left them "to endure / The life of anguish and the death of fire," Herbert speaks not only of the suffering of the people but of their religion "purloined" by Christians. With no reservation he also addresses the Jews in the second person, and, the antithesis of Donne, rebukes his coreligionists for taking the sweet sap of the nation and leaving them dry, of using their words as in the baptism (a rite most famously practiced by a pre-Christian Jew, Yohanan the Baptizer), while leaving the nation to "pine and die":

The Jews

Poor nation, whose sweet sap, and juice
Our scions have purloined, and left you dry:
Whose streams we got by the Apostle's sluice,
And use in baptism, while ye pine and die.

Soon after being initiated into ATO, I quit the fraternity, first for meals, and then formally I quit altogether. Ironically, two years later even ATO, a fraternity whose headquarters was in the South and had their exclusion laws written into their charter, pledged a few Jews, one from Lewiston, Maine, who was, I believe, a distant cousin. ATO was, like Sigma Nu, expelled from its national chapter. So ATO also changed its

Greek letters and went local. All these events made my nowhere stance even more absurd and reprehensible. What difference or advantage could it have been for me to seem to be a Christian? I wasn't. Yet I was not about to announce that I had lied on my college application and was a religious impostor. What I did was become an activist against discrimination. In my divided conscience, one part was working against and somehow trying to redeem the concealed other.

For those who didn't know my college application blank and my Quaker conversion of a sort, I was neither this nor that. No one asked or was concerned. I was for the most part passing anyway, and it was a nonquestion. And that no one was asking made it easier to keep the silence. Moreover, for my national protest, which would come in *The Nation,* my own affiliation wasn't an issue. Yet amid the labyrinths of identity and disclosure, there was some sanity outside these gloomy walls. I met a Greek woman, Helle Tzalopoulou, in New York. She was attending Wellesley. We began to go steady, and a few years later we were married in Paris.

Soon after we met, I said to her, gravely, "Helle, there is something I must tell you."

"So what's your latest horror?" In those days I was hitching down to Wellesley from Brunswick in icy winter, wearing only a sports coat without even a sweater or an undershirt. I would arrive frozen, but I did so because I had been told it's good for your health not to overdress in the winter. And it's true, I never caught a cold. Well, my revelation wasn't that the next weekend I was about to show up not only coatless but stark naked.

"I'm a Jew," I said.

"So what?"

This confession made no impression on my Greek friend other than her telling me—and she meant it—that some of her closest friends at Wellesley were Jews. At one of the dances, she introduced me to a handsome pair, a beautiful Israeli who was dancing with a Palestinian student, her fiancé, who was a student at Harvard. In Greece Helle had known only one Jewish family. The Germans killed most of the Jews outright, shipping them out of Thessaloniki on trains going north through Bulgaria to the extermination centers. Some died in the trains when the cars were filled with poison gas. Almost all the others died in the camps. Of the seventy thousand prewar Jews, mainly Spanish-speaking, five thousand were in Athens, where they were more dispersed and harder to find. One afternoon a father and his young daughter came to Helle's house, and the father asked them to hide their daughter for a day. He was a Spanish Jew from Athens. Helle's father, Dr. Tzalopoulos, a very good man, took the girl in. A day later the father came for his daughter. Father and daughter survived the war, and after the liberation they both came to thank the Tzalopoulos family. In those days of easy killing, harboring a Jew would have meant immediate arrest and worse.

A Letter to *The Nation*

In the fall of 1945, my second year at Bowdoin, there were a few more Blacks enrolled, one Chinese student, an Ethiopian, Zeléke Bekale, who became a close friend, and more Jews. While the vets had not yet begun to return in mass (more than 2,000 students in 1946), our numbers had grown from about 175 in 1944 to 600 in 1945. Discrimination was ever more repugnant, and there was at last a response.

Any social activity, from eating and entertainment to the famous Bowdoin house parties, was initiated in the fraternities. Those who were out were out. In a big school it wouldn't have meant much. But Bowdoin was smaller than George School when I got there. To live with twenty-two students who lived in exile within the college was appalling.

Personally, I felt deeply isolated during my first two years at Bowdoin. By now I was eighteen and already a junior. So I turned again to my Quakers and went to Mexico, first to work several months in an Indian village for the American Friends Service Committee (as I had done one summer while at George School) and then to spend the rest of the year in Mexico City. Living in a Spanish refugee orphanage, teaching private English lessons at night to make it financially (and often selling my blood at clinics), I also studied at the Autonomous University of Mexico, the old one, as they called it before it moved from downtown to the edge of the city. At the end of that marvelous year, I spent the summer at the French School in Middlebury (also taking one Spanish course). The seeds of becoming a poet had started that year in Mexico. For curious reasons, those seeds began to take root on the frequent all-night walks with my French and Spanish friends in the moon-green hills of Vermont and with the Spanish poets Pedro Salinas, Jorge Guillén, and Luis Cernuda of the Generation of 27, who, by the magic of literary cabala, were all at or passing through Middlebury College.

When I came back to Maine from Mexico in the fall of 1947, Bowdoin had changed dramatically. The student population was twelve times greater than the wartime group of underage students and 4Fs in 1944. The society had also changed. The non-frats at last decided to establish a local fraternity for the outcasts and called it Alpha Rho Upsilon (ARU), an acronym for "All Races United." I had mixed feelings. I agreed that students couldn't wait forever for the restricted fraternities to open their doors. At the same time, the new fraternity could formalize the status quo by creating an official ghetto for the outcasts, thereby releasing the fraternities from any need to change. Like the infamous solution for Blacks in the South, "separate but equal," it would definitely confirm separation and would surely not be equal. I thought it better to shame the administration into obliging all national fraternities with religious and racist clauses to go local, free of restrictions, or close shop. (Eventually, that's exactly what happened, but not for more than a decade after I had graduated.) In my last semester during the summer session, I wrote a letter describing the society of Bowdoin. It appeared in the July 17, 1948, issue of *The Nation,* on page 82:

Establishing the Ghetto

Dear Sirs: I can only take the forming of new inter-racial fraternities (commented on in your issue of July 3) with mixed emotions after reviewing the history of fraternities on the Bowdoin campus. During the war fraternities survived on skeleton crews. At Bowdoin, under the leadership of a few dynamic students—and also the need for survival—fraternities openly pledged a handful of Jews. They even accepted a Negro, the first move of this kind in Greek-fraternity history.

Soon after the initial gesture this radicalism waned, and old pre-war policies were reinstated. As a result, a new solution was sought, and soon with high hopes the Alpha Rho Upsilon symbolized "all races united." Here at least seemed some solution of the problem of the socially unwanted in a school in which 85 percent of the student body (white-Christian) were in fraternities.

But the establishment of A.R.U. clarified only one thing. It cleared the air completely of any further attempts to break down racial barriers and discriminatory clauses. Other Greek-letter fraternities simply excused themselves with "If Jews need fraternity life, let them join the A.R.U." So the ghetto was firmly established. All Races United came to mean "All Refuse United." What then is the solution? Certainly not setting up detention camps for displaced persons. Part of the answer must come from those "close-mouth" college administrations which permit fraternities to continue without removing racial clauses; the rest through students and a half-way humane approach to the meaning of "liberal education" in colleges.

WILLIS R. BARNSTONE
Brunswick, Maine, July 7

At first everyone was sore, both the administration and fraternities, including members of Alpha Rho Upsilon. But overnight the whole matter exploded. There were debates, school newspaper articles, statements by the administration, and endless talk. In 1946 when the vets returned in large numbers, the process of integration had been accelerated. They were older and from more diverse backgrounds and economic classes in large part because of the GI Bill, which paid their tuition and living expenses. The GI Bill alone dramatically democratized colleges and universities. There were enough angry vets to speed the death of the hateful "clauses." What had been accepted practice, a silence (and I knew the ways of silence from the mirror) was now open and controversial. As a result, during the four years I attended Bowdoin, nearly half the fraternities rejected national affiliations, went local, and took in Jews and Blacks. With that accomplishment, ARU itself became less a ghetto but one of the choices, with its own special history and purposeful background. Bowdoin evolved from the typical fraternity school to become a pioneer liberal arts college.

Coming Out of My Own Ghetto of Silences

I cannot say when I came out of my own silences. Let us say I made progress while at Bowdoin. I became half a Jew, meaning of mixed parents or a Quaker or nothing. I was anything but myself until I left. But the interior weight of discomfort and guilt remained long after I had left silence and dissembling behind. It's only natural. It is why I say that I can write this memoir of icy bigotry without pain, for the writing itself relieves me, almost pleasurably, of the last stains of hurt, conflict, and culpability. Today is different: you, reader, are different, and so am I.

Relief from quandary actually came very quickly.

As soon as I left college, there were no more *deadly* applications to fill in. I left most of that baggage behind. I was leaving for Europe and, without exaggeration, as a free man. A Jew, however, whether a believer or an atheist like me, is always a Jew for diverse reasons. Jean Paul Sartre, in his masterful short book *La question juive*, said a Jew is not a Jew because he thinks himself a Jew (excuse the gender, but it's Sartre, not me) but because others think him a Jew. Yet Robert Lowell, who for some years became a Catholic, could say when he became a Protestant again, "I was once a Catholic." A Jew can also convert to Catholicism or Buddhism, but he or she is still a Jew. There is an old tale about two Jews, one a recent convert to Christianity, the other a hunchback, who were passing a synagogue. "That reminds me," said the convert, "I used to be a Jew." "Really," said the other, "and I used to be a hunchback."

The great French philosopher Henri Bergson (1859–1941), my first idol among modern philosophers, wished to convert to Catholicism, yet in his courageous way he remained a Jew. Near death when the German armies entered Paris, the Nazis urged him to renounce Judaism and go through with his intended conversion. He refused, but not for religious reasons. He would not officially break off from Judaism at this abhorrent moment and further endanger the fate of his fellow Jews. When he died shortly afterward, he was buried, at his request, in the Jewish corner of the cemetery according to the Catholic rites.

As for my flirtations with concealment, I think when I left Bowdoin the mess was over. I won't swear to it. But the walk in the penumbra was over. I'm not sure what happened when five years later I applied to graduate school. That there are no scars of remembrance is a good sign. I may have left the religious blank unmarked. Or maybe Columbia didn't have such a question. And after I got out of the army, I applied under a new round of graduate school applications. I can't remember what I wrote on the blank for Yale in 1956. Was religious affiliation still on graduate school applications by then? I think there was not. But to come down hard on myself, I also have no memory in those early years of writing down "Jew." Sylvia Plath said in "Daddy," "I must be a bit of a Jew." In her good and mad poem, she, who was not a Jew, was more enlightened than me—if I dare use any light metaphor for the somber way of denial years.

It is strange not to be able to remember how I filled out a graduate form only forty years ago, when I clearly recall how I fabricated some evasion of religion affiliation fifty-eight years ago when I was thirteen. The emotional memory hook stuck. By 1956 I was cynical enough about those ghosts to think either *it's none of your business* or *go to hell*. Today, if asked, I'd write "Jew" and be pleased to do so. But who's asking? The climate is good. The war is over. Today they ask only for one's race and ethnic background, which information somehow is intended for good purpose, for achieving "good" quotas. *Plus ça change, plus c'est la même.*

Off to Europe, Where Old-Fashioned Bigotry Is Huge, yet Now Who Cares? Not Me

I sailed for Europe on the Queen Elizabeth in the autumn of 1948. My life would start all over again. That's what happens sometimes when you change continents. Especially if you can leave the darknesses behind and take with you the skills and thrills of light. Yes, and the kindness of hope. At twenty I had a lot of light. But I remembered enough darkness to give it balance. The shadow of emotion, the dusk, the wait for change, all that hunger and patience are also the bread of life.

The year in France was essential in every way. I learned French, took a Greek wife, became a wanderer and writer. Now that I was a Jew again, I could forget about it—or rather, leave it where it should be, a fragment, a gift, relatively easy. Eventually, when I began to do research on Jewish and Christian noncanonical apocrypha and pseudepigrapha, I took in those scriptures with frequent elation because of their fantastic, visionary spirit. But now I was a twenty-year-old American in Paris soon after the war, and I would stay five years in Europe and come back, as my brother noticed, not quite American. He said the color of my skin had changed, I walked funny, and I had no American clothes. He was wrong and right. I came back very much at home again, for I had found my profession. (Later on, I did manage to disperse another four years sneaking off to work in New York, Buenos Aires, California, and Beijing, but the return meant spending more than thirty years largely in one room, a cement block office with Turkish rugs on the linoleum and a real Picasso litho of a stunning Cretan woman on the wall above my computer, living off memory and imagination. This convenient workplace was the trade-off of the wandering Jew on continents and sedentary memoirist with a pen).

The trip over to Le Havre was slow as an ocean trip should be. The isolated time and space on a ship cleanse. An airplane confuses. Ocean liners are for destinations, for changing city and life. There is the intimacy of the crossing, born of transience, given breath and candor by the solitude of the empty deck at night and the sudden friendships. I was full of aspirations. To wander, to experience, to know, to write. And there are people who open up, who speak candidly and make dogmatic declarations, which they would not do were these floating days not days of passage. Like a vacation romance or adventure, these were buoyant hours separated from ordinary life, alien to implications of future responsibility. After dinner the ship orchestra played in the lounge and we tourist-class passengers had a great time. Passengers from the more sedate, duller second- and first-class sections would invade our lounge to enjoy our fun. In late September the ship was rocking hard on the Atlantic, and sometimes when the waters were very rough and tables slid from side to side, I'd rush up alone on deck to stare at the mystery of the endless ocean.

Rocking on the Queen

Deep in the hold we have no porthole, yet
I gaze, X-raying whales and a green squall.

The pitching of Elizabeth has set
the tables rolling, banging wall to wall.
I push up to the deck and wait for France.
At twenty I'm a character whom Plato
might keep for lunch—yet the Greek's reasoned trance
is not my Bergson dream. I'm a potato-
head says my Marxist pal. Norm's blind but grins
at me. Naive! As Europe nears, wet shade
washes my eyes with reverie. I dry
my face. Europe is full of women. Inns
of smart delicious lips. We dock. The maid
at l'Hôtel Flore pinches my pants and tie.

The night the boat train got to Paris, the taxis were on strike, so I stayed at a hotel near the rail station. I went up to my room, made friends with the maid, who was lovely (which is how I got my pants pinched), got hungry, and went downstairs to the bistro. Hard-boiled eggs in a brass holder sat on the counter. I looked at the mirror, put my beret on, which I had worn since Mexico, chose two eggs, ordered a filter coffee with cognac, and I was French and happy. In the morning I went to the Left Bank, carried my suitcase along Boule Miche, went one block down la rue Bonaparte, which led to the Seine and the clochards sleeping on the banks, turned right on la rue Jacob, walked a few more steps and entered the hotel.

Paris was a city where most of the time I walked. In fall and spring there was gold in the air, in winter coal. Each had its poignant smells. I confess that on the first day I already felt more at home and natural in this open city of a thousand faces than in my intense Bowdoin days and nights (perhaps I was reliving the freedom of Mexico City), even before I settled in my room facing the street.

My room at the Hôtel des Tours on la rue Jacob had a red carpet and a sink, was filled with sunlight, and was cheap. The sink with hot water was the only hot spigot I'd have in a room in five years in Europe. Ten dollars was all I needed to live well for a week, and that included hotel room, meals out, and entertainment. The red-nosed concierge knew one phrase in English, "no monkey business," by which she meant no *ménage à trois* in her respectable hotel.

"This is a proper place, only couples."

"Any married ones?" I asked.

"Yes, I believe there's an older Jewish couple who might even be married."

Next to my room lived two painters, a Czech couple, in a studio half the size of mine, and half of that occupied by tall canvases against the wall. The beautiful, sad woman, ironing clothes on her worktable, came directly from Picasso's Blue Period canvases. They were good painters, with their exile experience printed on their grave faces. Within days all my friends were foreign painters and writers—from Greece, South Africa, India. I was enrolled at the Sorbonne in a *certificat* in philosophy and a doctor in letters (like a master's) in French literature.

In the room next to me a young Dutch woman lived. She introduced me to Bernard Citroën, a tall blond Dutch poet who was into every Quartier Latin literary activity. That winter he started an Anglo-French bilingual periodical, *Points,* in which I published my first poem. *Points* did remarkably well at the kiosks, where disappointed women bought it up in the belief, as the French title implied, that it was a knitting magazine. Citroën, a Jew, survived the war in Holland, hiding for five years in a basement.

Paris has been for many years an alternative for black American jazz musicians, weary of America. The French appreciated their music. They loved it. It was an exotic romance, like African masks that inspired Picasso and Modigliani, along with new world cowboys and Apaches. It was also popular art, and a richness America could offer them. In performance art, Josephine Baker came early and was another legend. She also internationalized her racial harmony convictions by adopting and bringing up children from five ethnic backgrounds. Our top black novelists, Richard Wright and James Baldwin, also went to France. Like the jazz stars, they stayed there, continued their art, and died in France. The Beat writers also found a refuge in Paris. Later it was Tangier, India, and Katmandu. Even today the main street on maps and street signs in Katmandu bears the name "Freak Street." Jack Kerouac was also in Paris. Although I didn't know him personally then—we were together for one long pretty drunk weekend in the late fifties—I used to see Kerouac regularly hanging out in the cafés. He had his famous mechanical typewriter in Paris. He wrote and wrote on his contraption, which took an endless roll of paper, on which he typed his novels with great facility with his outrageously fast fingers.

With all the colonies in France, there were many African students. A generation earlier, Aimé Césaire from Martinique and Abbe Diamancoun Senghor from Senegal had invented the *negritude* literary movement. I was an early lover of Césaire's poetry. Only a few of Senghor's poems worked, I thought. Senghor's role was ultimately political (he became his country's first independent president). It was common to see African students with their French girlfriends. For all the complaints against French xenophobia, the black African did well in Paris. Many times I heard the French run down the Arabs by praising *les africains,* whom they said were *dociles.* These semi-compliments based on unfriendly comparisons with others, I received often during my three years in France. When people would ask if I were Catholic or Protestant, I'd say, *"Non, je suis juif "* (No, I'm a Jew). Inevitably, the smiling answer was, *"Mais monsieur, vous êtes différent. Vous n'êtes pas comme les autres"* (But sir, you are different. You are not like the others). You are different could mean you are not like other Jews, or in another context, not like other Americans, or whatever. None of these old French wisdoms bothered me.

I led the vagabond student life in Paris, moving from hotel to hotel, going to many meetings at the Sorbonne where the poets Paul Éluard and Louis Aragon protested against police brutality and deaths in the coal strikes or other outrages. In those days students of all colors were constantly carrying banners down le boulevard Saint-Michel only to be confronted by the police (*les flics*), who flew out of their vans in their batlike blue capes, raised *bâtons,* and rushed the protesters. The students screamed *"cochons, cochons!"* (Pigs, pigs!) and scattered. Some scrambled up lamp posts before being dragged down by the *flics* and tossed in the paddy wagons. Art Buchwald, writing daily for the *International Herald-Tribune* (a European privilege like good small bookstores and delicious filter coffee) had just done a column saying the French police used their clubs on civilians' heads astutely, knowing, as a good French cook knows, that you can't scramble eggs without first cracking the shells.

I liked my first hotel, liked to hear the roving street musicians coming down la rue Bonaparte to play and sing under our window for francs in newspaper packets that came pouring from the apartments like rain down on the performers. I liked to walk around the corner to the immaculate small plaza, la place de Ferstenberg where Géricault had had his atelier; and I especially enjoyed dropping in on the small galleries and bookstores at the far end of Jacob. The autumn air of Paris was blended smells of window houseplants, coffee, and smoke, and on Jacob the aromas were silently uplifting. It was enough to fill my spirit simply to look at those lighted store windows and their tasteful treasures. Yet I still moved to a cheaper hotel a few blocks away, which initiated a series of moves, each one unique. I went from la rue Jacob to l'Hotel de Langue d'Oc to the rue du Cherche-Midi, and finally la rue Vaugirard, when Helle and I were living together. This Vaugirard hotel room faced the Luxembourg Park and had the implausible name of l'Hôtel du Portugal and de Lisbonne.

Paris was a bowl. Grapes from many cities and continents kept it full.

La rue Jacob, 1948

War was fun for Guillaume Apollinaire,
sending letter poems from the trenches, yet
a bombshell came, gravely combing his hair,
but Guillaume healed in Paris, a cigarette
like a love ballad in his lips. I spied
life from a hotel room with a red rug,
hot water in the corner sink, and sighed
happy when the street singers used a jug
to catch the hailing francs. The courtyard reeked
with rising fumes of piss when evening rain
fell from the wine-blue clouds. Our sheets were far
too short. *Fin de la guerre.* Spanish flu creaked
into the poet's brain. We were young, zan-
y like Guillaume! who croaked with *La Victoire.*

In the early part of our century, there were many truly multicultural cities: Constantinople, Alexandria, Tangier, Algiers, Berlin, Vienna, Prague, Paris. Their cosmopolitanism, multilingualism, made them rich and fascinating. When ethnic nationalism and tribalism prevailed and the minorities were slaughtered or expelled (Greeks, Armenians, French, Jews, Germans from this short list), these world cities lost both their depth and their fine patina of culture. Paris has remained intact as a micro-world. The Spanish poet Federico García Lorca saw gypsies and Arabs in Spain, and Jews and Blacks in New York and Havana as a single metaphor for the gay poet he was. He loved his city of Granada but complained that after 1492, the year of the reconquest by the armies of Fernando and Isabela and the expulsion of Jews and Moors, this international city of Moors, Jews, and Spaniards (and earlier a city of Carthaginians, Greeks, Romans, and Goths), ceased to be a capital city of vital architectural beauty and thriving and diverse peoples in every contemporary field of learning. Then after the *reconquista,* Lorca complained, for three centuries it was not a metropolis of thousands but a homogenous, decaying, and diminutive village lost in Andalusia.

Yet Paris has hung on to its multiplicities. The city in Europe which for several centuries received the students, artists, novelists, composers, theologians, and philosophers not only from Europe but also from Africa, Asia, and the Americas has been Paris. In those "banquet years" of Guillaume Apollinaire (himself a Roman of Polish-Italian ancestry), the painters Apollinaire celebrated in his essays on the avant-garde were the Spaniards Picabia, Juan Gris, and Picasso; the Italians Modigliani and Chirico; the Dutchman Mondrian; the Russians Chagall and Kandinsky; and Soutine the Bulgarian. American writers, composers, and artists flocked to the city of light and street lamps before and between and after the world wars. The years I was in and out of Paris, there was no end to the *étrangers* artists. Gertrude Stein (1874–1946) had just died, but Brancusi (1876–1957) had his studio a few blocks from where I lived. And Tristan Tzara (1896–1963), the Romanian Jew who invented Dada, was everywhere. I was lucky to spend a long afternoon with him alone, while he showed me his books and rued the quackery of fame.

To be a youth in those days of Paris was the best lesson one could have in art. Its internationalism was extraordinary. The French, so famous for their xenophobia and bigotry, attracted and held the world in their schools, academies, and studios. Shakespeare came too. I saw *Hamlet,* in André Gide's translation, played by the greatest of the mime artists, Jean Louis Barrault, who turned a clumsy Danish prince into a graceful, acrobatic fencer. And what a fine smile the American actor John Garfield, sitting a few seats over, had on his lips as he got up at intermission and went out for a smoke.

In Paris I was discovering memories, especially, through the Greek I was living with, like the Greek poets Cavafy, Seferis, and Elytis, who restored an ancient past in their poems and raised the question of how to enjoy and live the art of the past without being crushed by its weight and its traditions. I thought the Jews and Greeks had the same wealth and problem. What to do with it all? George Seferis (1900–71) wrote in "Mythistorema 3" (*mythistorema* means both "myth of our history" and "novel"):

> I woke with this marble head in my hands;
> it exhausts my elbows and I don't know where to put it down.
> It was falling into the dream as I was coming out of the dream
> so our life became one and it will be difficult for it
>   to separate again.
>
> I look at the eyes: neither open nor closed
> I speak to the mouth which keeps trying to speak
> I hold the cheeks which have broken through the sky
> I haven't got any more strength.
>
> My hands disappear and come toward me
> mutilated.

Helle handled her past as Seferis tried. In this amazing early poem, Seferis understood the burden of traditions and that the only bearable, if painful, solution was to see a continuity—and ultimately a simultaneity. Not one ancient and one modern, but a synchronicity of archaic, classical, Hellenistic, Seleucid, Byzantine, Turkish, modern Greeces. And it is all there at once, since the memory of information from yesterday's newspaper is not different from a translated document from twenty-three hundred years ago. Sappho or the Chinese Tang eighth-century poet Wang Wei seems more contemporary, familiar, and intimate to me than the great majority of writers I read today. They are closer. Sappho wrote, "Some one, I tell you, will remember us." If the papyrus or paper survives or it is copied, someone *will* remember. In Paris I stole from Helle's Greekness and from George Seferis. It was all helpful in the growing of a person from the trap and accident of the few cultures or religions one is usually heir to:

Two Souls Meet on a Windy Night and Worry about a Marble Face

After the war when we were young and gray in heart,
I went to Paris to get exiled, kiss a soul, and hear the wind
blowing the urine fragrance along Bonaparte.
Stiff black coffee and warm bread were my early copains.
   Wind dozed among the lindens.
I let it share my bed. The bed was bare;
a torn red blanket under a gray bulb of maybe
   30 watts, if I can count,
sputtered high on the ceiling, blinking at my underwear
wrinkled and dripping on the sink edge. I read
   the philosophy of Auguste Comte
hard as I could at the Sorbonne until my prof,
Monsieur La Porte, dropped dead. *La Porte est fermée*
was cruelly scribbled on the door. I met a soul
one windy night. Paris embraced us with her laugh.
She was a Greek. She gave me an ancient statue that hurt
my arms. The cheekbones almost pierced the skin.
   It's so heavy, where can I put it down? I say
to her.
   Don't ever put it down, she says. We Greeks wake
   with a glaring
marble head in our arms. Hold it up or it will roll away.

One morning I was walking near l'École des Mines when I saw an East Indian hurrying in my direction. The young gentleman came up to me, saying, in singsong British English, "Sir, can you direct me to a students' kosher restaurant."

I was taken aback.

"A students' kosher restaurant?"

"Yes, sir. I am an Indian Jew in the process of migrating to Israel. I am strictly kosher."

"Are there many Jews in India?"

"Not many, sir. I'm speaking not of foreign Jewish guests or recent arrivals. We old-family Indian Jews are about 45,000 and most of us are going to villages in Israel which the government is building for us. I am waiting for my place to be readied."

Like the Jews from China, Yemen, Iran, and Iraq, the Indian Jews were descended from those Jews who, after Cyrus the Great of Persia freed the Jews who had been taken to Mesopotamia during the Babylonian Captivity (586–538 B.C.), didn't return to Israel but stayed in that part of the Near East or went further east to India and China. As a result of their separation, many of these early diaspora Jews did not have the Bible after Ezekiel, Isaiah, and Jeremiah until in the mid-twentieth century when, as in the case of the Yemenites, the stories of Daniel, Dreamer of Lions, became known to them.

"I can't direct you to a Kosher student restaurant, but you are more than welcome to share a meal with my girlfriend and me. She's a Greek and a good cook."

"Thank you, sir. I shall be most honored."

Changing Money on the Rue des Rosiers and Getting Married by the Grand Rabbi of Paris

Life in Paris was cheap with American dollars. After the war the dollar was gold in Europe. In 1948 there was still rationing in Paris as there was in London in 1952 when I began a year there. And the black market in France, as in most of Europe, was pervasive. Businessmen and governments traded on the basis of the true value of international moneys. But for visitors and tourists, the government set wishful exchange values in order to scalp money from them. Almost anyone living regularly in the country avoided the official rip-off. The black market, or parallel market as it was euphemistically called, gave the world value of currency, minus what the trader skimmed off for his or her trouble and risk. I changed money regularly at the Cité Universitaire, a complex of buildings far from the center of Paris, which housed many university students. My contacts were an American of Armenian descent who roomed with a Turk from Turkey. Only in Paris. It was like the Israeli and Palestinian couple at the Wellesley dance. A blessing and rejection of nationalism and the curse of those deep nostalgias of history and ethnicity that, alas, inevitably cultivate hatred and justify war. The Armenian and Turk were very pleased about their odd-couple status.

When I didn't go to the Armenian/Turk bankers, I crossed the Seine and went to a poorish neighborhood inhabited largely by recent Jewish immigrants from Eastern Europe, who were the reliable money-changers for those who lived in Paris a while. La rue des Rosiers (the street of the Rose Trees) was the principal street. There were my living cousins from the world my grandparents had left in 1887 when they emigrated from the Pale to find a home in New England. Here the money changing was done in the open street without subterfuge. French Jews had no part in it. They were in large part the established bourgeoisie. But these recent unwealthy immigrants had languages and connections. What I enjoyed most was the transaction. They were deals of affection and rites of proper behavior.

Before any discussion of currencies or rate, there had to be foreplay. Where are you from? What are you doing in Paris? What do your parents do? Are you having a good time? Do you have a girlfriend? Are you Jewish? While all this pleasant interrogation was taking place—the Greek peasants are notorious for going through the same rituals of friendship with a stranger—the trader would inevitably show some physical sign of good will. Often it meant that I found the older gentleman's hand feeling the texture of my jacket or almost caressing my necktie. Much more heart than a handshake. All this humanity would have a close equivalent in China with the spiffy street-corner Uigur Turks, who were the most trustworthy of money-changers. They insisted first on going to some Muslim restaurant to drink beer, wash the bowls by swashing them with beer and tossing the liquid on the floor, and then drink a few bowls before getting down to the pleasure of haggling. These Jews on rue des Rosiers seemed to come out of stories rather than earlier memory. They were not Hasids, but village folk or small town dwellers, probably like my ancestors at the end of the last century, now thrust by war and their miracle of survival onto the safe street of the roses to trade greenbacks for francs.

In the late spring Helle and I decided to get married. It took about two weeks of running from office to office. It's hard to get married or die on this planet, at least in the civilized countries. It takes so long to settle the paperwork, especially when you die, for which reason I prefer not to explore that darkness, since I'm not very good at handling papers. The American Embassy helped immensely with the official paperwork. We were given a list of thirty-three documents we had to obtain in order to be married civilly in France. The list included checks by the names of the offices where we should leave a few packs of American cigarettes for good will and godspeed. By the end of May we were all in order. On June 1st, 1949, we and our friends met in the office of the mayor of the sixth arrondissement, across the street from the Saint Sulpice Cathedral. It was a jolly wedding by a stout mayor from Marseilles, whose French rolled eloquently from his lips as if he were speaking Italian, and he wished us well and many French babies to roll around in the Luxembourg gardens. (Our daughter, Aliki, did not come until seven years later, in New Haven, but at least she was conceived in Périgueux, France.)

Our friends gave us flowers. Like the fool I often was, that same day I lost the key to my hotel room. So after celebrating at the Cité, around midnight we took a cab to Helle's room that now was in a proper bourgeois apartment. In the morning I brought the locksmith, got a new key for my own room, and left for class at the Sorbonne.

When we met at my hotel in the afternoon, Helle had a story for me. Her dignified landlady had confronted her formally with, "*Qui était ce garçon avec qui vous avez passé la nuit?*" (Who was that boy with whom you spent the night?)

"*C'était mon mari.*" (It was my husband.)

She was asked to leave that very day.

I don't love Paris

I don't love Paris. Maybe
it's the blue rain and I smell salt
when the sewers sing their cries
of the troglodyte. I love Paris.

It's the sun of three bluets
who whisper that my papers
are fake and I live in a room
on Cherche-Midi. The concierge

each night holds a black cat
on his shoulder. No kidding.
He laughs tersely and I am scared.
Nonetheless a blue first of June

in the Place de Saint Sulpice,
the sixteenth arrondissement,
I marry in the city hall
but I lose my key. No room,

we sleep at her place. Who is
this boy with whom you passed
the night? speaks the lady.
He's my husband. She throws us

into the street. I don't like
Paris. I love her tenderly,
all the artists who are starving,
the dirty rain, the sun blue.

The marriage had been arranged so quickly that I had neglected to write my mother about the forthcoming ceremony. Feeling guilty, I sent her a postcard a few days after the wedding. To make the shock a little less, I said we were getting married the next day, an almost irrelevant statement about the time, since she would receive the card at least a week after the marriage. As if this lie wasn't enough, I announced, "We will be married in a civil service. I don't want to go through the hypocrisy of marrying in a synagogue."

There was no need for my reference to the synagogue. It was extra hurt. After years of denial, I was going to be blatant.

A month later my mother and brother arrived in Paris to see us, and Vassili, Helle's father, came from Greece. My thoughts were that Mother was thinking, "Billy's done it again." We cared for each other immensely, but I often failed in areas of respectability. But though she didn't approve of my spending five years in Europe and of not advancing a profession (I was just beginning the long vagabondage), she was more than tolerant. I have no complaints. She had a right to her feelings.

We met at the George V, an expensive, fashionable old hotel we would never get near on our own. We were to meet in the lobby. Mother saw us and burst into tears. I had married a non-Jew. I was only twenty-one. I didn't know what I was doing. But before any of these thoughts that I attributed to her could materialize into words, she took an immediate liking to Helle and a similar affection for Vassili. Mother and Vassili were a pair, obviously caring for each other. They looked handsome together. In fact there was so much harmony between all these previous strangers that I almost felt neglected. Mother approved of them more than me. And with good reason.

My brother Howard always had a mature overview and appropriate solutions. He was the elder statesman. After the first days of looking at Paris together, he took me aside. He was seriously businesslike, yet intimately brother to brother, "Billy, neither Mother nor I care about any religious reason for your having a Jewish marriage in a synagogue. It might be hard on Helle, and we know this. But we do care about your being deprived of the inheritance your grandfather designated for you. In his will Zeda stipulated that you had to marry a Jew in order to be a beneficiary, and upon marriage to a Jew you would receive what now amounts to a bit more than seven thousand dollars. Get married in the Paris synagogue, whether you like it or not."

All this Howard explained carefully and formally. I took it in. My postcard renouncing a temple marriage was in my mind, but clearly, for my mother and brother, that was irrelevant. I hedged. I didn't know what to think.

"I'll talk it over with Helle."

"Of course." Howard knew what to say.

Helle was upset. She was as unreligious as I was. But in Greece, Greek Orthodoxy is the national religion (as we were soon to find out for bureaucratic reasons) and the Greek Orthodox Church during the centuries of Turkish occupation was Greece. They operated schools; they preserved the Byzantine culture and the identity. And many priests were hanged in carrying out that task. Helle could not throw away her Greekness, her *romiosini*. In the history of merging and diverging cultures, the word *romiosini* goes back to the Roman Church and to Constantine the Great, a Romanian, who was the first Roman emperor to convert to Christianity. In the second and third decades of the third century, he established Byzantium in Constantinople, a city named after him. *Romiosini*, meaning literally Romanness, has come to mean Greekness.

Though my first idea was to resist, after a while I agreed to have a Jewish wedding. I tried to persuade my wife that we should hold our breath for a few days. The prior rites consisted of bathing in a small pool in a courtyard near the synagogue and hearing some blessings. The ceremony of the *mikvah* pool, meaning "immersion pool," was the ceremony that later Christian Jews and Christians called baptism, from *baptizein* in Greek, meaning "to immerse, wash, dip." On his deathbed, Constantine the Great chose to be baptized by an Arian bishop, making him formally a Christian.

For us it would mean simply stepping into a pool, about three feet in diameter, in the synagogue courtyard and hearing a prayer chanted in Hebrew that neither of us understood. The ceremony is known to Christians through the *mikvah* immersions performed by John the Dipper (the Baptist), a pre-Christian Jew who gave water baths to other pre-Christian Jews.[1] The gesture was tough on Helle, as any symbolic conversion would be, but she went along with it. In the end the whole process was fascinating, but fascination was not what we, or especially she, was looking for. Some days later, Mother and Howard went off to tour around France. We would go through the ceremony, as actors on stage in return for our salary, before they returned. Ironically, Howard converted to Christianity at middle age.

Being a big shot, Howard had suggested that we speak to the grand rabbi of Paris. That, surprisingly, was not hard to do. We called and met the rabbi, who happened to be a Spanish Jew. He was tall, ascetically thin, very handsome, and altogether charming. He was amused by us. The instructions were few. We were to come back in about a week and he would handle it himself on a weekday afternoon. The chief rabbi made Helle feel welcome without imposing any theology or comparisons between Jewish and Christian beliefs. I suspect that he considered this a conversion of *convenance*, which it was.

In the nineteenth century, for more dire reasons, outstanding Jews, themselves or their parents, with obvious resentment, went through "conversions of convenience" from Judaism to Christianity: Felix Mendelssohn, Karl Marx, Heinrich Heine, Benjamin Disraeli. In the twentieth century, with citizen and voting rights widespread, conversion was not a necessary *modus vivendi*. And so earlier in our century similarly significant Jews, such as Ludwig Wittgenstein, Albert Einstein, Sigmund Freud, Elias Canetti, remained Jews; yet they couldn't remain in central Europe without becoming ghosts of death camp smoke, and hence they fled. Those European Jews who stayed, whoever they were, were exterminated or escaped death either by hiding or by passing as Christians.

The question, "Are you a Jew?" was a fatal query. During the Occupation, the Germans obliged all Jews to wear the yellow Star of David prominently on their clothing precisely so they might not merge invisibly in the larger society; that they might not pass as Christians and escape the claws of the hunter. There is a famous story told about Jews and the king of Denmark. When the order was given in Denmark to wear the star, the next day Christian X, King of Denmark, appeared with the Star of David sewn on his clothing in solidarity with his Danish Jews. The story, it turned out, was apocryphal. It is true, however, that the king strongly supported the Jews and opposed the occupiers. And it is also true that the Danish people (since there was no Danish government) in September and October of 1943 managed to secret virtually the whole Jewish population to Sweden where they lived till the war was over.

In the end, which was better? Nineteenth-century massacres, the ghettos of the disenfranchised, and ultimately the emergence of an increasingly free middle class, or, in our century, immense freedom, legal and actual, together with the murder of most of European Jewry in that massive perversion of the camps?

Our century is one of passing, of intermarriage, of conversions. During the Occupation, passing took on for some years the life-and-death blood problem of the Spanish Inquisition, with its racial "laws of cleanliness." If the unclean blood was there and there was any appearance, true or imagined, that the religion of the unclean blood was being followed, then came the stake, the fire, and the smoke of purification.

We went to the synagogue one afternoon, and Helle stepped into the pool. Thereafter, for our later purpose of probating a will, for a minute she passed as a Jew. By the mock conversion, we were meeting the legal requirements of my bigoted grandfather, whose will excluded potential Christians from his inheritance as a way of enforcing the Jewishness of his descendants. I suppose Zeda had in mind keeping the people pure and other such nonsense. The clause in his will against intermarriage was a mirror counterpart of the fraternity clauses excluding Jews and Negroes from membership and all pertaining privileges. The frat legalism was also in the name of purity. Helle's uncomfortable minute of passing as a Jew contrasts with half my high school and college education of passing as a Christian. A few words on a form or certificate, a hotel register, a school application blank for entry into the restricted arena, and then one forgets (if one can) and lives in a nowhere land with no attachments. The history of all kinds of forced conversions is a bitterness.

On the day of the actual ceremony of our new marriage *malgré soi*, which had its origin in Jewish bigotry, we went alone. We didn't have a *minyan* (from Hebrew for *number*), meaning ten male witnesses required for a communal service. The grand rabbi tried unsuccessfully to hold back a deep smile and then asked one of his aids to see who was walking out in the street. Within a few minutes we had our required ten middle-aged Jewish street people, most of them looking very shabby in the nice ways of Paris, and we were ready to go. After a very short saying and chanting of Hebrew scripture, we discovered it was over. The rabbi shook our hands and we got big, amused congratulations from our new street-people friends. We thanked everyone effusively. The men left together in a group (they had been lured in one by one, but now the jobless and the employed among them were united by their good mission) and took up their interrupted paseo in the alleys surrounding the temple.

We headed back to our room on the rue Vaugirard. By the time the bus dropped us off near our hotel, Helle's flirtation with ancient Israel was over. I still had my yarmulke in my suit coat pocket. It remained there in forgotten celebration for a long time, for in Paris I very seldom put on my one suit.

Having Fun at Gunpoint in Crete

Better to be poor in a white room with a wooden table by your bed for writing poems on and to wake in the morning to the first breakfast in the world with Aphrodite than to worry about getting fat from swallowing a billion dollars.

—PETROS STAVLOS, *Lessons in Greek Hygiene*

Working in Greece for the King

Married to a Greek—more than once—I wanted to know her country. I didn't know how long it would be. Love and bureaucracy made it last two years. In the beginning of the Gospel of John, John knew what light was. The evangelist John was surely not John of Patmos and Efesos (though Greek Orthodoxy claims he was) whose Revelation is saturated with Greek island light. The apostle John said, imitating the first lines of Genesis, with Greek logic, "In the beginning was the word, and the word was with God." He goes on to equate God with life and light. "The light shines in the darkness, and the darkness has not overcome it." I knew that Greece was the European country of light, of the mind, of the land, of history and civilization. And Europe was the child of Jerusalem and Athens. So Helle and I were a good ancient couple. Enough. We had to go and be saturated in the sun of Greece.

A year in Paris is good to have when one is twenty. Ernest Hemingway went there when he was twenty-one and stayed five years. He was married, poor, earning a living as a writer. He had some good things and some bad things to say about Gertrude Stein, who accused him of being a member of a lost generation. I also stayed five years, but I shared it with other countries. I could have happily stayed another year or two in Paris—my French was good, I was writing. But I was newly married and wasn't a newspaperman who could support my wife on newspaper articles. I suppose I could have hung on in Paris, as I did in Mexico—and each day in Paris the city and the friends meant more to me.

But Greece was not only a job. It was a light. I didn't know what kind of light, but it was a light I knew. And as John knew, it was good to live in and with that light. As for Paris, it was not only education, marriage, weddings. It was an atmosphere, a smell, a rain, and a delicate spring both in the Jardins du Luxembourg and in villages we explored at random, only to return to the deep air of the Paris atmosphere. Hemingway said it definitively in his letter to a friend in 1950: "If you are lucky enough to have lived in Paris as a young man, then wherever you go for the rest of your life it stays with you, for Paris is a moveable feast."

In September 1949 Athens was still a lovely city. Antiquities were everywhere and everywhere seen. The splendid medieval section called

Plaka lay alongside the Agorá, and under Plaka another ancient city (which still can be unearthed only by destroying the oldest living section of Athens). Downtown was eighteenth- and nineteenth-century small mansions and town houses. As in most cities of the ruined modern world, the earlier centuries have given way to tasteless apartment houses that age disastrously. Athens in the fall of 1949 was still beautiful.

While the buses poured their black smoke out then as now, one could still see the mountains of marble Pendeli and honeycombed Hymettos every day of the week. A few minutes outside of Athens it was all olive trees amid wheat fields, and every day I drove a half hour through those fields framed by the changing mountains and Greek skies. The olive trees have been axed, and all those wheat fields have been turned into cement, giving way to small industry and urban housing as Athens exploded and darkened in order to take in fifty percent of the nation's people. In the autumn of '49 every day was another gaze at beauty.

But the Balkans are a mess. Wars keep changing the borders and enraging one ethnic group against another, who is often identical except for—well, a religion, a change in dialect—who knows or cares what. The Greeks are nurtured on hatred of Turks, the Turks on hatred of Greeks, the Romanians on hatred of Transylvanian Hungarians, and everybody hates the Albanians. So civil wars pulse through each multicultural entity. I got to Greece when an ideological war was winding down.

Curiously, except for the major intrusion of the Germans who wiped out most of the Jews and half of the Gypsies in the Balkans, in this sector of Europe the largely Hispanized Jews in general had it better than elsewhere. Perhaps the Jews were too inconsequential before the greater targets to waste anger on. A wistful example of their advantage in being outside the rival ethnic powers was the civil war in the divided city of Sarajevo in the mid-1990s, when Serbs shot at "Muslims," Croats shot at Serbs, and Bosnian children filled the graveyards. The Spanish Jews of the city—not many more than a thousand survived the German cleansing—were the only people accepted by all sides. They handled the distribution of mail, medicine, and medical care at their own expense and in all neighborhoods. They were not specifically targeted by snipers, and by some absurd miracle, in contradiction to Tom Lehrer's refrain, amid all the civil enmity "nobody bothered to hate the Jews."

When we docked at Piraeus, Greece was just coming out of ten years of world war, German and Italian occupation, and civil war. Wounds of many kinds were fresh. The postage stamps still showed Cretan peasant women catching descending German paratroopers on their pitchforks, and in the countryside many houses still had numbers scrawled on the walls in witness of the hostages executed at that spot. The country was recovering from its diverse mutilations, the last of which was the civil war that persisted from 1946 to 1949, and it showed in the most obvious way: the unusual number of amputees one saw in the streets. Greece was exhausted, its economy only beginning to come alive, yet there was plenty of food and, except for some skirmishing in a few mountainous sectors of the north and in pockets in Crete, peace at last was real. The common people dressed poorly in patched gray clothes.

Despite the people's hardships, I confess it was a wonderful time to have been in Greece. No tourists, even in the islands. The arts were flourishing. The poets Yannis Ritsos, George Seferis, and Odysseus Elytis were writing their best work, for which the latter two would receive Nobel Prizes. The modern theater was international and good, and the production of ancient plays, in the Herodian theater under the Acropolis or at the sonorous theater at Epidauros, was mesmerizing. I was part of a Greek family. There is a saying in modern Greek that a husband comes from the village of his wife, so my village was Athens. However, before enjoying the treasures of modern and ancient Greece, or even of my new metropolitan village of Athens, I had to find a job.

Vassili, my father-in-law, took me around. At the American College at Psihikó, where there were no positions, they suggested I speak to the director at Anávrita, a new school near Kifissiá. This would be perfect, since in a few days we would move to a house on the marble mountain of Pendeli, only a short bus ride from the school. That same morning I saw the English director of Anávrita Academy, a school of thirty-two students, including Crown Prince Constantine, then nine years old (for whom the school was established), and I had the job. I was to teach French and English. Constantine was to become the popular young King of Greece, and then throw away his kingship by a series of mistakes and betrayals to the nation. But I knew Constantine as a boy.

The Queen would drop in on my class and we would chat about

poetry. She lent me the *Faber Book of English Poetry*, which I was glad to study. She was an attractive woman, more dynamic than her husband, Pavlos Glückberg, who was a member of the Danish royal family and King of Greece. By common consent, she was the boss. Publicly she was on many charity committees, and she initiated a campaign to raise dowry money for poor women who were without dowries, thereby helping to perpetuate the repugnant Middle Eastern tradition of women as negotiable property.

Morning in the Schoolyard

As always I was late. Nevertheless
the king was standing by the cypress trees.
They pushed me forward. On this lemon morning
    at Anávrita estate where I was
    teaching, Pavlos, King of Greece,
a tall heavy Dane, was shaking hands. The squeeze
I felt made me look up into a glare,
an iron look on the fat metal face of a weak
and sickly giant. Wind lifted his hair
just as our palms embraced. I smelled the Greek
    oregano and basil by the wall
and body odor of the guards. The king
grunted a phrase, a kind phrase. The press made
    fun of him,
O *Frederikos*, a dumb stand-in for a crafty Queen
    Frederika. But all
I knew at twenty-one was that slim
disputative queen gladly lent me her English books,
    and she, the loathed daughter of the Kaiser,
    pulled a palace on her string.

Often the Queen, her son, and I ate lunch together in the sunny dining area near the classrooms. My father-in-law, a strong antimonarchist had fed me his ideas about the unpopular Greek monarchy. But while monarchy had a bad history, since the new Queen was a German princess, maybe her presence in Greece might be the best way to reconcile or forget the scourge of nationalities. Enough is enough with ethnicities. There was already too much violence domestically between Greeks, meaning the fratricidal war. On everybody's lips and in the papers was the debate about executing captured *andartes* (Communist guerrillas), which had been routine during the conflict. The gruesome practice was carried on vigorously by both sides. When a village was taken by the *andartes,* as the first order of the day it was common to seek out and execute the most guilty civilians, meaning the village mayor, priest, and schoolteacher.

Being young and not very good about keeping my mouth shut, I said, "But it's terrible to execute prisoners of war, no matter who they are."

"They were not prisoners of war. They were thieves," the Queen said.

"Thieves," *"kleftes"* the common word for thieves, was an infelicitous way to denigrate the guerrillas, since in Greek history *kleftes* was the word the Turks called the Greek revolutionaries in the eighteenth century and even into the nineteenth century when large-scale war broke out in 1821. So her appellation actually endowed the guerrillas with patriotic Hellenic heroism. But in her defense, she made me feel it perfectly proper to argue. Clearly no one else in her entourage enjoyed that naturalness. The teachers were polite but obsequious. Maybe my youth and foreignness gave me privilege. In any case, I felt pleased to express opinions.

Sadly, the history of the monarchy in Greece has been catastrophic, culminating in the 1921 war with Turkey. Against the orders of the esteemed Greek prime minister Venizelos, Constantine II, who had been pro-German during World War I, managed to slip back into power and muddle Greece into what Greeks call the *katastrofí* (the catastrophe). He led Greek armies into Turkish territory. They were defeated, and there followed an exodus of more than a million and a half Greeks from Anatolia, including that of my family-in-law from ancient Greek lands. Greece shrank to half its size. In recounting this bit of crucial history— as one might the fall of Constantinople in 1453 or the earlier plunderings of Byzantium by the crusaders—I realize that these events, both the 1922 and 1453 catastrophes, are for Greeks like yesterday's happenings. And each country in the Balkans, in Europe, maybe in the world, has similar historical memories, which makes peace a sly abstraction almost impossible to capture for good.

I didn't last long at the school. One semester and then I was fired. I never knew why, but I'm sure I deserved that honor. So I spent time writing and painting. I was quite serious about painting until a friend from South Africa looked in one day at my studio and uttered a disgusted grunt. I stopped. But I wrote poetry, and l'Institut Français d'Athènes published my first book of poems. We knew many Greek writers and painters. My favorite was the composer Manos Hadzidakis, who usually worked all night and slept most of the day, so our meetings were usually at supper. I learned more about poetry from Manos than from anyone in Greece, from the poems he wrote for his songs or adapted from Greek folklore. Helle and I translated *The Other Alexander*, a novel by Magarita Liberaki into English, later put out by Noonday Press. It carried a wonderful preface by Albert Camus written for the earlier French translation of the novel. Meanwhile, the inheritance from my grandfather came through on which we survived for nearly four more years in Europe. These years gave me languages and landscapes, and made me a writer—who would continue, as here, to live as a writer off their memory.

María Tzalopoulou, Helle's mother, was a grand lady. She died a short time ago, at age ninety-five, in Queens. I feel her loss much more keenly than that of my own grandparents, whom I hardly knew, since I was a child when they died. And I cared for her over a period of four and a half decades. María had studied piano in Vienna. One evening in 1920 she was giving a private piano concert in her family's summer home on Pringipos, Princess Island, not far from Constantinople, which a young doctor in the Greek army, then stationed in Constantinople, attended. They talked, he proposed, and before the evening was up Vassili became her fiancé.

María had a strong character. And she could lose her temper without much effort. During the war, if the Greek army had used her, I think she might single-handedly have driven at least half the occupying armies out of the country. On a Sunday we were all invited to go to a small gathering of Vassili's medical friends. María said I should wear a tie because it was only proper to do so. She was rather proud of me. It was a hot summer night and I thought a nice open-collared white shirt would do. She got furious. She wasn't going to let her son-in-law disgrace her. When I refused, she shouted with contempt, *Sale juif!* (Dirty Jew!). I put on the tie, but at the party Vassili and I were the only ones wearing ties; our hosts persuaded us to take them off, which we did. Calling me a "dirty Jew" hurt my feelings, but it shouldn't have. María was the least anti-Semitic person possible. Like her daughter Helle, she couldn't care less that I was a Jew. But she would also call Helle a whore or an ignoramus if they had a disagreement about some trivial thing. Helle, quite used to this highly tuned musical instrument, took absolutely no offense at her occasional cacophony. It was María's way of being emphatic. Even she laughed at her excesses. She had no meanness in her. Though I wasn't in New York when she died, from all the daily reports I know how she suffered in her hospital bed from the oxygen mask she had to wear and all the tubes stuck in her after her stroke. And I feel pity for that strong woman and anger at the human condition that brings us into the world to take us out ignominiously and cruelly.

Vassili and I were always close. He was a dignified, quiet gentleman. Old-worldly, with no pretense, and very advanced in his profession. Vassili had published a volume of poems and stories before doing a book on internal medicine. I remember one sorrowful conversation. Though Vassili never said anything about my being a Jew, I think he thought it was interesting. I was primarily his son, an American, and he never once showed any resentment about the fact that I would one day take his daughter out of his country and we would live in Europe (meaning where Greeks go to when they cross the border) and in America. One afternoon we were sitting alone in the living room at the Maroussi house, waiting for dinner to be prepared. Some one hundred cypresses served as the wall around the vineyard in the middle of which our house stood. There was always a fragrance of evergreen and seemingly of marble, for we lived on the mountain from which the Parthenon was cut.

"It's true that Roosevelt was a Jew?" he said, questioning.

"No. He was Protestant."

(Roosevelt, Dutch name, like Rosenfeld in German, means "rose fields.")

"The du Ponts, the munitions makers, they were Jews, weren't they?"

"Yes, the du Ponts made explosives and everything else, especially plastics. But they weren't Jews."

(The first du Pont industrial figure was Eleuthère Irénée du Pont [1772–1832], born in France. He built a gunpowder plant at Brandywine Creek, near Wilmington, Delaware. His father's name was, innocently, Samuel du Pont.)

"But the great bankers behind Roosevelt were Jews?"

"I'm sure you heard this crazy Nazi propaganda during the Occupation. Hitler was making the Jews out to be the big shots in America and the vermin in Europe, all at once."

I felt uneasy. We never spoke more about Roosevelt the Jew, whom Vassili admired anyway as the American president who had turned the war around. This conversation took place in Greece only four years after the German armies pulled out. During the Occupation, the Greeks mounted a fierce resistance, which doesn't mean that no Nazi propaganda got through to the people and stuck.

White Islands and Northern Monasteries on Huge Stalagmites

We went north to Salonika by a long detour south—that is, by way of the Aegean islands, which is half of Greece, for they contain as much light as the rest of Greece, or perhaps the rest of Europe. To know Greece is to have lived in moveable light, from the iceberg light of Mykonos, the island of geometric forms whitewashed for the sake of blending with gulls and occasional clouds, to the mysterious clarity that hung over the medieval Orthodox monasteries at Mount Athos.

After my teaching job, Helle and I went to Mykonos, and we were the only *xeni* (foreigners) during our five months there. It was 1950. I taught English privately, learned to dance *rembetika* from Captain Andonis, who lived downstairs, and learned a geography of austere beauty and plainness that was to last a lifetime. We never had hot water. We usually had to fetch water from a well. I've never lived in such abundance. A few whitewashed rooms, a plain island table for writing, a mattress in the bedroom, and air and people. Every day was a feast, and I had no desire to leave.

White Island

My first day at the school for Constantine
I meet a peasant father with two hooks
(wounds from Albania) and the German Queen
of Greece who loans me her blue *Faber Book
of Verse.* But soon I'm fired and so begin

to loaf and write on islands. Mykonos,
the iceberg. I'm the only *xenos* in
the village, living with a Greek, and close
to getting jailed for working without papers.
The ship comes twice a week. Down at the pier
we all watch who comes in, but lemon vapors
of broiling fish seduce me. One white night
Captain Andonis slaps his heels. Austere,
he teaches me to dance, to live on light.

After half a year of living on and wandering the islands, we took to the country roads. On the long and beautiful way to Athos lay a thousand ancient sites, ports, villages, and cities. We began in the Peloponnesos. The first site was Olymbía (Olympia). No one lived nearby but a peasant hunter, who in the evening offered us a place to sleep on his floor by the fireplace, under animal hides which he spread over us to keep us warm. The winter freeze was only beginning to show cracks of spring.

In the morning at the famous but now empty site where Nero had once won a fixed chariot race to gain the laurel leaf of victory for his vanity, I spent a happy morning lugging an ancient lion head around in the cold sun. The lion's face had been left ignominiously stuck in blind soil with only its mane showing. About ten meters from his surface grave I found a low marble column and managed, with Archimedes' engineering help, to prop him nicely onto companion marble where he sits and gazes out to this day, chuckling at postcards that capture his now inviolable setting.

From Olymbía we bussed north to Mistrá, a Byzantine citadel and convent on a mountain overlooking the Peloponnesian orange-tree-covered plain of old Sparta. With solitary surprise we climbed up to this high refuge. The convent and church complex was the last Byzantine holdout to fall to the Ottoman Turks nearly a century after their capture of Constantinople in 1453. Now it breathed amid its cypresses, graveyard, mosaics, and attendant nuns. It had survived, indifferent to history and political rulers, with eternity its constant companion. But below, on the plain where the great city of Sparta had been, the city was gone, with scarcely a trace of even ruins from this warrior power that once had wasted Athens. Near its former site lay a net of tiny villages with old names and instructed memories.

From the Peloponnesos we crossed over the Isthmus of Corinth and reached Meteóra on the mainland, a center of fallen moon monasteries standing on natural pillars in northern Greece. We had climbed the steep steps at Meteóra to reach the monasteries on their stalagmite summits. Albert Schüpbach, a Swiss painter who was our traveling companion, was outrageously irreverent to an El Greco Saint Jerome-like father superior with whom we shared our provisions one stormy December night in high Meteóra. As we entered the fabulous building, perched in isolation on nature's tower mountains, we were greeted by the tall white-haired saint. Albert smiled and said, *"Bonjour, mon père,"* tapping the stern patriarch on the belly. After a flash of severe hesitation, the patriarch burst into laughter, and we were set for an evening of history and reminiscence.

Our room was a generous cell, with steel beds, a copper brazier that filled the room with a smoky blue haze, and walls painted yellow at some time shortly after the caesar Constantine left Rome to establish Christian Byzantium near the Bosporus. We had a small balcony that looked out at the wilderness of a black sky. I recall the monastery toilet next to our cell, a tiny closet extending precariously over the mountain. As you entered it, the walls trembled like a rocking ship. As I flipped open the cover to the wooden box toilet, the howling night rushed up at me. Sitting on its wooden box was like riding a gale of thunder and darkness.

Thessaloniki, a City of Peoples

With the Greco fury and colors in our heads, we took the dawn bus north to Salonika, that new romantic city on the sea. New by Greek standards, this *polis* (city) dates back only to 315 B.C.E. when it was founded by Cassander, king of Macedon, near the site of the ancient town of Therma (hot springs). Paul addressed his two epistles to the Thessalonians to members of the synagogue in Salonika, urging them to accept the true messiah. We were in the city that also had the aromas of Spain and Portugal for those wandering Jews from the 1492 Iberian diaspora. During the Second World War, when the Germans came down from Yugoslavia and took the city, they deported most of the Jews to their death in the camps.

The Matarasso family in 1917 (Archive of the Jewish Community of Thessaloniki)

Remembering this amazing city, I cannot help but reflect on its multiple populations, who themselves reflect multiple mirrors of Crusader Europe, Islamic Iberia, the Turkish Empire, and the last war of wars that erased its ancient Jewish presence. The Jews of Greece and elsewhere, like the Blacks in America or Africa and now increasingly in Europe, are the outsiders who do not demand or desire outsider status. To trace the history of one is to mirror the traces of the other. Tribal nationalism is unique to no grouping, and it must also include Jews and Blacks. But these "peoples," if I dare use the charged word, are the eternal other, marked by body or idea that make them different. And from difference come beauty, fascination, slavery, death. And from difference comes nations or families or gangs or peoples who easily conquer and kill each other because it feels good.

Hatred is joy. Murder is sexual ecstasy, as Camus and Melville show in their favored alienated criminals Meursault and Billy Budd. The record on otherness, from nations to the crippled and blind, is not up for the Nobel Peace Prize.

> It is a joy to feel sun
> sweeten the face
>
> of the exotic dancer
> and the hungry child,
>
> but deeper down,
> people love to hate.
> That sweet hatred
> I weave on flags
>
> and maps to cover
> the eyes of infidels.

> —KEFA THE MAPMAKER

Greeks and Jews and Blacks and Russians

Once I landed in Greece with its diaspora Greek Jews from the classical and Hellenistic periods, its Romaniot Greek Jews from the Byzantine centuries, and its Spanish Greek Jews from the 1492 expulsion from Spain, the Jewish question changed. Jews and Blacks are not local neighborhood presences without historical mirror. Jews and Blacks, like all peoples, are worlds, despite their tribal self-identifications; they are infinitely mixed worlds with ever-changing histories and emphases. The Jew is not only from old Mulberry Street and the upper West Side, nor is the Black only from the South Bronx, Harvard, or New Orleans. The Jew and Black are everywhere. Think of Aleksandr Pushkin (1799–1837), father of Russian poetry, whose great-grandfather was Abram Hannibal, Ethiopian slave, who became Peter the Great's favored general. Pushkin, proud of his mother's grandfather, was writing a historical novel about him at the time of his death. In the 1950s in New York, Aleksandr Sergeyevich Pushkin would have been considered a Black, or, had he not come clean, a Creole-tainted Anatole Broyard, who lived his literary life passing as a white.

I remember one afternoon in 1975 in Jorge Luis Borges's apartment in Buenos Aires. The writer was all jokes and laughter. He was delighted to discover that in addition to Spanish, Portuguese, English, and Jewish blood, he had black ancestors as well. "Look here now, I am a world," Borges spoofed. "Maybe one day I will be famous, like a tennis player." According to Argentine demographers, around 1900 ten percent of Buenos Aires was black. By the end of the century there were none. On this relativistic planet of changing names, identities, and secrets, what happened? Clearly, as the Jews disappeared from the Jesus family and the Jesus movement, so the Blacks ceased to be among the white Argentines, except in Borges's memory.

In reality, Jews were commingling with Greeks from the first blur of erudite speculation. They both learned to write by adapting versions of the Phoenician alphabet, itself a version of Egyptian hieroglyphs.[1] So we have Greek *alpha, beta, gamma,* and *delta* and Hebrew *aleph, beth, gimel,* and *daleth,* which recall Egyptian sign pictures for ox, house, throwing stick, and door. The Greeks and Jews confronted each other most decisively when the Greek armies of the Seleucid Antiochos IV and the Maccabee brothers faced off over hegemony in Israel. And eventually, we hear the Jew Paul (Shaul) of Tarsos speaking Greek in the synagogues of Greek lands, hoping to come out with new converts. After the Roman destruction of the Second Temple in Jerusalem in 70 c.e., Jews as well as

Christian Jews were expelled from the holy land and went in great numbers to Greek-speaking cities. But the emerging Christians kept the two holy books about the Jews as their own. And thereafter, Jews and Greeks were united. Jesus would always be known as the King of the Jews.

The Jews and Greeks were also united by the survival of the Gospels in Greek, which are four narrations of the life and death of an Aramaic-speaking Jew, Yeshua ben Yosef, crucified by Pontius Pilatus for sedition. Similarly, all the first Greek saints of Jerusalem, Saint Peter, Saint John, and Saint James, were actually Aramaic-speaking Jews, whose names were Kefa (Paul called him Cephas in Greek), Yohanan, and Yaakov. Beyond the borders of Israel most of the Jews in Egypt, Asia Minor, and Europe spoke Greek and had inhabited Greek lands since the sixth century B.C.E. when the Persian Cyrus the Great freed the Jews of Babylonia from captivity. Hence, this commingling of Greeks and Jews, in language, geography, shared culture, and religion, goes back to the archaic, classical, and Hellenistic periods of Greek civilization.

That early Christian pot contained a confusion of Jews, Greeks, and Romans, a fine combination for radically exciting ideas.

Jews, Greeks, and Romans in Alexandria

Jews, Greeks, and Romans seemed always in conflict and always profoundly influencing each other. We see this in beautiful Alexandria, with its population of Egyptians, Greeks, and Jews, and its contentious Roman rulers, who fought each other for possession. Alexandria was the center of Hellenistic civilization and Jewish culture. There lived the largest Jewish community in the ancient world. There lived Archimedes, Euclid, Longinos, and Plotinos. It was a city of poets and grammarians and the Library Museum with its 700,000 scrolls. By the second century B.C.E., the Greek Jews could no longer read Hebrew. So on the harbor island of Pharos, meaning "the lighthouse," where the giant lighthouse dominating the sea was one of the Seven Wonders of the World, seventy scholars in seventy days miraculously translated the Hebrew Bible into Greek. This was the famous Septuagint version. Its title means "seventy."[2] In the New Testament, composed in Greek, most of the citations from

Old Testament scriptures, from Genesis and Isaiah, are not from the Hebrew Bible but from the Greek Septuagint of the Jews.

Among the Jews of the city was the great philosopher Philo of Alexandria (30? B.C.E.–C.E. 45?) who platonized Jewish thought, making Platonic ideas accessible to both Jews and gentile believers in the new Messianism (Christianity). As Hillel, the foremost Pharisee teacher and philosophical parent of Paul brought the notion of platonic eternity into Judaic thought, so Philo categorized platonic speculation, and, through his four steps of understanding, provided the ladder of ascent for much of Western mystical speculation.

Cavafy and His Poem "Of the Jews (A.D. 50)"

In his poem "Of the Jews (A.D. 50)," the modern Greek poet Constantine Cavafy (1863–1933) described the mixed passions that separated and held the peoples of his Alexandria together. He recreated classical Alexandria in his poems for its own sake and as a metaphor for his personal sensual and historical purpose. With amazing cunning, he revealed the duality of pious Judaism versus secular Hellenism. Cavafy's poem is a clear metaphor for two diverging identities and beliefs. Ianthis, son of Anthony, has a Greek name and is a painter, poet, runner, and discus player. He is the perfect classical Greek figure, excelling in the arts of the mind and body, but he is also one "of the holy Jews." As an emblem of Greek and Jewish worlds, Ianthis reveals the richness of these conflicting diversities that were, despite public protest, inextricably mingled.

Of the Jews (A.D. 50)

Painter and poet, runner and discus-thrower,
beautiful as Endymion, Ianthes, son of Anthony
was from a family friendly to the synagogue.

My most honest days
are when I leave behind the aesthetic search,
when I leave behind beautiful and hard hellenism,
with its paramount focus
on perfectly made and mortal white limbs.

> And I become the person I wish
> always to remain—of the Jews, the holy Jews, the son.
>
> His eager declaration: "Always
> to remain of the Jews, the holy Jews—"
>
> But he did not remain that way at all.
> The hedonism and art of Alexandria
> held him, a devoted son.

This intensely diverse and innovative first century also gave rise to trauma. While the struggle of Jewry for civic rights and freedom was often successful in Roman Alexandria, in the year 37 the Jews were massacred. On too many occasions Jews fell to the Roman sword or were burnt alive by some Greeks who, as Josephus documents, resented their presence in the multiethnic city (*Bellum Judaicum* II, 18.7–8). In 115 the Jews in Alexandria and in Cyrene (a strong cultural center in Cyrenaica in Libya) revolted against the Roman emperor Trajan. On this occasion they were supported firmly by the Egyptian masses. The revolt spread all over Roman North Africa. It was born of a messianic dream of establishing a kingdom of heaven in these lands, freed from the yoke of Rome. When the rebellion was finally put down in 117, the Jews in Egypt were decimated and their quarters devastated. Communities would rise again later, but it was never the same. For the Jews, imbued as they were with classical and Hellenistic thought and deeply involved in the Alexandrian institutions such as its fabled Museum Library, their very existence was now mayhem. Rome's revenge extended to Cyprus, where Jews were in all parts of the island. "The entire community was exterminated."[3]

But from all this destruction and sorrow came at least one major benefit. After Trajan's consuming embroilment in North Africa and the islands, the Romans ended their attempted penetration into Eastern lands, that is, into Babylonia and the Parthian Kingdom, which had become a haven for diaspora Jews. There, in Babylon, then under Persian rule, was formulated the famous Babylonian Talmud, a rabbinical book of instructions and commentary on the Bible consisting of Mishnah and Gemara.

Romaniot Jews in Byzantium

Despite so many untoward events, most of Jewry still lived in Greek-speaking lands under the Romans. By the third century, some one million Jews represented a tenth of the peoples in the Roman empire.[4] The fourth century saw great changes. Constantine the Great had a vision of crosses in mid-battle and became the first Christian Roman emperor. Classical "pagan" culture yielded to the new moralities. Emperor Theodosios I razed the great Library of Alexandria. As for the Jews in Byzantium, the seat of the new Roman Empire, the situation was bad. Christians had at last found legal rights, but the Romaniot Jews, as they were called, did not. By the time of the Crusades the restrictions, the forced migrations, and the mass murder were a fact of despair.

With the Fourth Crusade in 1204, the Venetians sacked and seized Constantinople, splitting Byzantium and establishing their own states in Macedonia, Thrace, and Greece. This was the first of Western plunders that prepared the city for the eventual conquest by the Ottomans in 1453. Now most of the Byzantine lands, except for Epirus, Nicaea, and the Trebizond area on the Black Sea, passed from Greek hands to the Franks, or the Frangi, the Greek epithet till this day for the Crusaders and even Europeans. The Venetians brought with them the *serenissimo,* later called the "ghetto," from the name of an island near Venice where the Jews were forced to live. The *serenissimo,* a beautiful word meaning "most serene," was imposed in Crete, Corfu, and many parts of Greece. With its severe constraints, the economic life of these noncitizens withered.

The Sephardim in Muslim Spain

By contrast to the travail of Jews under diverse Christian rule, in the Muslim world, particularly in Islamic Spain under the enlightened Ummayad Caliphate of Córdoba, the Sephardic Jewry enjoyed centuries of freedom. There was an extraordinary flourishing in letters and the sciences, and the Jews were welcomed into public professions and high governance. This resurgence reached into every field in what was called "The Jewish Golden Age."[5] The magnificent Jewish poets, Judah Halevi from Tudela (c.1075–141) and Solomon ben Judah Ibn Gabirol from Málaga (c.1021–58), wrote in Hebrew verse but followed Arabic prosody and versification. These poets were preceded by "the David of his age,"[6] Samuel the Nagid (Shmuel HaNagid in Hebrew, Samuel Ibn Negrila in Arabic; 993–1056) from Córdoba, who was also vizier of the new taifa (city state) of Granada and leader of Granada's armies in battle against Seville and Málaga. He rebuilt the old Moorish fort, the Alcalá Alhambra (al-Qala al-Hamra or "Red Castle"), which dominated the new city of Granada only recently established on the Darro River, and his son Joseph laid out the gardens around the Alhambra. The philosopher Maimonides from Córdoba wrote his *Guide to the Perplexed* in Arabic, in which the most important philosophy in Europe was then composed. In his *Guide* he presents a rational proof of the existence of God, based on an allegorical exegesis of the Old Testament.

But peace was always precarious—a habit of the world—and Samuel the Nagid himself led Muslim armies of his taifa victoriously against other rival taifas; so too there were terrible reversals even in Muslim Spain. In 1066, under the newly arrived and fanatical Almoravids Berbers, there were anti-Jewish riots in Granada, with loss of life, including the killing of Samuel's son Joseph, the architect and editor of his father's poems. Victor Perera gives us a poignant account of the sequel to the Granada slaughters: "By the end of the twelfth century, thousands of Jews had fled north to the Christian kingdoms of Aragon and Castile, which offered them sanctuary in exchange for vassalage and the payment of feudal taxes."[7]

In the fourteenth century the severely repressive Almohad Berber rulers, who followed the Almoravids, killed or expelled Jews from many Andalusian cities. At first the Jews, many of whom were highly educated, bilingual merchants and other professionals, were handsomely welcomed in the North and given privileges from state and monarchy. But conditions changed. Toledo, the early capital of Spain, with a large Jewish community, was for centuries famous for its multilingual school of translators and contributions to greater European culture. The high moment in Toledo was the thirteenth century when, as Perera notes, "The Castilian king Alfonso the Wise recruited Christian, Jewish and Muslim sages to compile an encyclopedia of astronomy, entitled *El Libro de Saber (The*

Book of Learning)."⁸ Moreover, in 1261, for the first time in Christian Spain, under his Code of Seven Parts, Alfonso guaranteed the Jews the freedom of worship and civil safeguards. However, "a Jew who cohabited with a Christian woman was condemned to the sword." But in 1391, incited by the preaching of an incendiary friar, Vicente Ferrer, Toledo's Marrano converts (the Marranos, meaning "swine," were Jews forcibly converted to Christianity) were executed in huge numbers or driven back to Muslim lands.

There is an irony in the obsession with *limpieza* (clean or untainted blood), which later under Isabela la Católica was to be a legal prop of the Inquisition and its auto-da-fé. There was probably not a noble family in Spain which by this time had not intermarried with Jews, including that of King Fernando of "Isabela and Fernando," whose maternal grand-mother was a Jew. Yet Fernando was particularly cruel in upholding the laws of purity, rejecting the pope's pleas for mercy for those seized by the Dominican friars, who, as earlier in France against the Cathars, carried out inquisition police work. Prodded by Fernando, the inquisitor general Tomás de Torquemada (himself of *converso* ancestry) "relaxed" (burned) thousands of *conversos* and "reconciled" at least 40,000 more to life confinement in prison.

Toledo had been a city of synagogues, the "Jerusalem of the West" as Salonika was later to be called the "Jerusalem of the North." Soon after the fires and slaughter, there remained only two synagogues. One was the small austere gem that became the convent of Santa María la Blanca, now a museum; the other was the grand Sinagoga El Tránsito, built by Samuel Halevi Abulafia as a mirror of Alhambra architecture, which became a church in the Alcántara Military Order.

The last Moorish stronghold in Granada fell in 1492 to the Spanish armies of Isabela and Fernando. In the spring of the same year, Isabela la Católica signed the Edict of Expulsion for Jews. She gave them three months to convert or leave. Huge numbers fled to Portugal, where they soon encountered the bitterness of the Portuguese Inquisition, which also ordered conversion or expulsion. Those who refused conversion, perhaps half, went mainly to Morocco, Italy, the Balkans, and Holland.⁹

On July 31, 1492, the Ottoman Turks filled more than fifteen ships in Andalusian ports to bring the first wave of 20,000 Jews to Turkey and to lands in Turkish control. Catching the common chaos of Jews and Muslims undergoing forced conversion and then exile from Spain, Khaled Mattawa writes, recalling a vanished past in Iberia of three peoples and their structures:

> And when they speak to me in Spanish,
> I say Moriscos and Alhambra,
> I say Jews rescued by Ottoman boats.[10]

Spain lost its most industrial, educated, and hard-working class, and thereafter the nation slid into centuries of economic turpitude. New World gold could not replace the industry of the expelled Jews and Moors. Turkey gained. The sultan Beyazid II is reported to have remarked, "How foolish of the monarchs of Spain to impoverish their empire while enriching my own."

Jews and Greeks in Thessaloniki

Under Islam in Turkey, the Jews again prospered. In the Byzantine period, it is true that there were places and moments when things improved. In the eleventh century, Byzantium recovered Thebes and Thessaloniki, and Romaniot Jews were permitted to enter the production and dyeing of silk. But these moments did not last. In nearly two thousand years after the great diaspora of 70–71 C.E., the only safe and constant haven for Jews was in lands controlled by Muslims in the Near East, North Africa, Spain, and Turkey.

After 1492, with the great exodus of Jews from Spain, the Sephardim brought their Latin language, Ladino (Spanish), into North Africa, Italy, Holland, the Balkans, and the formerly Greek lands that comprised the Ottoman Empire. They came with their professions and their cultural nostalgia for Spain. Borges has a sonnet on old Spanish Jews who remember Toledo and an earlier legion of Roman soldiers (under Titus in the Jewish War of 66–70 C.E.) that pillaged and burned the Temple. He captures the nostalgia of five centuries for their home in Spain:

A Key in Salonika

Abarbanel, Farías or Pinedo,
Hurled out of Spain in an unholy sweep
Of persecution, even now they keep
The doorkey of an old house in Toledo.
At last, from hope and terror they are free
And watch the key as afternoon disbands.
Cast in its bronze are other days, far lands,
A weary brilliance, a calm agony.
Now that its door is dust, the instrument
Is a cipher of diaspora and wind
Like the other temple key someone flung high
Into the blue (when Roman soldiers bent
And charged with dreadful flames and discipline)
And which a hand received into the sky.

Most of the Turkey-bound Jews settled in Constantinople, the most vibrant city of the Greeks, as it had been since Constantine the Great. But by the mid-sixteenth century there was a huge influx into Thessaloniki (Salonika), breathing life into the city. Salonika became one of the richest trading cities in the world. It was called the Mother of Israel, and so it was for four centuries. In the sixteenth and seventeenth centuries there were more Jews in Salonika than English in London (where no Jews were permitted to settle until Oliver Cromwell's brief reign). During this period the Jewish population varied between a third to two-thirds of the city's cosmopolitan inhabitants, which included Christian Greeks, Serbs, Armenians, Bulgars, and Turks. Kemal Atatürk (1881–1938), the founder of modern Turkey, was born and raised in Salonika. The main language of the city, in commerce and culture, was Spanish. By 1900 the Greek Jewish population of Salonika was approximately 78,000;[11] the Christian Greek population, 40,000; and the Bulgarian, 5,000. Salonika dwarfed Athens in population and vitality.

The Greek War of Independence of 1821 was disastrous for Jewish communities in the Peloponnesos, where the revolution began. The Jews of Mistras, Kalamata, and Tripolis were massacred, decimated. The few survivors moved north to the cities of Volos and Halkís, still under

Ottoman rule. After the Second Balkan War in 1912, Greece finally regained possession of Thessaloniki as its ancient historical city. The fortunes of the Greek Jews plunged. There were anti-Jewish riots. Newspapers printed articles making the traditional charge against Jews of ritual murder of Christian children during the Passover in order to use their blood for making unleavened bread. Three-quarters of their property was expropriated.

Jews had been living in Greece since the Babylonian Exile, before Alexander the Great came down from Macedon; and by the time of Paul, every Greek city in Asia Minor and Europe had a Jewish population. Now in ancient Thessaloniki, they were becoming highly restricted outsiders, and life was precarious. A series of mysterious fires, the first around 1900, then a terrible one in 1917, wiped out half the Jewish quarters. The city's thirty-two synagogues were ashes. After the 1921–22 war between Greece and Turkey and the arrival in Salonika of large numbers of Greek refugees from Asia Minor, the Greek Jews began to leave in larger numbers for America, France, and other countries. Then, on June 23, 1931, the fascist National Association of Greece (Ethniki Enosis Ellados) attacked two hundred fifty Jewish homes, burning them to the ground. There was again a large exodus.

On the eve of World War II, there were 56,500 Jews in Salonika, still a third of the city's population.

Facts on the Slaughter

During World War II German armies came down from Yugoslavia and took the city, confining all the Jews to two quarters to facilitate the subsequent slaughter.

The human details of the last years of the Jews in their ancient city are horrible. In the summer of 1943 during the Occupation thousands of young Jewish men were stoned and jeered and were tortured publicly, as a spectacle, in the main Elefthería Square of Salonika. ("Elefthería" ironically means "freedom.") Some had fled to other cities on the mainland and on the islands. Soon 45,649 Jews were trucked away from the city and sent by trains to die in Auschwitz. The Bulgarians rounded up

Deportation of Jews from Kavalla, March 1943

4,200 from Kavalla, Drama, and Komotini, and delivered them to the Germans, who sent them to the extermination camp at Treblinka. Only 216 survived.

The Jews of Athens, less than four thousand, fared much better. They were well integrated into the community, and half of them survived. While the puppet Greek Prime Minister Constantine Rallis announced that the Salonikan Jews were subversives and deserved their punishment, the Greek archbishop Damaskinos, at peril to his own life, did everything he could to arrange for concealment and escape for his Athenian Jews. Many in Greece (among them my Greek family) risked fortune and life to hide or find escape for Jews; others were indifferent or ignoble.

In Corfu, whose Jews dated back to antiquity, "the mayor declared a public holiday on the day the Jews were deported."[12] Of two thousand prewar Jews, 185 survived the camps; almost none survived from the old community in Crete with its famous synagogue in Haniá.[13] But on the large Adriatic island of Zakynthos, the archbishop and mayor were ordered by the classically educated German commandant to bring him a list of the Jews who lived or who had taken refuge in Zakynthos. They returned the following morning with a sealed letter. When opened, it contained only two names, that of the bishop and the mayor. They saved all the Jews on the island, many of them escapees from Salonika and Kavalla.

One sorrowful event to me as a teacher relates to the Aristotle University of Thessaloniki, which for some years before the war tried to persuade the Jewish community to move its cemetery, the largest and oldest Jewish cemetery in Europe. The request was politely refused.[14] In late 1942, in a desperate move to ransom the 9,000 Jewish men of Thessaloniki who had been sent to forced labor camps, the community council made an agreement with Dr. Max Merten, the German military representative, to relinquish their 2,000-year-old ancestral graveyard, though Jewish law forbids the disinterment of the dead. Every piece of marble and brick was used as building material: the marble of the tombstones was used to repair churches damaged in the Italian air raids, to build swimming pools for the German officers, and as doorsteps for homes. The university annex was built on the land which had held a half-million graves. The men came home, but it was a temporary reprieve. In 1944 they were among the 45,649 known Jews from Thessaloniki who were deported to Auschwitz and Bergen-Belsen. Today the Spanish and Hebrew names remain visible on many of the stones.

The murder of Jews in Greece and Eastern Europe was directed by the Nazi ideologue Alfred Rosenberg, who supplied Hitler with his theory of "the master race." His immediate enforcer for the "Rosenberg Commando" was SS Major General Jürgen Stroop, who had also supervised the destruction of the Warsaw Ghetto in May 1943 and the dynamiting of the Great Synagogue of Warsaw.[15] Alfred Rosenberg was executed as a war criminal in Nuremberg in 1946. Stroop was executed as a war criminal in Warsaw in 1951.

In Greece the disappearance of northern Jews was recorded on water.

But in April 2003, exactly sixty years later, the prime minister of Greece, Konstantinos Simitis, declared April 29 to be thereafter a national holiday to commemorate the Greek Jews of Salonika.

Thessaloniki and Absence

Today, the Jews in Spain and Greece are few. In both countries events took care of the Jewish problem: from Spain of 1492, expulsion and exile; in Greece of 1943, deportation and execution. Now, in their absence, in Spain there is a romanticization of all things Sephardic, from Spanish songs of the Jews of the Near East, in frequent concert, to Maimonides and rebuilding of historic synagogues in Córdoba and Toledo. Spaniards often speak with proud nostalgia of their Jewish blood and names that prove a medieval family ancestry. So too in Greece the romance of Greek Jews and their music has begun to take hold. In the last few years a best-selling CD was recorded by George Dalaras, Greece's international performer, singing traditional Greek and Sephardic songs with the Israel Philharmonic Orchestra. Similarly, there have been popular recordings by contemporary Greek and Turkish musicians, playing together with the purpose of ending centuries of stupidities and separation and of showing artistic and spiritual commonality.

But as for other popular, educational, and political acknowledgment of the long history of Jews in Thessaloniki and other Greek cities, there is a terrible record of absence. Of the some 69,000 Greek Jews slaughtered by the German occupiers, there have been few public words or gestures of their existence.[16] Nevertheless, according to records, 12,897 Jews served in the Greek army fighting the Italian and German invading armies, and thousands fought in special units of the Greek underground.[17] By war's end, about ninety-five percent of the Jews in Greece were dead. Thousands of Christian Greeks also died as soldiers, in the underground, and as hostages. For the latter there are monuments, stamps, histories, memorial days, and abundant literature, that is, the full and appropriate attention for the nation's fallen. But the Jew who fell, fell into nowhere.

Were the 45,649 known Jews from Salonika or the 2,000 from nearby Kavalla not also Greeks? Did their religion make them non-people? Did Jews not also fashion Greece's modern event and ancient intellectual history, among whom we think of Philo of Alexandria, Paul of Tarsos, and John of Patmos? Look at faces in pictures of those who disappeared in the Greek holocaust. Are they human? Is otherness or difference or tribal nationalism or religion—who can pinpoint it?—such that these poor victims of barbaric behavior should be officially forgotten, as yet unmentioned in any public school text? One cannot know what has passed through the minds of authority. I prefer not to take silence as tacit congratulation to killers for their ethnic cleansing. But, alas, I am persuaded that these silences eloquently signify that the death of these many Greeks is of no concern.

Some have protested.

In 1999, at the insistence of Greek historians, consideration was given to noting in future textbooks that once in the city of Thessaloniki there had been a Jewish presence. It is good to remember, or, as so many have stated, in the future we are lost. All the Jews are gone now, except for twelve hundred from here and there who have come back to the city. That fabled Salonika, the only Jewish city in Europe, the Jewel of the Balkans—are these epithets a sin and anathema to recall?—has disappeared forever.

Days and Nights with Odysseus on the Way to Holy Athos

> Who knows the Holy Mountain of Athos
> has stepped on the earth of heaven.
>
> —PIOTR AMBÁROV, *Diary of a Russian*

The way to Athos was an odyssey. A small *kaiki* took us there. Each morning the gales threw our black sails against the sun and we slid ahead almost invisibly. With bad weather we made only a short distance. From Salonika to the peninsula required four days on the sea. At night we anchored in tiny harbors or camped on abandoned beaches. One night we slept in a lodge. At dawn the sky took on the colors of a bloody Barbary fig.

On our *kaiki* there was a village storyteller, and all through our Homeric voyage, he told his tales to us. I shivered under a coarse red-and-black wool blanket, listening to war adventures, village dramas, and comic and dirty stories. He was a worthy teller of tales during our sea voyage, and his audience eagerly took in every word.

Only one person on the little craft was not a peasant—an engineer from Salonika. A tall, slender Greek with an angular face that would fit well on a chapel wall next to an icon of the Panagyía, he introduced himself to me with friendly formality. By his Spanish name, Alejandro López-Pinedo, I realized he was a Greek Jew.

"What part of Greece are you from?"

"Thessalonki."

"I thought the Jews of Salonika were dead."

"If I'm not mistaken, I'm still alive."

"How did that happen?"

"I'm not sure, but I was young and strong enough, and I guess lucky. But almost all of us, my friends and my entire family, were gassed on the train. I was on a cattle car that went right to a camp. And I lasted. What can I say?" He looked at me quizzically and threw up his hands.

"How many of you are left in Salonika?"

"A handful. But that's passed. And we're passed."

"What do you mean?"

"A world is gone. I remember, but it's gone. Now I'm a Greek, hardly a Jew. I'm also a survivor, but a lonely one. There is a small Jewish community now. Less than a fiftieth of us from Salonika got back. What I learned about Judaism, I learned in the camps. The camps were a long, unbearable agony because hope was beaten out of us. We saw too much, and there was nothing else. Here in Salonika there is little to remind of the Jews, as if five centuries of Spanish Jews in this city never were. The old quarters are unrecognizable." He slipped on his glasses, looking at the waters. "And before the Spanish Jews, for two thousand years were Greek Jews, here and all over the Eastern Mediterranean and Anatolia. Salonika always had a Jewish presence, since Alexander's time. But today it has no real connection with prewar times when I was a child or when I was in the camps. I am a man of voices that remain in me," and he touched his chest, "who can't speak to each other. I can't decipher them, but I hear them, often enough, like a far, rumbling aftershock. I hear my Spanish tongue in me, though I never speak or hear it outside. I don't know whether I still have it to use, but it still speaks to me in deaf whispers."

Alejandro paused, and we said nothing.

Then he said, "My past is an unreal memory of a memory. The civil war is almost over. And I can only go on with the present. That's why you find me on this adventure boat. We're both imitating captain Odysseus."

The civil war too was already almost a memory. There were only some isolated skirmishes, especially in this remote part of Greece. After we landed, I did have a military escort for the last miles of the trip. With soldiers in front and behind, we went on muleback through the snow, forest on one side where the *andartes* were operating, sea on the other, until we came to the actual monastery walls. It was López-Pinedo who had told me how the walls went up around the two Jewish sectors. I was thinking of Thessaloniki as I rode on my mule, freezing in the December breeze off the sea.

Mount Athos is a community of monasteries on the southern tip of the Halkidiki peninsula in northwestern Greece. Restricted, alas. No women have ever been allowed to visit or live in the areas, much less in the monasteries, of Athos. Women are the Jews and Blacks of gender. That bigotry against women has a Judeo-Christian religious origin, going back to the Garden for its justification. But an incident in the Garden, of Eve choosing to defy God's hegemony by choosing the fruit that gave both her and her mate knowledge cannot alone explain a uniform history of depreciation of women in the West or any place else. Surely there are many explanations. In Athos the prejudice against women simply intensifies, in this holiest of places, on this holy mountain (Hagion Oros), the essential sorrow of Christianity and virtually all religions, which see women as property, as child makers, as servants to their husbands. So the lonely monks who come to Athos never again set eyes on a living woman, though quite a few females, like Mary, play significant roles in icons and on wall paintings and mosaics.

There are also no permanent residents on the mountain who are not of the Orthodox faith. But within that already wide category, this medieval metropolis has sketes and monasteries representing Bulgaria, Romania, Serbia, and Russia, scattered on the southern part of the peninsula. The monks have their plots of land to grow vegetables, fruit, and olives, and are largely self-sufficient. They chop wood in the forest that slopes down the peninsula into the northern sea.

The first night I spent in Zografou, a Bulgarian monastery castle hanging over the sea like a mountain in Tibet leaning over an abyss. My hosts treated me to cold beans, bread, and vinegared wine, and I opened a can of sardines of my own to share with them. Sleep came early and mountain deep. My bed was a thin straw mattress on a wood bench, and not too wide.

The next morning I began roaming the pathways. I met a Russian hermit prince as he came walking around a tall hedge. We exchanged greetings. The prince looked like Tolstoy (on Mykonos I had been close to Tolstoy's grandson Alexander, the French linguist) and spoke impeccable British English. We went to his little hermitage and shared some bread and liqueur. It was all strangely matter-of-fact. He was perfectly at ease in his hermitage and had no regret for lost estates or homeland or sophisticated company. This was 1950, thirty-three years after the revolution in his native country that made him an exile in a remote mountain Eden. I wondered what lay behind his imperiously good manners, his cheerful resignation and wisdom. As in a story by Borges, when the seeker finds the jaguar with the invisible script on it or the Indian god in the desert or the poet with the word in the Chinese court—here the author, Borges, stops, since no one can sanely blurt out words of truth. The unknown, if it is worthwhile, must remain unknown and not be cheapened and confined by explanation and summary. So I assumed there to exist that huge spirit, with its keys and enigmas, into which the Russian hermit might retreat or experience at will. Perhaps it was my desire that the spirit be there. In any case, here was a man serenely himself. He was a prince in his own hermitage.

In the evening there was a ceremony at Vatopedí, a Greek monastery. The monks were wearing magnificent vestments. The chapel was incense, icons, gold brocade, silver chalices. It was very dark and yet brilliant, the singing faces lighted as in a mannerist tableau. My eyes fixed on one beardless monk with gold hair who sang like a bullfrog or angel-woman to the Pantokrator. In his orange robe and the long uncut hair characteristic of all Greek clergy, he was clearly a shining intruder, not quite man or woman or angel among the dark-bearded friars. His eyes were fixed on the ceiling as he and the others sang the Byzantine hymns for Christmas. I cannot explain why, but when I looked at the angelic figure staring through the ceiling, I felt an immeasurable aloneness. I wasn't sure whether it was his isolation with his God or my remote witnessing.

Going Muleback in the Snow on the Holy Mountain of Athos during the Greek Civil War

Going muleback in the snow to the monasteries on the holy peak, I see
some rebel *kleftes* hiding from the drawn
weapons of the soldiers. When they spot me,
they fade. The forest groans. Once with the monks
they give me vinegared wine, bread, a bed
of straw on wood, and guide me to the crypt
where oil lamps by the icons show the blood
of converts sworn to parables and script
about some Essenes from the wilderness
who scorned the Roman weapons and were drunk
with faith and towering awe. Light gilds the hair
of one young beardless monk whose gaze and dress
call ancient zealots to their rebel prayer.

These Greek Orthodox monks, mainly of the order of Saint Basil (my father-in-law Vassili's saint-day name), had gone as far as they could—to a mountain at the bottom of a peninsula—in order to shun the world. Entranced as I have rarely been by ceremony, by the sonorous illumination of the singing monks, I thought of a much more extreme form of utopian community: the Essenes in the desert, practicing celibacy, wearing only white garments, healing by way of laying on of the hands, believing in the immortality of the soul (a platonic rather than Jewish notion, which the later Christian Jews took over by way of Greek influence), pledging preservation of the sect's secrets, and believing in baptism and of a messiah who might be just then coming out of the desert. The Essenes were clearly one of the more apparent bridges between Jews and the Christian Jews who had found the Messiah and called him by his Greek name, Christ.[18]

For a month I lived in Athos, going from monastery to monastery in that utopian peninsula, including a few weeks of pleasant solitary confinement and intense reading at the Russian skete, where I had my meals in an empty dining room under the blessing of great, life-size photographs of the Tzar and Tzarina, the ghosts who presided over the great uninhabited chamber.

My encounter with the second and third Jews in Greece took place some years later. The episode of speaking to Moses Morales still touches me, and being a happy pedant and hoarder of language incidents, I think the anomaly of our conversation may have overshadowed the human one. I hope not. Kyrios (Mr.) Morales was a ninety-year-old witty, articulate accountant in Athens, whom I went to one year to prepare my income taxes. We talked. In Greek and English, but mainly in English, which he liked to practice. When he began to go over the accounts, he switched into Spanish. I assumed he was a Spanish Jew. After all, he was counting in Spanish, so I began speaking to him in his own tongue.

"I no longer speak Spanish," he interrupted me.

"But how can you say that? You're counting in Spanish."

"That is correct. You have noticed that I am counting in Spanish."

"Then why do you say you don't speak Spanish."

"Because I do not speak it. I count, but I don't speak. I wish also I spoke. But I count in Spanish because I feel I can count *only* in Spanish, my childhood language, and many of us count only in our first language. Or we give in to that belief. But I'm ninety, and I've forgotten my Spanish since I haven't spoken it since I was a child. Maybe a day will come after I retire, and I'll go to Spain and remember."

So we had a good long laugh, and he kept counting in Spanish until he finished our accounts.

Helle's father, Vassili, came from Mólista, a tiny village in Epirus in northwestern Greece, which no one, except for family, visits. It is run-down but beautiful, and I remember spending hours standing on stools in a small Byzantine chapel where Stathúla, Helle's aunt, directed me in replacing the candles that were burning along the walls and on candelabras. When Vassili became a doctor, he returned to the mountain village a few times a year to treat the sick, free of charge. He loved the region, and his book of short stories was based on Epirote incidents, many of them a retelling of gossip and legends told him by his younger half-brother Apostólis, who was a hunter, a lazy café habitué, and a master story-teller. High and lonely in the mountains and overlooking a plain that separates it from Albania, Mólista was by then an almost empty village, deserted by the young who went to work in the cities, inhabited by a few old families who remained and a few stragglers who have come back to retire in the good mountain air. Helle had wanted me to know her father's birthplace, so we stayed in the stone house of her grandfather. Our window faced the mountains and looked directly on spooky, unvisitable Albania, Southern Epirus, which was mainly Greek inhabited, where at that time, given the sweetness of nationalities, the Greeks and Albanians lived in their mysterious prison.

Overlooking Rock Meadows of Forbidden Albania

That night it rained a thousand years and when
my heart was soaked, Mólista windows turned
to sleet. The cold intensified. Again
between your breasts I read you poems we earned
in Greek because this mountain cottage near
the Albanian border was a single lamp
and moon-coarse blankets smelled of wool winter
and candles. "Don't expect to sleep." Souls damp
with longing blare like sirens. We were still
because we had the speech of solitude.
A thousand years is nothing for a pound
of rain together. We made love. To fill
the soul with bread and olive oil is crude
and wonderful. Night gossiped while we drowned.

After the high village we went down to Hades. By the river Acheron, now a very narrow river with a few rowboats tied up on the bank nearest Hell, stands the prehistoric temple, in good condition, that Homer describes as where Achilles descended to find his father. We went down the old marble steps one flight into the underground basement, damp with the dead, but keeping its deeper secrets intact as do Troy in Turkey and Knossos in Crete. And also in Epirus we went to the capital city of Yánnina (Ioánnina), founded by the Byzantine emperor Justinian in about 527 C.E. Early in the nineteenth century, Ali Pasha, the "lion of

Yánnina" described by Byron in *Childe Harold,* governed an area including Albania and Epirus, independently of the Sultan in Constantinople. Ali Pasha was a brutal, romantic, cultured figure. By one of his many structures overlooking Lake Yánnina is an exquisite synagogue. During the Occupation the Germans used it as a stable. So it was desecrated, but it was not burnt as was the great synagogue of Frankfort on the evening of Hitler's Kristallnacht, November 9, 1938, when viewers witnessed in newsreels around the world the huge fires that enveloped Europe's old and most significant synagogue and saw its dome and building in black clouds finally collapse into veins and bones of death across the streets. This horrible event, meant to terrify, signified that the Jew's Vatican palace was gone for anyone who cared to care. That night of murder and broken crystal was the first loud step to the camps and ovens.

Here the few thousand prewar Jews of Epirus, who date back to classical Greek times, were sufficiently isolated to resist becoming Hispanized as were the other original Jewish populations of Thessaloniki and Athens, so they had their own popular songs and folklore as well as their own religious practice. They knew no Spanish. Of these original diaspora Jews, only a handful survived the Occupation. Folklorists study their song (a dissertation on Epirote Jewish song was recently completed at my university), but the people have disappeared. When I went inside the synagogue, with its blue and orange colored walls, I was guided by one of the survivors. I noticed the tattoo on his arm.

"Where did you get the tattoo?" I said to him.

"Auschwitz."

"How did you survive?"

The short man looked at me severely, almost aggressively, and declared, "*Dioti O Theós ton íthele*" ("Because God wanted it so").

There were other survivors, including Eva Victoria Perera, who wrote from the island of Andros, where, as in Zakynthos, there were those who with false papers and friends made it.

Day Breaks on Andros, 1944

When all at once dogs bark from the cobblestone
labyrinth in my nightmare and donkeys clop,
more burdened than ever, and the roosters panic
with church bells, footsteps, a screaming lamb,

I think, they know who I am, and they'll take me away . . .
at last, they've identified me, however narrowly.

Cerberus howls his unwanted welcome;
the doves grunt with the weary souls
in the underworld.

Then just as suddenly I wake, a taste on my tongue
like something spoiled. The red hibiscus flowering
outside the window spins a second among sunrays,
then stops. A gust of wind.

I'm on the island, safe for now.

I reach for my glasses on the nightstand,
put them on, and the room's colors shift into focus.
Then I turn my head slowly on the pillow,
almost afraid to reassure myself.

My daughter is asleep, there on the small bed
next to mine, her lips moving a little,
her braid coiled along her neck, her hand resting
on the chest of her doll.

I remember it is Easter Sunday and the scream
I heard was the lamb carried off to be slaughtered.
Today I will celebrate, too, posing as a Christian,
and I will call out with the rest, *Christos anesti!*
Christ has risen.

We've been passed over. I allow
sleep to lay its heavy body on mine
and I sink beneath it for a few more hours,
still and dreamless.

—EVA VICTORIA PERERA (TR. ALIKI BARNSTONE)

The Madness of a Jew Trying to Marry in a Greek Orthodox Church in Crete

At the end of January we were all back in Athens. By February, bureaucracy had caught up with us again. Helle and I had been married civilly in Paris. The American government recognized this marriage and gave Helle a visa in her passport to enter the United States. The Greek government also recognized that I was married to her; but since we did not have a religious marriage in the Greek Orthodox church, and Orthodoxy is the state religion, it didn't recognize that she was married to me. Therefore, they would not issue her an exit visa for foreign travel. In those days only Greek students, businessmen, and diplomats were granted exit visas. This onerous restriction was an attempt to prevent hard currency, meaning dollars or English pounds (the drachma was virtually worthless in the international market) from leaving the country. It did succeed in reducing foreign travel by its citizens. Few knew whom to bribe.

In our case the most obvious way to circumvent the visa problem was to get married in a Greek Orthodox church. I had reservations, but if this was forced upon us, what else could we do? For another kind of personal bureaucracy, Helle had been willing to marry in the synagogue—not joyfully, but, as everything she did, with grace and good will.

Vassili called the Athens bishop, who had once been his patient. I sat near him in the room facing Tzortz street, where just a few years earlier there had been so much shooting during the December uprising.

"My son-in-law, an American, wants to marry my daughter in the church," I heard him saying on the phone.

"How can he be your son-in-law and marry her again? Isn't that bigamy?"

Vassili laughed. "No, my bishop, they were married in a civil ceremony in Paris. Now we want a church marriage."

"Very good. I will do it myself for my doctor friend."

"Thank you. Oh, by the way, he's a Jew."

"No thank you. It's impossible." And he hung up.

"That was short and sweet," Vassili told me. "So much for the bishop." Vassili had no more love for the clergy than he did for the monarchy.

"What next?" I asked.

"Go to some other city, as you did for your visa to get into Greece. But not as far as Genoa."

I had not been able to get an entry visa for Greece in Paris, and so stopped in Genoa a few days to do it from there. I took a ship from Marseilles to Genoa. My first night in Italy I spent in the kitchen of the *pensione* where I was staying, chatting for hours after supper with the cook and the maid. It was my first exposure to the Mediterranean sun at night, and all this seemed more natural in Italy than it might have been in France or America. I was always grateful that visa trouble led me by ship to that Italian kitchen, forcing me to spend my first hours in a country I love almost as much as Greece.

Now, after a year in Greece, we were making plans for leaving. At least for the possibility of leaving. I was glad to have to stay in Greece longer. A second year was already getting language, friends, and places deeper in place. But without a Greek marriage, Helle couldn't leave the country, so we were looking for a Genoa in Greece where we could solve our papers problems. Crete had many advantages, and one straight road connecting everything latitudinally. Besides, there was the labyrinth at Knossos and Minos. It would have been a calamity to snub the Minoans, who leapt over bulls and whose women, beautifully depicted on the labyrinth walls, had a colorfully fancy Asian dress, more erotic than the conventionally draped women you met on a black-figured or red-figured classical Greek vase. So we took an overnight boat and rocked our way like Allan Bates on his way to meet Zorba. Our destination was Haniá, a Venetian port city, with snaky streets and Greco-Italian mansions.

Haniá had suffered no damage from modernity, and except for the capital at Iráklion, which was ugly and shabby in those days, the blitzkrieg of misused Bauhaus architecture had not straightened out the island with obtrusive ugliness. I think of Lhasa in Tibet, now two percent old magic and ninety-eight percent prefab progress. Of course I'm also a child of modernity and think the sensitive austerity of the Rothko Chapel in Houston, which my brother Howard designed, is a great building; but that same brother very early tipped me off about the flattening abuse of bad modern architecture. For all its bad politics, Greece (unlike Spain) has saved its islands, which were austerely imaginative thousands of years before modernity rediscovered geometry; the Cyclades are intact, even the most overrun places like Mykonos and Santorini gleam white, in Cubist architecture, in the sun and moon.

Red is the color of Haniá, another memory from Italy. It is a distinguished occupation to linger in this stunning city, to meditate in its harbor cafés and walk the cobblestone amphitheater curve of the port itself. Give me a pad, an ink pen and some colors, or just a few books, and I'd be happy to spend any week of my life there, without moving from my stone harbor seat or, if necessary, my standing feet. I did that, days at a time dry brush drawning in the Yucatan, and I'd like to do it again in southeast Asia. But we couldn't give in to dream pleasure. We had a marital mission, and we left the lovely city quickly, taking a bus going west.

Off we went to our Greek wedding.

After a few hours we were dozing. Even the beauty of Crete will not keep you awake all the time, although to shut your eyes when traveling through that land is folly. Suddenly we heard gunshots, and pellets came flying into the open windows.

"What is it?"

"Walnuts," Helle said.

"Walnuts?"

"Everyone out of the bus," a man was ordering the driver. He was carrying a rifle.

"A baptism."

"Do they make war when they baptize?"

"No, they eat and they dance."

So all the passengers on the bus got out, joined the circular Cretan dances, made lots of noise, sat down and feasted, and an hour later we were on our way again. We are having fun at gunpoint. No one complained.

Crete was lovely in that moment when spring comes. It comes not quite as early as in Andalusia, that is, in December when the Málaga almond trees blossom, coinciding with the coldest moment of the year as well as with the winter solstice. But we were in Greek February, and all the fruit trees were frolicking serenely. In late afternoon we asked the driver to let us out at some small village. We stopped at one that looked nice. We didn't know the name.

The road lay above the village, which extended down a long fertile valley and eventually to more meadows and the sea. We started along the sloping main village road. Before we knew it, there were cries from women: "*Xeni!* (Foreigners!) Who's going to put them up?" We didn't get very far, since people insisted on drawing us into their open doorways and feeding us mezedes, coffee, and water. As in China, water is a fundamental drink, though in China it comes in thermoses and is hot. Greece is the country of cold fresh water.

The fact that we were *xeni* and therefore had to be treated with special generosity is particular to Greece but not uncommon in Spain, Italy, Turkey, and what was Yugoslavia. The opportunity to see the other and not feel threatened inevitably awakens the best, the pearls to grow and glow in their shells, and all good things. When fear comes or history intervenes, preknowledge or prejudgment (from which "prejudice" derives), then it may be war. The Greeks, who are so naturally curious, as are the Tibetans, and like to enjoy the light, have a cunning excuse for their hospitality. If you don't treat a stranger kindly, that stranger may turn out to be a god, an angry and vengeful Athena or Zeus; or, if you are in Tibet, the ruby-colored Amitabha, Lord of the Lotus Clan, who because of your stinginess will keep you out of paradise. So kindness is good news. If we could arm the armies of the world with walnuts, dance, and banquet lunches in the middle of an olive orchard, we might joy them into the energy of life, rather than the filthy blood of death.

Three sisters and their mother all in black finally cornered us. We had to stay with them. We couldn't argue. We went inside. The bareness of the living room, the large white wall spaces with a few choice pieces of furniture, make Greek houses beautiful. The nakedness of the outer geometries is repeated in the interior. There is a natural taste. The interiors of Greek peasant houses and sophisticated new ones are designed to make plain internal sculptures of light and wall space match the exterior play of lines. In this house, however, there was a dramatic digression. The living room mirror was covered, a black cloth draped over it. A death in the family.

The sisters' brother had been through ten years of war, from 1940 through 1949, and was never wounded. War and more war in Greece. War as the fruit of nationalities, peoples, differences. When the differences abated and peace came and tourists from all the wartime nations mingled again, the brother at last came home for good and "with the good," which is the Greek epithet for arrivals and departures. One day while picking olives from their olive trees, he slipped off the ladder, fell the short distance to the ground, hitting his head against a rock, and was instantly killed. God or his assistants who had chosen him to survive a decade of public murders failed to be there when he slipped to the earth and under it.

So there were three sisters and the mother, already a widow, all in black. But we were guests, foreigners, friends, and had to have a good time. That was the law of hospitality that transcended every bitterness and coarse custom in the world. They killed the rooster and prepared a special chicken dish for us. After supper we played *távli* (backgammon), at which I was no good but for which Helle had an avid talent. We didn't tell them our mission of marriage and how we were already married. Yet if we had explained that the government was obliging us to do something ridiculous, they would have been in sympathy and fully believing.

In the morning the sister who was silent was up earliest. She brought the ironing board into our room and began to iron the family's clothes. Her name was Elektra. She had an amazing beauty. Her eyes were large and peaceful, her classical nose fashioned by Phidias, strong but more gentle that the Parthenon sculptor's faces. The black dress set off her marble features. And when she smiled, there was a quiet eroticism of the sea.

Elektra said nothing. We didn't speak to her but did exchange glances. One of her young sisters had told us casually when I stepped outside to eat an orange for breakfast, "Elektra didn't speak." They didn't know if she was smart or dumb, but she had never really spoken. She was not deaf and had no apparent speech defects. At the market she pointed at what she wanted and pronounced numbers, very clearly and naturally, and calculated with no difficulty. Numbers were her only spoken words. The family was so adjusted, as was Elektra herself, to the beautiful woman who was unspeaking that they scarcely noticed, or didn't appear to notice, anything out of the ordinary. We left this family reluctantly. Elektra kissed us both.

We took a bus to one of the towns and stopped at the first church. Everywhere it was the same: You must spend six months studying how to be a Christian and then come back; or Nothing doing; or We don't know what to tell you; or Wait till the bishop comes and we'll ask him.

The Greek Church had no experience, or didn't in my uncomplicated case, in marrying a Jew to a Greek Orthodox. I suppose I could have lied and said I was a Christian, which might have altered possibility and speed, but I wasn't keen on passing in Greece. After lovely weeks of failed attempts at our third wedlock, we sailed back to Athens with no marriage certificate. A will and a visa had tried to change the religious labels that came with our births. Yet Helle was still a Greek Orthodox and, in the confusion of empty abstractions, I was still a Jew.

So I stayed in Greece a second year. The visa blocked us, but, like the abortion in France, someone said a few words and there was a solution. Instead of going futilely through the Church and the ministries, which we had done, we discovered that a travel agency in Sýndagma Square could obtain an exit visa in twenty-four hours—provided you bought your ticket through them. They knew how and had the connections. Years later, though I got into China for special reasons during the tumult of the People's Great Cultural Revolution for having done a book of Mao's poems in English that Nixon read from in Beijing, others met only silence when their applications were sent in. In 1972, with China in chaos and Tibetan monasteries large and small becoming rubble, the journalists hung out in Hong Kong, usually at the Peninsula Hotel, waiting for travelers' tales—usually a chosen physicist or astronaut or an Albanian or Pakistani—to reveal glimpses of the secret nation. Yet only a few years later some discovered the key of entry into even forbidden China. A few Hong Kong travel agents had connections with ministries and could obtain a visa within twenty-four hours or less into mainland China if you purchased your train or plane ticket through them.

Once you're inside Greece, or in any country, you're there, and whatever happens happens. However, when you go into or out of a country, you are changing and moving into the other, and the experience usually has little to do with a residence in the nation. So the last moment of entry or exit is always a mystery, not always pleasant, often scary, and reflects another reality that one hopes is only momentary. But that reality above all represents difference. It reflects the difference initiated at the descent from Babel. Thereafter, humanity spoke babel to each other, distinct tongues, and the world was richer and poorer, prouder and more suspicious, for difference in tongue is an ultimate distinction. Yet the language itself is only a reflection of other differences, since with good will one can go and be anyplace. But the insecure human condition can make ordinary speech communication impossible. And so the sword, bullet, and bomb replace the word, and death replaces a shared table of coffee and yogurt.

A Black and White
Illumination

When Abraham left Ur, a thousand years earlier the Sumerians had already invented the Swiss watch with its reliable sixty seconds and sixty minutes. Then to the same region came *A Thousand and One Nights,* and who could ask for more adventure and pleasure? Yet more came. From Baghdad to Córdoba in Spain, Islam played with law, philosophy, and the metrics of poetry like a sun becoming a flower out of the desert with arabesque shapes and a multitude of faces. And in that same walled city of Córdoba lived a Jew, Moses Maimonides, who wrote in Arabic about the perplexity of the soul. Those were good days and nights, when even across the straits to the Atlas Mountains where the Berbers lived, amid all that diversity, the sun shone with welcome.

—BOUTROS TOLA, *Here the Lion and Lamb Ate Breakfast from the Same Blue Ceramic Plate*

Friendship in Tangier with a French Baroness Who Told me I Had Killed Her Lord

After Greece, we went to Spain. Spain was another image of Greece. The periphery of Europe, centuries of Islam, women in black and white-walled villages in Andalusia, Spain's great Greek-island province. Both farm and city workers were hungry and under tyranny of men in three-cornered hats, men in black dresses of a severely intrusive church, gray armed men waiting to inspect the arrival of each bus from village to village, and all joined, tight like shit and ass (to use the Catalan expression) under the fearful mystique of one man, Generalissimo Francisco Franco. Spain's lands and its popular culture and architecture were still intact by the preserving nature of poverty and injustice. While the differences that make people kill each other are more often between nations or religions, Spain suffered from the worst divisions, a fratricidal civil war. After thirty-nine years Franco died, and by then the divisions were largely healed between good people and maybe bad on both sides of a war that should never have taken place, as no war should. But there was no absolute change until the caudillo died. The mystique of the enemy is transcendental.

Tangier lay across the waters from Andalusia where we were living. It sat near the other shoulder of the Pillars of Hercules that held up the sky over Africa and Europe. Tangier was an international city in 1952, not to be returned to Morocco until 1956. I took a bus to Algeciras where Molly Bloom said *yes, yes*. Then to Tangier. The Zócalo Chico (the main square in the city) reminded me of Mexico, except that the smell of kef, a hemp narcotic stronger than marijuana, was in the air. Kef was legal and available at all kiosks. In the Casbah, usually next to the whorehouses, there were tiled stores with open doors where men, usually older ones, sat on elevated tile platform benches smoking their kef pipes.

I had to wire New York for money that should have come through in four or five days. Fortunately it didn't, which gave me the necessity and privilege of staying a month in the city. In the Casbah I found a hotel room. At night there was a strange singing, which I suspected was rats. The landlady said it was swallows singing in the attic, but one morning when I woke up to find a rat jumping out of my shoe by the bed, I thought it best to find another room. I wandered that city from street to street. The Beat Generation was in and out of Tangier in those years, though I ran into no one, not even Paul Bowles. But I did meet another exile class, in some ways their opposite in that they had money and titles. Yet they were so very much outsiders that they, like the Beats, had wandered to this free-market port so they could also live as they wished to.

The cabal of wealthy titled Europeans who lived in tax-free Tangier formed a community much like the group described in Thornton Wilder's book *Cabala,* where the wealthy are portrayed in their elaborate decadence. I had two friends in this Tangier society: a French baroness and a French count. I spent many days with the baroness. She took me for an afternoon to a walled-in mansion in the Casbah where our Arab host entertained us with talk and platter after silver platter of cakes piled in high geometric shapes. The art of food presentation was abstract and reminded me of designs on *azulejos,* the wall or floor tiles. As the essence of Chinese calligraphy goes through architecture and wood engravings in China, so the writing, wall designs, jewelry, and shapes of delicious foods in North Africa have its austerely beautiful curving tradition. The wife of our generous host had rooms on the floor below. Because she was a woman, the wife of the family could not be seen, even in a veil, by anyone other than core members of the family. My host explained the custom.

The baroness also took me to the count's house, really a museum of small and massive sculptures he had collected in Burma and Cambodia in the 1920s, when his comrade André Malraux was up to similar uncertain ventures (Malraux faced arrest for his art hunting). The count was a boxer, aviator, and archeologist. But most clearly, despite the photographs and other evidence of those other professions, what came through was his wonderful battered face, bald head, and iron build of the boxer with the cultivated gentle voice.

The baroness, in her late fifties, was svelte and elegant. I liked her speech, which was as shocking as she could make it, and extremely witty. Her religiosity bothered me, however. I didn't take her on. One day she asked me, "*Vous croyez en Dieu, n'est-ce pas?*" (You believe in God, no?)

"*Non.*"

"What religion are you?"

"*Je suis juif.*" (I'm a Jew.)

"You killed our Lord."

I recall that I said to her that she believed in a Jewish Lord. This oldest of questions I didn't pursue. Should Jesus or Yeshua and his mother be held guilty of crime, since they were Jews? It's too terrible to continue the discussion, which others would say is theological, but which in practice has distinguished Jews, not as the first Christians, but as the *other*. The baroness and I saw each other another time. Why not? She was not expressing an original idea. There is no end to recrimination in the world. To end antisemitism, one must begin, Jew and gentile, to understand its origins and then, just as quickly as possible, go on to think of everyone and oneself as ordinary. There should be no age-old debts to the past, no matter who holds the receipt.

I was obliged to cook for myself until the bank transfer came through. A pathetic cook I am. I bought an alcohol stove and ate boiled eggs, boiled potatoes, and hot cereal. I stayed healthy and was even proud of my stinking cooking. The odor was raw alcohol. As I moved away from the cabal, I found increasing delight in climbing towers where one could order tea and look at the Atlantic Ocean, look at the sun mirror that extended into an infinity of beauty. There I sat for many hours, writing, thinking. I was very much alone among diversities. I was glad to be the wandering Jew. It's good to be the infidel. I wish everyone had that joy. If I was different, then I represented the world, as every single person does. There is no world but only single people. Jorge Luis Borges expressed that message of lonely singularity that is universal and ordinary, in one form or another, many times.

In "Eleanor Rigby," John Lennon sang it.

A Tower in Tangier

Some place among onions of pain I lose
my nerve. Gone is the table in that tower
on the west coast of Africa I used
to climb to in the afternoons, where hour
on hour I'd smoke, sip tea, and look at ships
fall off the glass of fire into a throat
of stars. Back in my room a bone rat slips
along the walls, singing the infant note

of swallows as I boil the milky smell
of oatmeal on the green alcohol flame.
The green casbah moon floats over the square
like a knife patient in the dusk. I came
to climb jail steps to you. The Moors in prayer
yell from the towers. I climb, crazed, infidel.

"Sound Out Your Race Loud and Clear"

God got weary of mist and spiritual plenitude and so descended to a U.S. Army barracks where he enjoyed a bagel with lox and cream cheese with some Sunday Jews, and then, feeling guilty about his invisible skin, went to a black Sergeant at Camp Gordon, Georgia, who gave him a haircut that was long overdue. From all this experience, God lay down, again weary, but now in ecstatic dream about the diverse world he had cooked up out of nothing.

—PIERRE GRANGE, *On God's Redemption*

A Jewman in the U.S. Army

When I was a student at SOAS (School of Oriental and African Studies) in London, a Canadian painter who lived near us in Chelsea told me, "So you're going into the army. I can give you a bit of advice to save your neck."

"What's that?"

"Keep your mouth shut about what you do."

"What are you talking about?"

"It means don't tell them you're a poet."

John Camden and his wife were an unusually proper Anglo-Canadian couple, both of them painters, the wife more talented, though it was John who earned his living in London from his work. This was 1952. The Korean War was on, a stalemate, but I expected to be called up as soon as I got back to the States. My draft board was disinterested in my letter that said I held Quaker views about peace. If I had said I *was* a Quaker, there would have been grounds for alternate service.

"What's wrong with being a poet?" I asked.

"Willis, you're an idiot."

"I don't disagree, but be more specific"

"Listen. I was in the Canadian army. When someone asked me what I did on the outside, if I told them I was an artist I got a dirty look. As if I were a faggot."

"But being a faggot isn't as bad as being an artist," I said, "so maybe they were upgrading you."

John wasn't through with me.

"After I had enough with the artist routine, I started to tell people I was a painter, and they figured I painted houses. And pretty soon I just said I was a house painter."

"So you're a fake. I never thought you were an artist."

"What I'm saying to you is once you're in the army, don't tell anybody you're a poet. I got it for being an artist. If you say you write poetry, someone will haul off and sock you."

"Thanks."

I thought he was nuts.

I had published two books of poems in Europe, one in Athens in 1951, one the next year in Málaga. I never felt unease about being a poet in those years of wandering Europe. In the army, as it turned out, when I began to publish verse in the *Stars and Stripes*, I received praise from my superiors—from Major Bradley, who was in a French course I gave on the base, and from Sergeant Anthony Molino with whom I used to have a beer or two after work. It pleased me a lot to have their approval for the poems. I was a lousy soldier. A slob, I made a lot of people laugh at me. I never got the hang of spit polish. When I was stationed in France, Sergeant Green, my protector, who was black and had green eyes, was cursing me up and down after the colonels halted in their march through the ranks and began to circle around me, scowling and taking notes in their little notebooks about my terrible haircut, my Ike jacket in which I drowned, my beltless droopy trousers, and my less-than-glittering boots. I wasn't a creep, or maybe I was. Green said he was going to lock me up in the quarterly room at the next inspection, for my sake and the army's.

As for being a poet, the only place I consistently was told by my buddies to skip "the poetry stuff" was when I became a professor. My cronies were not bigoted against the poem— they taught it for a living. But they knew that being a live poet in a literature department wasn't helpful. My really close friend, Peter Bondanella, said, "Keep it to yourself. Just shut up about writing poetry." He always kidded me, and I loved him for it. But they were right and well-intentioned. However, by then I was not into denial. If a herd of professors had a bad feeling about live poets, what could I do?

One of the inane things I did in my early years was "to deny," not the poet, but the scholar in me. I failed to publish a book I thought was good on Antonio Machado when a fine publisher made an offer. I cared for Machado and owed him the best literary study I could come up with, but I was a myopic, small-spirited coward. Or at least overreacting to the academy's prevalent dictum to shut up about writing poetry or appearing "creative" rather than "serious," to use the clichés. The world is filled with sorrows and agonies, and isn't this dilemma pitiful and all too common? As the years went on, both sides in me, the misnamed "scholar" and "creator," have fed each other. Their assumed conflict, at least for me, is false and invidious.

How can anyone fret about the privilege of being able to write poems? Even to do so in secret for a secret reader who may not be there. In the academy, if they find out, no one hauls you off and slugs you for writing a poem. As with much of the old days' icy bigotry, the writer's identity in the academy has radically changed, and, on a different level of consequences, as decisively as religious and color biases. Note the growth of creative writing programs. But I would be lying if I didn't recall that being a poet in the university was more problematic than being a poet in the U.S. Army.

With this preparation, patient reader, if you are still here, hear now about the glories of the U.S. Army. And many of these glories were black glories, since, as in my childhood, circumstance put me into the intimacy with more than the pinkish-white folk.

A Touch of Freedom

The first thing the armed services do is humiliate you. It's good for character. When you take your physical, in my case twice—in Syracuse and in the damp basement bowels of a government building in New York—you are immediately told to strip. Then you stand in line for a few hours, naked, cold, and wondering. You linger in a circle around a series of offices. No towel to cover your shame. When it's your turn, you snap to and dart in and out of an office where someone grabs a part of your body or sticks a piece of metal against you. But there is one spiritual happening. The illuminating moment came when I was ordered into the office of a young navy officer dressed in splendid white. He was a shrink of some kind. He didn't ask me to sit. Bored and curt, he asked just one question. "Do you like men or women?" Then I was out and back in line.

When you become a soldier, you enter a dictatorship. There is the army and there is the outside. The army gives you security. You have a job and will get your pay on the chosen day, you will eat regularly, and unless you sock someone who's a rank above you (which will land you in barbed-wire city), you will sleep at night in a decent narrow bed. If you are completely asocial by army standards, though you might manage fine on the outside, you will spend a lot of time in barbed-wire city, receive an "unfavorable" discharge, or spend time in a federal pen.

The army, like death, is also the great equalizer. In its absolutist yet democratic way, it fundamentally makes everyone the same, whether they came in rich or poor, educated or barely literate, white or black. When inducted, and during most of the time for those who live on base, all sleep in the same barracks bed in a row—just as, in an army cemetery, death sets everyone sleeping in the same nothingness of eternity—in clean, spit-polish rows, each lot fairly and accurately in place like a checkerboard.

The "democratic" equalizing profile of the army has diminished now that it is *professional* (or *mercenary*, if one is unfriendly), for the draft in my days took all classes, all races, all religions, and within seconds made them the same, officially making one's origin irrelevant. Once Truman desegregated the armed forces in 1948, the miracle of the great bulldozer took over and flattened out difference. So a black career sergeant in 1954, when I was inducted, could live in the fully segregated South as a free man or woman, with a spouse of any color, thanks to the social laws of military dictatorship, as long as he or she was on base. Outside it was hell, and dangerous. While even in the army a Black did not escape every "civilized" hurt and insult that began when the slave ship took its human cargo aboard, no place in the South or the North offered an African American the career and domestic privileges that were routine in the services.

There are three ways to do things, you soon learn: "The right way, the wrong way, and the army way. And until you get out, trooper, you do it the army way." The army way doesn't like *differences* and disrespects the *other*. When the other is outside and is the enemy, it will be fought when the order comes to fight. And your deep philosophy will be that you're just doing your job. When the other resides inside the army, if it opposes the army way, it will be punished. The gays at last are making a little progress, but very little. They have been the internal other.

Fort Dix: "I'm Black and My Balls Are Made of Brass"

> I am black yet beautiful,
> daughters of Jerusalem,
> as black as Kedar's tents,
> as lovely as Solomon's tapestries.
> Don't look at me with scorn
> because I am black,
> because the sun has scorched me.
>
> —from The Song of Songs

Immediately upon being inducted in New York City, I was sent to Fort Dix, New Jersey, across the Hudson and discovered that I was an "enlisted man," not an officer. I knew I was not an officer, but I never reconciled myself to the army lie that a conscripted man is an enlistee. The army way of describing has its own truths. The last time I had spent a night in New Jersey was when, as an eleven-year-old Boy Scout, I spent the day marching in circles, cooking—or rather burning—potatoes in an open fire for supper and sleeping in army-type barracks. In the Scouts I learned to march, use semaphore flags, and take orders. So I was really an experienced old-timer by the time we hit Fort Dix. We went into a barracks depot where clothing was thrown at us. Then we sat on our bunks or circled the barracks on beautification details, picking up cigarette butts, and learned military order number one: "Hurry up and wait." Our wonder and gossip was interrupted by frequent shouts over the bitchbox (the speakers outside or in the barracks) to fall in. These were informational, and we got to know our temporary leaders while we were still officially on "casual status." The no-place, no-know situation went on for days.

One morning right after chow in the consolidated mess, we got the order to fall in. A corporal, a short black paratrooper sculpted in steel and clearly tough as nails, shouted our nonconsequential orders for the morning. The orders were to wait for the next orders. We waited for the real message, and it was worth waiting for, though it was brief. He warned us: "Troopers, I want you to know my balls are made of brass, and when it storms, they **THUNDER!!**

"Dismissed!"

All this baroque fanfare of celestial machismo took some thirty seconds. The corporal was followed by a sergeant with an Italian name, a lanky, leaning figure whose deep voice was full of hesitation as he searched for the right army terminology. What was wrong with him? He was searching for a word. He was almost embarrassed, which we had learned, men in authority were not. Finally, he blurted, "All *Jewmen* fall out and report to headquarters!"

I fell out. Standing next to me was a black kid from Harlem whose name was Sammy and who seemed to know everything. "What's up?" I asked.

"It's Jewish holidays. A three-day pass. We're going to be able to get back to the city."

"Sammy, you Jewish too?"

"No, but I want the three-day pass."

So Sammy and I went to headquarters. We weren't supposed to get dog tags till we were actually in Basic Training, which was to begin the next day, but since we were being sent off base, they issued the tags in advance for the lucky Jewmen. At the office, I discovered the standard argot the sergeant couldn't come up with, "Jewish personnel," a dignified designation. Sammy and I picked up the dog tags, both with a Star of David on them. The tags, we were told, were to let the diggers know, if we fell in combat and were torn apart, our ID card destroyed, *who* we were (by the ID number) and what symbol—a cross or a star—to put in the grass above us when we were set underground in an army-issue casket. Sammy kept his Jewish Star of David dog tag throughout his army career, and we both got the same surprise orders when we returned to base after our holy holidays.

The gang of Israelites showed up at Dix around six p.m., Tuesday evening, just before the seventy-two hours of religious meditation ended. Next morning we learned that our group had already started Basic Training and that since we had missed the cycle, we were being sent someplace else in the country to be recycled. There were a million rumors. An hour later we learned it would be Camp Gordon in Athens, Georgia, where a new cycle for enlisted men was beginning. I thought it fine. The army was becoming exotic. Adventure, travel, the South. Since we didn't possess anything but our street clothes and some army garb that barely filled a duffel, it was no problem to pack us onto an army transport plane and shuffle down to Gordon. The plane was like no other, even more shabby and noisy than the Russian planes I later flew in over the Chinese Gobi. The seats were bucket, all facing backward—safer, we were told, for purposes of survival if hit by enemy fire and we needed to come down in a hurry.

"Sound Out Your Race, Loud and Clear! Caucasian or Negra!" Yelled the White Sergeant in Segregated Georgia

I had never been in the South. In a few hours we were looking at it through our porthole windows.

September in Georgia on a hot runway. The tar was almost bubbling and stuck to our boots. The sun was a ball of fire. The drippy air was bloated with moisture and infested with huge bugs greeting us as we deplaned. They were angry miniature hand grenades, buzzing around our heads. Nevertheless, I had a slightly heroic feeling as we stepped out of the plane painted the same color as my brown boots. I felt very happy. We lined up, about a hundred of us, in eight or ten rows. White sergeants moved quickly among us, shouting us into place. When we were finally properly lined up and still, the order came.

"Duffel bags at port arms!"

This was an awkward maneuver. As we struggled to balance the sluggish sack, came a second order:

"Sound out your race, loud and clear! Caucasian or negra!!"

I was furious. The sergeants were suddenly white sheriffs. A Puerto Rican next to me was confused. We sounded off.

"White!"

"White!"

"Negro!"

"Negro!"

The yelling took two interminable minutes. Then we were bussed out to Camp Gordon. We all sat together. The Blacks didn't have to sit in the rear, although we were in the South, where that was still the rule.

To remember what the South was like, I found an old clipping from 1960, reprinted in *Time* magazine, when segregation was officially over.

An Ecstasy of Hatred

> 'Nigger lover, nigger lover,
> nigger lover, Jew.
> We hate niggers, we hate you.'

Chilling snapshots from the civil rights battlefield: "Each morning the women gathered in an ecstasy of hatred on the streets of New Orleans, where two schools had been ordered by U.S. courts to integrate. They shrieked like harridans, cursed, kicked and clawed at the few who dared brave their lines. . . . When police shooed the women away, they went to a hospitable neighbor's lawn, where self-styled 'cheerleaders' chanted their favorite doggerel: 'Nigger lover, nigger lover, nigger lover, Jew. We hate niggers, we hate you.' In front of the shabby public-housing apartment where [one integrationist family] lives, a crowd of children . . . piped: 'All I want for Christmas is a clean white school.'"

—December 12, 1960, *Time* (from "25 Years Ago Today")

This inauspicious reception made us apprehensive. I already had some buddies. We made a few cracks about it on the bus. The black recruits were angry. "What are those mothers up to?" they kept saying in different versions. I took this hell-week gesture to mean "You niggers, and you nigger lovers, remember, you're not in the North." The cabal of sheriff sergeants had this cunning tactic in mind. Ku Klux Klan? Who knows? Those not in the circle could be worse. The true old South was outside the base, which for half an hour a group of noncoms re-created in an army company of recruits on its way into camp. They wouldn't have dared to do it on base, because they couldn't. We were green, and they were white. And no black noncommissioned or commissioned officer was around. In precise fairness to the army, there was nothing in my next three months at Gordon that in any way duplicated this blatantly disgusting drama of racial intimidation.

In fact, I wish to tell a more surprising and positive story that has a different color to it.

Boot Camp in Georgia

"Yeah," shouts the corporal, "all Jewmen fall out!"
A black kid and me, we go to pick up
our 3-day pass from Dix. "What's it about?"
"Jewish New Year." They fly us with our pup
tent, boots and duffel down to Georgia where
still on the airstrip a white sergeant blurts,
"Sound out your name and race!" We're in the fair
sweet South. "I'll squeeze that bastard till he squirts
white piss," the black kid whispers. I get stuck
three days on K.P. God what grease! I feel
good here. No anti-intellectual crap
of campuses. I catch pneumonia but heal
fast and they treat me good. Have friends and rap.
I don't have to kill. It's peace. What the fuck!

We Jews among the recruits soon were dispersed. Most of the guys were seventeen- and eighteen-year-old volunteers from South Carolina and Georgia. I was twenty-six, but tops in the exercise tests as a result of diving training. The army is very physical, and my closest to getting into a fight was breaking up a fight between a black guy and a Puerto Rican—one flashing a knife, the other wielding a chair. Maybe they thought they were in the movies. I was sure they would both get socked into barbed-wire city, and I used my Spanish to talk the Puerto Rican out of it by grabbing him, shouting at him, and pulling him away. This was a saving face for the combatants. But no heroics. This incident took place late in the evening in front of the canteen at Fort Devins, Massachusetts, where I worked on a newspaper, and I was surprised how good my standing became in the eyes of my fellow editors when I told them the story the next morning.

Our company of two hundred men occupied a line of barracks. Each barracks had double bunks and a private room for the master sergeant who was our barracks leader. We had a can, meaning the toilets and showers. Both were wide open. The showers were along the wall, and in the middle of the rectangular room was a row of ten toilet stools, standing lonely, with no partitions between them. Before breakfast the sarge would come through screaming at those of us who were still sitting on them.

"Snap shit, trooper! We got a formation to make! Snap shit!"

Those of us who had some college tended to be less gung ho. I thought a lot of things were funny. We were quickly getting incredibly strong. Long marches, every kind of exercise. We didn't get enough sleep because we were usually out on the target range at daybreak, leaving before dawn as we got into December, and the officers said we wouldn't get over our colds until we could get a real rest after Basic. But the chest colds didn't prevent our bodies from taking on muscles. Our sarge, who was a splendid guy, pushed us hard, but was then sweeter than he was supposed to be in the evenings when he showed us how to clean our M1s and gave us pep talks and hints. Whites and Blacks liked sergeant Riley a lot, and he was black. And they hated Captain Ken Anderson, a crazy White who made the national newspapers for things he did to us, like his punishment for a trooper who fell behind in a long march. He forced him to dig a pit and get into it and have our buddies bury him up to his chin and put a small wooden cross in his open mouth to show that he was really dead. The captain had a hearing for these excesses and got off with a reprimand. He did do one thing, which they shouldn't have nailed him for, since we thought it was a gas. If someone fucked up, he made you climb a tree and swing from a branch and scream "I am a shitbird." That always raised our morale.

One afternoon during a five-minute break during a long march, I leaned against a tree and fell asleep immediately. A second lieutenant bashed his helmet down on my helmet and I woke with a jolt. He was swearing at me. The crash of metal thundered in my ears but didn't hurt. I couldn't bring myself to feel intimidated. I thought the guy a fool and not a good officer. If I had a key with me I might have offered to wind him up after his tiny explosion. Instead, I said something nutty.

"Thanks, sir, for being my alarm clock."

From the first week on I discovered that if I had any problems—and I slipped through my two years amazingly trouble free—it was never gratuitously caused by a "negro personnel," which was the approved title in those days for a black soldier. Generally, the African American soldiers made the transition into the military with more warmth and less posturing than many of the Whites. They didn't lose personality and turn into military puppets, performing mechanically and gratuitously cruelly. And they kept my spirits high and human at unexpected moments. In parts of America I feel like a stranger. It's then that I hold my breath and remember myself in the Mediterranean or someplace lost in Asia. With the black soldiers I didn't feel foreign or wish myself elsewhere. They were fun. And in the army fun was sometimes the only remedy against depression, madness, and boredom, the three gray notes in the military flute.

As for racism, I learned an essential and surprising lesson. Racism exists because it is allowed to. Army law forbade its existence in the ordinary ways that it thrived in the segregated South outside the camp gate. Formal segregation was out. Within seconds of getting into the barracks routine, the least-educated guys were not only gung ho army, as if they had no memory of any previous existence, but they immediately accepted, as the army way, the breaking down of all the essential taboos they had been nourished on in the Deep South. Whites and Blacks shit together, slept in the same room above and below each other's bunks, were assigned details together, were bossed and harassed by Whites or by Blacks and thus, in turn, harassed Whites and Blacks indiscriminately when they had a chance to do so. I remember few events I would call nasty racism. The ugliness I remember had to do with contact with Whites off base.

Holy Communion of Bagels and Lox for Jewish Personnel

On the first Sunday in Camp Gordon we had our only obligatory religious service. Local ministers came on base to officiate. After that Sunday, attendance was optional. Sergeant Riley gave out the orders: "White personnel go to the right. Negro personnel get in the middle. Jewish personnel move over to the trees. When you're properly assembled," he shouted at this big semi-circle, "we start moving. At ease, men."

Soon the white ministers from town arrived and went to the Whites and divided them up according to denominations and marched them off.

I'm not sure where they went. Riley marched his Negroes away. A corporal took us Jews, leading us all the way across the camp, which, holding some twenty thousand men, was much bigger than our Basic Training area had revealed to me. It was a wired-in city. On this nice Sunday we took an almost informal march to a far barracks. There, once inside, we found waiting for us some volunteer Jewish ladies from Athens, who smiled and offered us coffee and bagels with lox and cream cheese. Sammy, of course, was with us. His Harlem bagels had to be more Jewish than the good-intentioned tasteless soggy rings of dough we were eating. We hung around for forty or fifty minutes and then were marched back—to my regret, I must say. That was my only religious experience in the army and it tasted okay, because it was so funny.

I wasn't a complete fuck-up, but I was often in trouble. One morning they picked me out of morning formation to be a "volunteer" server at breakfast. That wasn't bad. You ate well. You just had to wait till everybody was served. I dished out pancakes. When I saw on the line one of my buddies who had come down from Dix on the same plane, instead of giving him one pancake I intended to put two pancakes on his dish. In my haste and clumsiness, I got three pancakes on my fork, and as soon as they hit his plate he was off to the next server. When the last server, who was the mess sergeant, saw the plate with three pancakes, he screamed murder, and I was on KP for the rest of the day until ten that night. The next day was my regular day anyway, which meant going a second day from four in the morning till ten at night. The KP pushers were never happy with me. Then on Sunday, a day of rest when there were no regular assignments, an officer came through the barracks looking for volunteers. Everyone ducked under the blankets. He nabbed me. So it was three days in a row. I was dead. My job was pots and pans, and the pans were enormous and filled with grease, which was my duty to make clean. I was missing my belt, and my pants kept slipping down, so I pushed my belly against the sink most of the day, which caused a greater quantity of grease to cover me from waist to boots.

At about four in the afternoon, one of us dared ask the mess sarge, who was a terror from my home state of Maine, for a break. It was a mistake.

"So you guys need a break. Okay. Take twenty, in the leaning rest position."

So we lay on our bellies on the dirty kitchen floor, pushed up to the leaning rest position (as in preparation for pushups) and then held the position as long as we could. When one of us broke, we had to do ten pushups and resume. This was the stuff I was really good at, so I didn't bitch as much as the others. But my moment was coming. About an hour before supper the mess sarge, who seemed to hate me, which was a normal pose, ordered me to put a bar of soap in one of the four-gallon pots boiling on the stove. There were three pots on the stove, and he didn't say which one. It was a big bar of detergent-strong soap and smelled bad. I went to the stove, opened the lid, and dropped the bar in. Just as it hit the water I saw that the pot was filled with boiling carrots. I was back scrubbing pots and pans in a few seconds, and then my crime registered in my conscience. But I knew the sarge would kill me or I'd be on KP for the next two years if he realized I'd ruined the carrots for the whole mess hall.

I said nothing and scrubbed. That evening I didn't eat carrots. And strangely enough, none of my friends complained about them and no one died of food poisoning.

This was my luckiest night in the army.

Black Barbers Brought on Base to Cut Black Men's Hair

The most poignant morning in the army happened on a Saturday when we were due to get haircuts. At Camp Gordon that work was done by local barbers who came on base. It was one of those things that helped the town economy. The Whites were taken to tents where white barbers sat us on chairs and quickly scalped us. But they wouldn't touch a Black. So Riley told all the Negro personnel to follow him. He was upset, but it was an upset of centuries. He led them to one of the tents that had a Negro barber who scalped the Negro personnel. It wasn't much, but it was an act of southern segregation, naked and impure, on base.

In the North at least they would have properly murdered anyone who tried to pull such a stunt.

When I got out of Basic, I began to meet a wider group from all ranks. I knew a lot of black noncoms who were married to Japanese and German women, and they were all in Georgia. Of course they couldn't leave the base together. If they walked down the streets as a couple, they'd be jailed or worse. But they were safe on the camp grounds. So that's where they lived and were concealed from the communities of the South. It was an anomaly that the U.S. Army was the only place in the South that permitted the crime of interracial marriage. "Miscegenation" is the hideous official word for that crime, and "mongrelization" is the hate term. Like everything else, interracial marriage was perfectly normal on base because it was the army way.

Captain Hammond, Baritone, and the Children of the Périgord

In Europe the American soldiers were the minority (Whites and Blacks alike), which was good; and I must say that my assignment in France was terrific. Most of the GIs didn't want assignment in France because the story was that the French were frogs. So after our ship, the U.S. Patch, crossed the Atlantic and dropped us off at Hamburg, and I requested France rather than Germany, I easily got assigned to an American air resupply unit in southern France, in the gastronomic city of Périgueux, with its Byzantine church and *douce France* gentle countryside of the Périgord. Most of the American GIs in Germany slept in pup tents out in the fields and were in constant field training, winter and summer. They were Cold War border troops. I preferred the rooms I rented in town at the home of a French family, where eventually my daughter Aliki was conceived.

My work in France, where I spent a year and a few months was cushy. I was the camp interpreter, a French teacher at night for the University of Maryland overseas program, and a one-person editor of a small weekly newspaper I put out to sabotage the dignity of the military profession. I read a lot of French novels. My closest friend was Captain Eldrich N. Hammond, who was the base chaplain. He was a handsome officer with a magnificent baritone voice that brought us together. He was also black. He was well liked, though I learned that there was a word to denigrate all black officers. The envious regular army bigots called them "carbon copies." I learned that expression in France.

Captain Hammond turned my life around in many ways. As the Quaker had earlier led me into obscure Nahuatl-speaking Indian villages where we did Peace Corps–like operations, Captain Hammond led me into the charities in Périgueux, which meant raising money for orphans and for a children's hospital. In the army it was unusual for an enlisted man to be close to an officer, regardless of their backgrounds on the outside. It was frowned on. Music originally brought us together. I had written some songs (words and melody), and at the Christmas Fund Committee concert he sang one of my songs. I had never heard one professionally sung, and I was thrilled. Hammond worked with Father Roumagne's children's choir at St. Joseph's College. The choir sang Bach, Gruber, Negro spirituals, and Spanish songs. Then the Captain sang Berlin's "White Christmas" and Barnstone's "Come with Me Golden Bird." The program, which took place on December 2, 1955, at Headquarters of the Périgueux Quartermaster Depot, ended with "Somewhere a Voice is Calling" and Verdi's "La Donna e Mobile." (The program had a slight misspelling, thereby giving the Donna a companion named Mobile. It read "La Donna & Mobile," which in French made phonetic sense and was a natural error, since "&" in French is *et*, the same sound as Italian *e*.) After Hammond sang my song, he asked Private First Class Barnstone to stand, and I stood up very straight before the American and French audience.

Afterward we were together often. In those days there was a glass ceiling for black officers. Less than seven years earlier, the U.S. Army was officially segregated, the black troops being led mainly by white officers. There were no regular black sailors in the U.S. Navy. Just cooks. While there were few high-ranking officers of color in the army—a few colonels but no generals—as an opening field, the army still represented an opportunity for advancement that few corporations offered to educated Blacks. Hammond was an idealist and so was I, but he had known the rough side. As a Jew what I experienced was a historical memory of terror, not a lived one. Had I been born in Poland in 1927 rather than in Maine, I would have almost certainly had an early transformation into smoke and soap, with plenty of preparatory terror. We didn't talk about race and religion, but about everything else. It was enough that we were friends. We were solving problems of the world and soul in a wishful fashion. He was like my childhood idol Leah in that natural dignity pervaded everything in his character and actions. I don't think I've ever been accused of poise and dignity, and if so it was a mistake.

Hammond did tell me once, "Willis, it's a lot easier to walk the streets of France as a Negro soldier than flit about back home. I know they're looking, but it feels better."

The concert was only one of the events he arranged. We became very close to a French order of nuns, Les Soeurs de Nevers, who ran an orphanage and a children's hospital. Our base "adopted" the orphanage, and each month at payroll we solicited contributions to buy presents and food for the little kids in La Maison Notre Dame de la Misericordia. The building, built in 1821, was in real need of repairs, and our carpenters from the base got days off to renovate some of the rooms. We actually did enough to get unexpected French and American newspaper attention. On the front page of the January 11, 1956, issue of *The Courier-Journal* in Louisville appeared a story by an American reporter in France. It was embarrassingly flattering, but it did reflect the diversion of our colorful ways. Henry Brinckerhoff III, was a buddy I teamed up with:

> Brinckerhoff, a 1954 Yale graduate, works closely with Pfc. Willis Barnstone to solve as many of the orphanage's problems as possible. Their most recent promotion was a gala variety show at the Casino de Paris, the largest theater in Périgueux. Replete with cowboy songs and low comedy, the performance delighted the Frenchmen and raised $400 for the orphanage. In addition to the American soldiers' contributions, La Maison Notre Dame de la Misericordia is supported by private donations, church collections and a fund from the Périgueux City Council.
>
> Brinckerhoff and Barnstone, a New York City poet who speaks fluent French, are favorites with the children. Barnstone's wife, Helle, a painter, spends her afternoons helping the nuns and finding out what the orphans need.

The usual French provincial reserve toward uniformed strangers has never been a problem for Brinckerhoff or for the Barnstones, because they are known as the children's friends.

—Alan Levy, Périgueux, France

Captain Hammond—I never addressed him as Eldrich—worked out an arrangement for me to auction off contributions from army personnel and the base itself that was to be held downtown in one of the city buildings. I could handle the French. I tried to get hold of every unused typewriter, adding machine, telephone—anything that would bring in some francs. The auction was to raise funds for the children's hospital run by the Sisters of Nevers. In preparation, the captain took me to meet the mother superior and her assistant, who asked me whether I would like to visit the hospital. The next morning they picked me up in their own black Citroën and we went about twenty kilometers into the country where the very attractive new hospital was. I went alone with them.

We looked through many wards. In one ward there were only seven girls, all about the same age, eight or ten, and they were all in a coma. They had cancer. Because they were so young, the disease had not ravaged the freshness of their skin. And the room, whose glass walls faced the Dordogne valley, was radiant with morning sun. The young girls were exquisitely beautiful and they would all soon die. They were peaceful, although the cruelty of uncontrolled, insentient cells was following its terrible natural law and bringing those faces closer to their place under the dead earth. I see them as clearly today as I did on that morning. One of the girls, whom the sister called Annemarie, was her niece.

A Girl in a Coma in the Cancer Ward at the Nuns Hospital in Périgueux

Through bright air above the Dordogne valley,
A sunny and womanly soft meadow of castles,
Morning light passes through tall glass walls
And spreads like cotton cloth in the corridors.
The nuns hospital receives the daylight as a blessing,
Its modern rooms lit with a happier cleanness
Enveloping the children from the Périgord
Whose ravaged bodies linger in daytime sleep.

The nuns like white clouds hover near a child
As her breathing weakens on this full morning.
She is unknowing as we what the light means,
Why she must disappear so soon in the earth.
Sunlight reaches through glass walls to her bed,
Sunrays quiver on the sheet drawn near her chin.
Her room high on the soft and unfeeling hill
Is filled with radiance of an almost joyful light.

My young mother had died of cancer a few months earlier. In 1994 I remembered them both, the young girls and my mother, lingering near the good sunlight that, like death, has no bigotry toward whom it shares company. For religion and race, sun and death are perfectly equal in their treatment. This coupling of the source of light and life and the abstraction of its absence is strange, since death removes the knowledge and even the picture of sun.

A Sunny Room at Mount Sinai

Mount Sinai Hospital. My mother lay
in a good corner room with lots of sun.
In Périgueux, the children's ward, one day
I saw a young girl in a coma. Sun
came through glass walls; the child was beautiful,
her face freshened with youth. Only inside
the cancer stormed. I saw the nun place wool
soaked in cold alcohol on her. She died
that afternoon. My mother's gown was loose
and she told us that awful things were done
when testing her downstairs. I see her eyes
today. She too was fresh and live. Some juice
lay undrunk by her pillow. A surprise
of pain. I left the room and she was gone.

People murder for differences. Nature also kills but asks no questions and acts apparently without discrimination, although human actions such as poverty, neglect, ignorance, and violence can quicken the deadly hand of nature. Nature counts time, which is its mindless ally in healing and killing, and then, ready or not, nature acts to erase consciousness. The payment for our birth is death, which is unalterable. As to murder, which is history, no, it is not acceptable, whether by state, religion, greed, or passion. But natural death? Why in the world don't litigious nature and evasive God read and honor the dictum "Thou shalt not kill"? Well, silly rhetoric. Illiterate nature is a program, following natural law, and God is unaccountable, and there is no answer.

An army is an instrument for killing in the name of one thing or another. That power to kill is justified by many clichés—conquest, defense, democracy, peace, God, freedom, duty. However, I also found at least one sterling benefit of military dictatorship: the abolishment of local laws and customs of bigotry. And because of army chaplain Hammond I was given the chance to help children, who are the vulnerable and innocent among us. In children is the first morning of existence.

Mumbling about Race and Religion in China, Nigeria, Tuscaloosa, and Buenos Aires

In the late sixteenth century, when the Italian Jesuit missionary to China, Matteo Ricci (1552–1610), met in Beijing a delegation of Chinese Jews from Kaifeng, the Jews were overjoyed after two thousand years to find a fellow Jew who shared their Bible, though his had a few brief books added to it, and though they and Ricci didn't look exactly alike.

—BAN WEILI, *Early Diasporas to the East*

Ma Ke, a Chinese Jew with Whom
I Shared Suppers in Beijing

In *Jews in Old China* (1984), Sidney Shapiro, a Beijing journalist/ writer and permanent resident in China, speculates on the first migrations of Jews into China. He notes that some claim it goes back to the sixth-century B.C.E. Babylonian Captivity, when, upon their liberation by Cyrus the Great in 538 B.C.E., the Jews migrated to many areas in the Middle East and as far as India. Others speak of Roman or medieval times. There were surely several migrations.

The center for Chinese Jewry was Kaifeng, in Henan province, where a sizeable Jewish population settled in the twelfth century. Matteo Ricci, the Italian missionary in the late sixteenth century, speaks about meeting a delegation of Jews in Beijing. A high point of Jewry in China seems to have been in the eighteenth century, about which much has been written. Israel Epstein, the old editor of *China Reconstructs*, told me in Beijing in 1985 that in the 1930s he went to Kaifeng and met with a gathering of Jewish families. Epstein, born in Poland, had lived in China since the age of four, with a seven-year interlude in the States as a newspaperman and taxi driver. He had been married to an English woman with whom he escaped to Hong Kong when the Japanese troops were near. Eventually, he was jailed under the Japanese and again for five years during the Cultural Revolution. He spread his captivities around without prejudice.

From 1949 on, and even a few years before "Liberation," October 31, 1949, the day the armies of the Revolution entered Beijing with Mao as their leader, there was a small but very active community of foreigners from England, America, and Australia, who as Marxist ideologues had come to China to work for the Revolution. They became Chinese citizens, usually took Chinese wives, and usually worked as editors, journalists, or teachers of English. At least half of them were Jews. Although some foreigners attained high positions, and my friend Israel Epstein was honored with a dinner and speeches on his seventy-fifth birthday by the paramount leader Deng Xiaoping in the Great Hall of the People, they all spent their time in Chinese prisons during the Cultural Revolution, without changing loyalties, and were obliged to live in foreigners' quarters, which were special hotels like the famous

Friendship Hotel, where temporary "foreign experts" and old-time residents mingled. An exception might be the universities, but there too, as at Bei Da (Beijing University), there are separate pleasant dormitories built for foreign visiting professors. Even the venerated teacher and intellectual John Winter, friend of the intelligentsia, who had been in China since the early 1920s and died near his hundredth birthday at Bei Da after the Revolution, couldn't live with the Chinese. In the People's Republic of China racial segregation was absolute, without exception, based on the politics of being a foreigner or a Chinese. The one exception were the overseas Chinese returning for visit. They occupied an uncertain and changing treatment, since the government couldn't make the easy connection of foreigner, hence other race. They were generally treated as second-class Chinese, and housed in special hotels.

Despite the suspect idea that the Chinese consider all foreigners barbarians, which in one form or other is the rule for all national identities with respect to the *other*, and the stupid politics of housing segregation, I always felt not only at home but privileged in a personal way among the Chinese. And I'm not alone in that response against the old cliché of xenophobia. Nevertheless, the Chinese are, except for the "minorities," overwhelmingly Han Chinese—some ninety-three percent of the population are Han. And there are ways in which foreigners can never be Chinese. Even the isolationism is changing as multinationality condominiums become popular in the new economy, where money changes the habits of tradition. The official separation of Chinese from foreigners in all matters of housing (and here "foreigner" includes permanent foreign guests) is in part a political practice of spy and information paranoia picked up from the Soviet model, and in part the prevailing provincialism in a nation of essential racial homogeneity. The Japanese, who are not only homogenous but insular, treat their Koreans with blood disdain, although Japanese culture came by ship from China and Korea, and the earliest Japanese inhabitants (not meaning the more ancient highly ostracized "aborigines" of the northern islands) also came by water from the Korean peninsula. All peoples share the same stupidities with respect to nationalities and race.

Israel Epstein told jokes. But a joke episode, he insisted, really happened when he visited those Kaifeng Jews in the 1930s. After so many centuries, the Jews of China were completely Chinese in appearance. When he met the families, he announced that he too was Jewish. They replied, "You don't look Jewish." He said his name was "Epstein." They thought a bit and said, "Epstein doesn't sound Jewish." He told them his given name was "Israel." *"Haode* (better)," they said.

My young professor friend Ma Ke and I sometimes ate together at the random table sittings in the Friendship Hotel in the spring of 1985. Professor David Crook, the English historian, introduced us. Crook had mentioned that Ma Ke was one of the rare Chinese Jews in Beijing. Ma and I spoke about his being a Jew in China.

"I really don't know anything about what a Jew is other than I am one," he told me. In the past I kept it a secret, because they are against religion here. I'm not religious myself. But I am curious what it means. It is a mystery to me to be a Chinese Jew now."

"How is it perceived now officially?"

"It's not bad. There is a saying that Jews are smart, and the Chinese think themselves smart and like that distinction. With the Catholics they have a political conflict because there are Catholic churches and a clergy in China, but they don't care or know anything about Protestants or Jews. It's all foreign religion. Right now there are some Israelis in China, agriculturists working with the government, even though we don't have diplomatic relations with the state of Israel. There's a secret under-standing. I've been told it even gets into the foreign newspapers."

Except for that one conversation, we always spoke about other things. Like most of the professors and students I knew, he was interested in going to study in America one day, where the streets were paved with gold-colored Ming tiles. One evening after a pleasant meal, he said, "Willis, with my being a Jew, do you think if I have a chance to go abroad, I should take an appropriate Western name?"

"Ma Ke, what do you have in mind?"

"What do think of 'Maurice Kaufman'?"

Olaudah Equiano Bouncing around the Globe as a Slave Sailor under a Quaker Captain Until He Settles Down in London as a Distinguished Writer and Abolitionist

> Again I saw all the oppressions that
> are practiced under the sun. And
> behold, the tears of the oppressed, and
> they had no one to comfort them! On
> the side of the oppressors there was
> power and no one to comfort them.
>
> —ECCLESIASTES 4:1

My two favorite writers from Africa are Cavafy and Equiano. Constantine Cavafy (1863–1933) was the Greek poet from Alexandria who restored antiquity to modern poetry and who hoped that one day one such as he, a homosexual, would have an unconcealed place in the sun. He too was *different*.

Hidden

From all I did and all I said,
let no one try to find out who I was.
An obstacle was there and it transformed
the actions and manner of my life.
An obstacle was there, and often it stopped me
when I was about to speak.
From my most veiled writing—
from that alone I will be understood.
But maybe it isn't worth going through
so much care and effort to discover who I am.
Later, in a more perfect society,
someone else made like me is certain
to appear and act perfectly free.

—CONSTANTINE CAVAFY, 1908

The second, a sub-Saharan writer who also hoped for a place in the sun everywhere, was Olaudah Equiano (1745?–97), a Nigerian memoirist whose personal biography as slave, sailor, explorer, and leading abolitionist in England made him one of the great memoirists. His may be the most keenly compassionate and telling document composed about the black and white races. A third writer whom I read with excitement is the African American Yusef Komunyakaa from Bogalusa, Louisiana. He is the vernacular nightingale of contemporary American poetry. He is Yusef—not Yosef the older son of Yaakov and Rakel, not the husband of Miryam mother of Yeshua, and probably no relation to Joseph II, the Holy Roman emperor (1765–1790), who was a contemporary of Olaudah Equiano.

Equiano was one of first African writers whose name survives. There were surely many other African writers whose penned manuscripts eventually disappeared into the invisible library for unpublished authors. But whether he was first or thousandth, we are lucky to have this master of prose whose life was the global map of his age.

Olaudah Equiano was the literary progenitor of African writers, their archetypal model and ancestor. He achieved this status, not for being one the earliest black Africans of whom we have both the name and truly substantive work, but because, as a major and majestically modest writer, he is the source, the imitated one. Chinua Achebe in Africa, Caryl Phillips in the Caribbean, Toni Morrison and Alex Haley in America— all have found their ancestor in Equiano's great autobiography, *The Interesting Narrative of Olaudah Equiano, or Gustavus Vassa, the African, Written by Himself* (1789). To the twentieth-century reader, the baroque title (supplied by the printer) is intriguing and patronizingly informative. The "Written by Himself" postscript was typically appended to titles of works by slaves. We read *Narrative of the Life of Frederick Douglass, An American Slave, Written by Himself* (1845) and Harriet Jacob's *Life of a Slave Girl, Written by Herself* (1861). The addendum assures a skeptical nineteenth-century reader that this slave author (unlike the normal illiterate slave incapable of serious authorship) composed the autobiography all by him- or herself.

Equiano was born in Nigeria, perhaps as early 1745, in an Igbo village called Isseke. When he was eleven or twelve, he was kidnapped by African slave traders and sold to white slave traders whom he described as having "horrible looks, red faces, and loose hair." He was then shipped to Barbados in the West Indies and later to Virginia where he was bought by Lt. Michael Henry Pascal, an English naval officer, who gave him the name Gustavus Vassa. He served Pascal for years on his ship, during which time his master had him educated both on sea and on shore. Despite this good treatment, Pascal eventually sold him to an American Quaker from Philadelphia, Robert King. Equiano worked on King's merchant ships and earned enough money to buy back his freedom. Thereafter, he had many adventurous voyages: he went to Central America, where he spent six months with the Miskito Indians, to the Arctic as a surgeon's assistant, and around the Mediterranean as a companion to an Englishman. After visiting Smyrna, he accumulated a knowledge of Islam and the black Muslim movement, which entered his writings and informed his antislavery work.

Equiano describes everyday life in his village, from washing and warfare to the transmigration of souls and the punishment for adultery. He writes like a dramatic anthropologist, one with a great heart. In his writings on slavery, he records how slaves are collected through battle or kidnapping, and the motives for this commerce, which is to trade them to African traders for European goods. Equiano's descriptions amaze in detail and measure, and we discover that women, including his own mother, fight in battle. While he censures the practice of slavery in his homeland, he mitigates the practice by condemning the much crueler customs in the West Indies, which he himself suffered:

> When a trader wants slaves, he applies to a chief for them, and tempts him with his wares. It is not extraordinary, if on this occasion he yields to the temptation with as little firmness and accepts the price of a fellow creature's liberty with as little reluctance as the enlightened merchant. Accordingly he falls on his neighbours, and a desperate battle ensures. If he prevails and takes prisoners, he gratifies his avarice by selling them; but, if his party be vanquished, and falls into the hands of the enemy, he is put to death: for, as he has been known to foment their quarrels, it is thought dangerous to let him survive, and no ransom can save him, though all other prisoners may be redeemed. We have firearms, bows and arrows, broad two-edged swords and javelins: we have shields also which cover a man from head to foot. All are

Olaudah Equiano (Gustavus Vassa)

taught the use of these weapons; even our women are warriors, and march to the field, a red flag or banner is borne before them. I was once a witness to a battle in our common. We had been all at work in it one day as usual, when our people were suddenly attacked. I climbed a tree at some distance, from which I beheld the fight. There were many women as well as men on both sides; among others my mother was there, and armed with a broad sword. After fighting for a considerable time with great fury, and after many had been killed our people obtained the victory, and took their enemy's Chief prisoner. He was carried off in great triumph, and, though he offered a large ransom for his life, he was put to death. A virgin of note among our enemies had been slain in the battle, and her arm was exposed in our market-place, where our trophies were always exhibited. The spoils were divided according to the merit of the warriors. Those prisoners which were not sold or redeemed we kept as slaves: but how different was their condition from that of the slaves in the West Indies! With us they do no more work than other members of the community, even their masters; their food, clothing and lodging were nearly the same as theirs, (except that they were not permitted to eat with those who were free-born); and there was scarce any other difference between them, than a superior degree of importance which the head of a family possesses in our state, and that authority which, as such, he exercises over every part of his household. Some of these slaves have slaves under them as their own property, and for their own use. (8–10)

The memoirist also describes the creation of the world, the human pleasures of the pipe-smoking monotheistic God of his Igbo tribe, the passage of souls after death, and the fascin ating rites at the grave, which include terrifying cries. He again particularizes custom by making his mother a participant:

The natives believe that there is one Creator of all things, and that he lives in the sun, and is girted round with a belt that he may never eat or drink; but, according to some, he smokes a pipe, which is our own favourite luxury. They believe he governs events, especially our deaths or captivity; but, as for the doctrine of eternity, I do not remember to have ever heard of it: some however believe in the transmigration of souls in a certain degree. Those spirits, which are not transmigrated, such as our dear friends or relations, they believe always attend them, and guard them from the bad spirits of their foes. For this reason they always before eating, as I have observed, put some small portion of the meat, and pour some of their drink, on the ground for them; and they often make oblations of the blood beasts or fowls at their graves. I was very fond of my mother, and almost constantly with her. When she went to make these oblations at her mother's tomb, which was a kind of small solitary thatched house, I sometimes attended her. There she made her libations, and spent most of the night, and the ceremony of libation, naturally awful and gloomy, were heightened by my mother's lamentations. . . . I have been often extremely terrified on these occasions. The loneliness of the place, the darkness of the night, and the ceremony of libation, naturally awful and gloomy, were heightened by my mother's lamentations; and these, concurring with the cries of doleful birds, by which these places were frequented, gave an inexpressible terror to the scene. (10)

Interesting are the references to the Jews: "We practiced circumcision like the Jews, and made offering and feasts on that occasion in the same manner as they did" (11). And he also compares the cleanliness and purification ceremonies to that of the Jews. His main parallel, however, is his comparison of his people to the Jews before they reached the Land of Promise. The analogy with the release of Israel from bondage was to become a commonplace of black literature, particularly in the American slave narratives. Equiano goes so far as to suggest that his "Eboe" people may have been originally Hebrew and proposes interbreeding as the reason for their darker complexion (14).

All these memories are based on that of a young boy of eleven or twelve. When he became enslaved, his work to gain freedom lasted years, and he expressed his dismay each time his hopes were frustrated. Often he called on death to liberate him, as he did when he arrived on February 13, 1763, at the West Indian island of Montserrat, where he was resold to a Quaker merchant:

At the sight of this land of bondage, fresh horror ran through all my frame, and chilled me to the heart. My former slavery now rose in dreadful review to my mind, and displaying nothing but misery, stripes, and chains; and, in the first paroxysm of my grief, I called upon God's thunder, and his avenging power, to direct the stroke of death to me, rather than permit me to become a slave, and be sold from lord to lord. (63)

In the Barbados he tells of good gentleman lords and the worst. The treatment is so cruel and severe that "a Negro's life is said to be there but sixteen years." There are many accounts of the condition, but a typical one conveys enough:

It was very common in several of the islands, particularly in St. Kitt's, for the slaves to be branded with the initial letters of their master's name; and a load of heavy iron hooks hung about their necks. Indeed on the most trifling occasions they were loaded with chains; and often instruments of torture were added. The iron muzzle, thumb-screws, &c. are so well known, as not to need a description, and were sometimes applied for the slightest faults. I have seen a Negro beaten till some of his bones were' broken, for even letting a pot boil over. Is it surprising that usage like this should drive the poor creatures to despair, and make them seek a refuge in death from those evils which render their lives intolerable. (71)

After much instruction on miserable founderings of slave ships and diverse evils, Equiano became a free man by means of toil and intelligence. And he continued his life on the ships in great adventures all the way alone above the Arctic Circle, where he was trapped in ice off of Greenland. London became his permanent domicile, and soon after establishing residence, he made speeches all over England to decry slavery. In 1790 he submitted a petition to Parliament calling for the abolishment of slavery. He worked closely with white abolitionists, especially with Granville Sharp, whom he alerted to the murder in 1783 of more than a hundred slaves on the *Zong*, a slave ship. Meanwhile, he was writing his memoirs, and in 1789 published his *The Life of Olaudah Equiano*, which was extremely popular in his time, going through eight English editions. In 1791 his narration was published in America, and it was subsequently translated into German and Dutch. Through the nineteenth century his book was frequently reprinted. A year later, 1792, he married Susan Cullen, an English woman, from whom he had two daughters.

In a letter to the Queen "on behalf of my African brethren," he argued a sensible reason for abolishing the slave trade: good business. In his letter he suggests that it is a waste to deplete the rich continent of Africa, twice the size of Europe, of its working inhabitants rather than to exploit it for its natural resources in minerals and agriculture, which can only help English industry. In brief, "a commercial intercourse with Africa will open an inexhaustible source of wealth for the manufacturing interests of Great Britain, and to all which the slaves trade is an objection" (168). He speaks to the Queen as a humane economist:

> The abolition of slavery, so diabolical, will give a most rapid extension of manufacturers, which is totally and diametrically opposite to what some interested people assert. . . . Population, the bowels and surface of Africa, abound in valuable and useful returns; the hidden treasures of centuries will be brought to light and into circulation. Industry, enterprise, and mining, will have their full scope, proportionably as they civilize. In a word, it lays open an endless field of commerce to the British manufactures and merchant adventurer. The manufacturing interest and the general interests are synonymous. The abolition of slavery would be in reality an universal good. (168–69)

In his enthusiasm for capitalist gain, he does set limits, however. Those who will suffer by freedom will, he writes, and not without satire, be "those persons concerned in the manufacturing neck-yokes, collars, chains, hand-cuffs, leg-bolts, thumb-screws, iron muzzles, and coffins; cats, scourges, and other instruments of torture used in the slave trade" (169).

Equiano had a good memory. He never forgot his childhood and the brutalities and indignities he suffered as a slave, yet he could write, without overt irony, "I consider myself an European"; and indeed, he thought his a favored life. As proof of his luck we may remember that his Igbo name, Olaudah, means "favored by heaven." He dedicated his years to the cause of Africans and, for our immense benefit, to the art of autobiography. We would be poor without his testimony. His work is the marriage of literature, history, anthropology, and folklore. Though slavery is now rare on the planet, murder and war is commonplace everywhere, including Africa. As in antiquity, it is race, tribe, religion, and as always, those external signs that distinguish us from the other yet cause conflicts.

. . . Some of us grow ashamed,
   peering up from the rat's hole
     in the belly of the Ark

till we're no longer the same
   women & men. Like Sheba
     & Solomon, who asked

hard questions, we know
   that if a man is paid
     only a stud animal's

fee, he'll butt his head
   till the stars rain down
     & kill some stranger.

—YUSEF KOMUNYAKAA ("At the Red Sea")

Yusef Komunyakaa, the Black Nightingale Singing on Paper with the Richness of a Sweet Potato

"I wanted to talk to you about color in America, because in France, you know, it's different."

"Yes, all those jazz musicians who went to France and to Scandinavia," Yusef was saying.

"Did I tell you about an evening in 1972 I spent in a hole-in-the-wall boîte at the Peninsula Hotel in Hong Kong, listening to that deep bass singer of the original Ink Spots singing 'If I didn't care' and playing the piano? He was the last of them. When I was a kid, I used to hear the Ink Spots on the radio."

"Willis, please tell me more about those Chinese jazz musicians at the Peace Hotel in Shanghai," he said, urgently. Yusef's religion is jazz.

"Another memory I have. I see a woman before me, sitting with her three friends in our after-lunch class in Périgueux. When I was a soldier in southern France, I taught English to some of the French women working at our base. In our practice-English conversations I asked a beautiful young woman where she was from. Her name was Josette. She said, "My mother's from Marseilles. My father was a boxer. He came from Martinique, a Negro." She smiled. It was no confession. She was French. There was no question about her being a white or black French woman. In America she would be black if she acknowledged her Martinique father."

"That's exactly the difference between the U.S.A. and many other countries," Yusef said.

"Yusef, a few questions?"

"Yes, okay."

"Tell me about color."

"Color is flexible in the African American community."

"Flexible?"

"My step-grandfather, we called him Daddy Red, had a blue eye and a gray eye. His real name was Wesley Pittman. So, in the black neighborhood, we had people who were almost pure African and others who could pass for white. And that's the situation within many African

American families. William Du Bois says the problem in America is a color problem. And it's interesting to look at Du Bois's photograph, and realize that my step-grandfather was whiter than Adam Clayton Powell or Du Bois. And yet color was never discussed within my family. I suppose the imperatives of culture defined black or white within the Southern matrix."

"When did you discover you were black?"

"I probably discovered it when I was six. My closest friend was John Whalen, a little white boy in Bogalusa, Louisiana. We played together. We created rituals. We discovered things in the woods. And in a way we tortured nature by trying to find everything we could about birds, frogs, and eggs. There was a cow pasture that stood between my house and his. When school started, I had to put on my short pants and he had to put on his. I remember it was a little sailor suit. A chasm that became a psychological abyss spread between us because we went to separate schools. He was bussed past my house to the white school. So bussing isn't new either. Bussing in the South had been used for decades to achieve segregation."

"Did you ever see him?"

"It broke the friendship."

"It's like you left?"

"And stepped into the next world."

"My next association with color came about in my observations of color consciousness within the black school system itself. That has a lot to do with the 'bad hair, good hair' syndrome, where the light-complected children were treated better than the dark-complected ones. It was like a psychological caste system that really wasn't discussed. And one has the feeling that this is something passed down from the slave hierarchies."

"Why didn't you discuss it?"

"For the same reason that we took segregation for granted. We forget in order to create the same crimes against ourselves."

"To create the same crimes against ourselves." I repeated.

"We are informed by early experiences, and sometimes one has to make a very conscious decision against those early experiences or we can't break them. It's my opinion that racism is not passed down only through language and laws, but through body language. When the young white child is walking the street with his or her mother and the mother clutches her purse tighter when she passes a black man, it's a signal to that child. Does that make sense? I've come to the point of thinking of racism as a mental illness, because it affects the whole chemistry of personality."

"Can we say of the 'brainset?'"

"Yes, brainset. I don't know if psychiatrists talk with patients about this? But they should. Just growing up where I did, there was a certain tension in the air, not talked about. It was there. It was part of the elements. One breathed it. One lived it. There's an element of dualism, because there were great moments of celebration as well. I grew up in an extended family. 'It takes a village to raise a child' still prevailed. That was realistic to me. Consequently, I could be embraced and chastised by neighbors."

"Who were the neighbors?"

"The close-to-me ones were Bee and Lo, who were like my other mother and father. They didn't have children of their own. All of us very involved with baseball, with the Brooklyn Dodgers. They had a great radio. It became a shrine. I remember their enthusiasm for Jackie Robinson and Roy Campanella. At the time, I didn't really realize it had to do with race and identity. They were two players who had broken the color barriers."

"It was the beginning of extended integration?"

"Yes. It also made my body aware because at that time I became very involved with baseball. I loved the physicality and the energy that propelled me across the playing field. I loved the precision and the surprises. But it was also connected with the celebration and exhilaration of those two people sitting around the radio."

"You talk like a pro, Yusef."

"Cut it out. It's interesting, because I've not thought about these things as much as I have this morning. By the way, Lo is short for Lorenzo. He was in World War II. You know the black and the Japanese-American units were among the first to rescue Jews in the concentration camps? I remember Lo's photographs in uniform—and the photos were always placed in a central location, part of that visual shrine. For these were individuals who were able to get out of their environment, at least momentarily, were able to go to other parts of the world, to see and experience things of a larger landscape: the imagination as well as possibility. I think those photographs healed, or at least served as a backdrop of my own imagination.

So I grew up as a daydreamer. It wasn't difficult to imagine myself in Mexico or Japan. I grew up with the expression, 'You can dig your way to China.' It was a metaphor of my daily and intellectual activities."

"You went to high school in Bogalusa?"

"Bogalusa, yeah."

"What kind of school was it?"

"Typical working-class school, segregated. But the great thing about that school was that individuals who grew up in Bogalusa, some of our brightest minds, chose to return. They had a mission to impart everything they had learned. In a way they were sending out young warriors to deal with the flux and the psychological debris. Here were people very much connected to education in a revolutionary way. But if we think about the idea of education in black America, it has always been seen as a subversive activity. It wasn't that long ago when it was a taboo to educate a black person. We can think about the writings of Frederick Douglass. We can go to Frances Harper's 'Learning to Read' in 1872. Although the ballad has sentimental and simplistic passages, it's a very subversive poem:

> Our masters always tried to hide
>   Book learning from our eyes;
> Knowledge didn't agree with slavery—
>   'Twould make us all too wise.

We took a break and went to Li Fo, a Chinese restaurant down on the square. Yusef doesn't own a car. It was spring in December. He likes Li Fo because the Chinese food is good and they always play jazz in the background. We ate and talked for an hour. Then I picked up my pen again, ran out of ink. Yusef lent me a better one.

"When I was fourteen I wanted to be a minister. But I felt I had to be aware of the biblical texts. So I read the Bible through twice."

"Both Testaments?" I asked.

"Old and New Testaments. I was very taken by the Old Testament's use of imagery. The Old Testament is surrealism."

"In a way all religion is. Is that because of the fantastic?"

"It has a lot to do with the fantastic and takes us out of the world we are living and breathing and carries us to an imaginary terrain so we can make incomparable leaps into other dimensions. It ties us to the universe. So things don't seem so distant. Especially growing up as I did."

"You mean you were locked in, and without the fantastic it was impossible to get out."

"Yes."

"Yusef, did you see a tie between Jews and Blacks?"

"I grew up with the idea of Jews as central to the black American experience in the same sense that they had come out of slavery and challenged the hierarchical definition of themselves. I think within the black Baptist Church, the Jewish people were always seen as revolutionary. They always challenged the system's ideas and phobias."

"A common bond of victimization?"

"No, a challenge to it. I grew up with people who didn't see themselves as victims. They had a certain audacity to challenge their own potential to become good at what they strived at: brick masons, carpenters, farmers."

"You sound like Walt Whitman."

"Well."

"What do you think of Whitman?"

"I like Whitman because of his inclusion. He includes common people in his vision. He's connected to place and has the ability to traverse the American landscape. The length of his lines seems like they were shaped by the railroad. If I have a problem with Whitman, it is those moments, as in 'Song of Myself,' where Blacks become exotic. The poem 'Ethiopia Saluting the Colors,' with the former slave sitting beside the roadside, presents a person disfigured and dehumanized by exoticism.

Actually, today I see there is an exoticism of Asian women, as if they are concubines in colleges across the nation. Most times, we like to think that campuses are centers of enlightenment."

"I got my wake-up call about racism and bigotry in college," I said passionately.

"Colleges fix the status quo among other things. And so often the best minds never come near the gate. The university has become an elaborate trade school. Some people only attend because they envision better jobs. That has nothing to do with a liberal arts education."

"That makes sense," I say. "Go to college to learn to think and feel. That's primary."

"I am drawn to that larger canvas of human activity."

"You hope a campus turns into a canvas? A canvas is much bigger than a campus."

"With distinct nuances. A canvas can withstand nudges to the brain. One can dance with the colors! For some reason I visualize an artist who can dance and paint at the same time. That's why there's so much light on the canvas."

"Talking about art, how do you feel about being a poet today?"

"For me it has been a process of discovery. It's not what I know that gives being to a poem, but what I am willing to discover. What I am willing to earn and learn from the outside and from the interior. My poetry is fed by need. I would be writing it if I were a brick mason or a plumber."

We took a walk around town, went into *Caravan*, a new Asian popular art store, and then walked back to his place. Tea and a few more hours of talk. But I didn't pick up my pen again. We were talking about some contemporary black writers, Stanley Crouch, Cornel West, and others. Many. I remember, but it's enough. I will forget the details and that's okay too. I've learned to be glad for a past that lingers. I feel good to have had that patch of us together, talking and not wanting to stop, and of drinking as much tea as I used to drown in in China. As I was about to leave, I kept walking into the wrong rooms. There must have been a purpose in that evasion of the way out. I felt strange when I left.

But I was stunned with well-being.

A Diversion Down to Argentina

The matter of what one recalls and how is fascinating. It reminds me of a conversation I had with Jorge Luis Borges in 1975 in Argentina. I thought afterward I had forgotten it all. But curiously, things stay, good and bad ones, deeply. Eighteen years later I wrote a book of memoirs of the years with the Argentine poet,[1] and half of it was the year on la calle de Paraguay, across the street from Borges on Maipú. And I had no notes.

This diversion is important for understanding what memoirs are about. I remember a morning I spent with Borges at the St. James Café in Buenos Aires, and we spoke for hours about only Milton and Dante. We were speaking more quickly than usual; there was not a moment's pause. It's the speed and intuition of that morning that took me back from Yusef Komunyakaa to Jorge Luis Borges. Milton and Dante entered the morning of the world that day, their first day, and Borges discovered them. His observations were spontaneous, brilliant, yet as if articulated on a page with the greatest care. There was electricity in the air around the several images of Borges "and his others" in the corner mirrors next to which we sat. (Borges could never have been a bigot or killer, since he was always with or looking for his *others*, the different ones.) Dante seemed to come out better, as Borges's first poet of the world, as the poet who, unlike Milton, didn't believe in any of those beautiful and absurd religious myths. Yes, Dante was magnificent because he invented that mythology of the *Inferno, Purgatorio*, and *Paradiso*, which perfectly served his narrative poetic imagination. But ultimately, Borges loved and learned more from Milton than from Dante. His comparative love of the poets is detailed in his own sonnets, and somber blind Milton who knew more than the surface of things came out a bit brighter than the maestro of the long song, Dante.

By the time evening came, I began to feel melancholy. Borges and I had gone back to his apartment for lunch, had worked together on some talks he was going to give at Michigan State, and were about to leave the building to go to Maxim's for supper. Down in the ground-floor hallway, just before we stepped onto the broken pavement outside, I confessed that I was depressed.

"What makes you say that, Barnstone?"

I explained that in the morning at the Saint James I was usually happy. I felt rich then, and now deprived. While the ideas of our conversation remained in my mind, most of the phrases were already hazy; in some weeks, months, even the main turns of phrases and arguments would surely fade. After a few years I would remember only that we had a remarkable discussion about two poets. I was greedy.

Borges put his arm around my shoulder and puzzlingly, with para-
doxical consolation, said, "Remember what Swedenborg wrote—that
God gave us a brain so we might have the capacity to forget."

I thought of Borges as a character invented by an Argentine named
Jorge Luis Borges. Borges himself wrote a sonnet about Cervantes, who
is the dream of Don Quijano (Don Quijote), and if you pushed him I am
sure he would have agreed with his favorite author Kafka that Quijote
was actually dreamt up by Sancho Panza. So the author of *Borges and I*
switched identities with the ease of a great actor in verse. This slight-of-
hand artist was accused in his life of being a Jew because during the world
war he spoke out against the murder of European Jews. Argentina
practiced "pro-Axis neutrality," as it was called, and after the war, under
Juan Perón, it became the main sanctuary for Nazi war criminals. Borges's
answer to accusations of being a Jew was that he had always tried to be.
So he might have called himself a Muslim or gnostic, or any of his
favorite heresies. He married his life companion, María Kodama, on his
deathbed. María's father was a Japanese chemist. One afternoon Borges
informed me with delight that he had discovered that he had *sangre negra*
(black blood) in him in addition to the Spanish, English, Portuguese, and
Jewish (the latter he claimed on his mother's side). So my preferred
author was all things we are, we were, and we will be.

Feeling His Midnight Arm, 1975

Especially after midnight when we walk
around the city—Borges loves to stroll
and spin around his cane and stop to talk
and talk, and never stop—he spends a whole
hour comparing Hopkins to his Milton. No
taxis, another strike, the hospital
once more filled with young *montoneros* who
fight the police and lose and we are full
of midnight books. We move again. This team
of arms. He's blind and eighty and I'm half
his rascal wisdom. All this spoofing in
the night. As dawn informs us, we must laugh
back to our flats. Our night over again,
I'm sad. Borges' dead eyes are fixed in dream.

Saying a Hebrew Prayer
at My Brother's
Christian Funeral

A funeral is a sad gathering, telling the worst. It is bad, not because of praise and love, but because a funeral enforces the myth of death, that Sappho is gone, that mother and father have died in our mind, which is where they were and are and will live. If I jump off a mountain, which is not happy for me, I may live deeper in you. Beings, like atoms, are not easy to store locked from their spirit, underground in February Siberia. Beings are sexually cast into biological time. And air gives them mind time and sometimes white air inside of soul time yearning to be everywhere. Think of their breakfast time, yawning and taking in caffeine and fruit, and how they are ticking in you, ticking, a loose god in you now burning.

—KIM BILLYSU BARNSTONSU, *History of Our Myth*

Saying a Hebrew Prayer at
My Brother's Christian Funeral

By the time I write this, like Olaudah Equiano, of African origin, who said "I consider myself a European," I, whose vague origins I have learned (not remembered as Equiano did), can say I am American. But I have learned to remember the unknown things, even if they are imagined:

Peddler and Tailor

My grandfathers come to me in an old film:
peddler and tailor going to the New World.
In the Old World the image blurs, unknown.
My bones, nose? I must be a bit like them.
Old photos say, look, here you were with a
black hat, white beard, dark faith in the one God.
But they stood dully in the light that day
in Lutz. They were despised. It wasn't odd
a century ago to flee. They wandered here
in steerage, climbing seven flights, and sat
in safety in their tenements. I hear
a plane, a wasp groaning under the sun.
Below I'm undespised and free: the son
peddling a soul and wearing no black hat.

I think I'm free, and that's enough. Other than that, I don't know who I am. Insofar as I was born accidentally as a Jew, not by choice but by the probable will of ancestors, I accept this condition of being a Jew—a very vague and confused notion that makes it more interesting—with delight. I am not into denial or affirmation. This memoir is not a book about affirming Jewishness. Not at all. I think I'd rather affirm being a Chinese or Greek or Nigerian. I would be just as pleased if accident had made me any color or religion, and I hope I would be as enthusiastic about any other ethnicity, since such newness and differences appeal to me now as a dictionary of learning.

But I started out by learning denial. My well-intentioned master was my brother Howard, and he learned it from his early times and all the centuries before his early times. He was not alone. He had more problems than I with it, and I think my sister is right when she said it helped kill him. It certainly was a big factor among the complexities in his suicide. We have come full circle, I sorrowfully relate. In suicide we return to denial of the self, now within one's own self, which invites its destruction.

My Brother Needed to Pass Like the Spanish Saints of Jewish Origin. Here Are Ancestors Whom My Brother, Not by Inquisition but by a Deeper Knife of Fire, Emulated

The history of the Spanish Jews who remained in Spain after the 1492 expulsion was precisely the history of passing. If you didn't pass, or passed "insincerely," you might be tested by the tribunal of the Inquisition at an auto-da-fé and burned at the stake. In the instance of Spain's three greatest mystical and religious writers, Santa Teresa de Jesús, Fray Luis de León, and Saint John of the Cross (two Carmelites and an Augustinian monk), all were from *converso* (forced convert) families, meaning Jews who had converted and thereby had the right of remaining in Spain following the *reconquista* and expulsion of the unconverted by Isabela and Fernando. Only in our time, and especially through prodding by English Hispanists and some Spanish figures like Américo Castro and Rafael Altamira, have literary historians not glossed over its Renaissance and Golden Age writers of Jewish background. In effect, by concealing the "tainted blood" of converso writers, historically they were causing or permitting them to pass. In earlier biographical references to Saint Teresa, Teresa was inevitably said to be of pure Castilian *estirpe* (stock) on both sides, meaning no Jewish blood. In his masterly book on Saint John of the Cross (John's father was a Jewish silk merchant), Gerald Brenan devotes a chapter to Saint Teresa. Teresa was from Toledo, the medieval capital of Spain and a city of Muslim, Jewish, and Christian cultures. Before 1492, under the pressures of the day, the Catholic saint's parents converted from Judaism to Christianity. But after a notoriously bloody massacre of the hated conversos in the late fifteenth century in which many were killed and thrown into the Tagus River, her parents thought it safer to convert back to Judaism, and did so. Conversos, not practicing

Jews, had been killed in the massacre. The Inquisition was soberly concerned with an accused's passing, of passing with no glance back, which it insisted on in order to avoid the fire.

My Father, Who Never Tried to Pass, Succumbed to Denial of His Being and Passed from Life

After my father's suicide in 1948, when I was eighteen, my brother, nearly five years older than me, took over the role of father in the family. It had happened earlier, when my parents were divorced. Now he was also in many ways my mother's husband. They went on vacation together to the Bahamas. They water skied. They went out together. They were close.

I loved my father, and I never remember anything other than that love. He was fifty-two when he jumped from the roof of an office building in Colorado Springs. It was a beautiful late May morning.

Father on Glass Wings

Death calls from Colorado spring. The phone
tells me you jumped: angel with dizzy stone
arms, floating on glass wings. But you don't land.
Childhood. We're selling watch straps, store to store,
sharing a shabby Greystone room. The floor
is spread with schoolbooks. As you take my hand
we ride downstairs for papers: SNEAK JAP PLANES
SMASH PEARL HARBOR!! I've got Latin to do
but we walk Broadway. Dropping through spring-blue
sweet air (I was in Brunswick's tedious rains),
you shattered in the gutter. You'd be gray
by now, I guess, and coming up the stairs
is my young son I love the same old way.
He can't see you. I won't know his gray hairs.

I've never forgotten him. It's strange how strong love and memory can be! And in many countries where I've lived there are recurrent dreams of meeting him in an obscure place that no one knows, where we can be together. And when I become suspicious and ask how we got there, what he did after he fell, I wake, and so remember the dream but lose his vivid image. But sometimes the dream is just a denial that fifty years have elapsed. All the dreams are denials that he died or that he is still dead:

Walking Around the City with My Dad

We are walking underground, great mosaic walls,
    a subway with huge corridors,
      lonely and secretive and no one there

but us, but who cares? I look long into his face,
    stop, who cares what age we are?
    We're back walking, and here in Boston or

New York. Maybe New York, don't recognize the stops.
    We've got our shoulders locked together,
    wondering where we should come up for breakfast.

Then Dad takes off. For business. Be right back. Leaves
    a phone number I stuff in my shirt
    pocket. We don't have cells, so I am looking

on every wall for a slot phone, a lonely wall
    with no phones but there are ads now
    and I guess the best way is for me to fly,

I have my license, he does too, and the small plane
    is just upstairs in a treeless park.
    I worry. He might be flying back to me,

and we could lose each other. I'm just a beginner
    but I haven't had an accident
    yet. Go into the park. Dad is there,

his smile big as a fat hot dog at a Giant game,
    seventh inning the Polo Grounds,
    when we saw Mel Ott raise his right leg

before the homer. Dad, Dad! I look at his face
    and won't calculate the years. No.
    Why should I? He takes over now. "I'm starving,"

he says, So we walk down the skyscrapers
    by Maiden Lane. They're very warm
    and close this morning. The window

is glass sun by our table. The waitress in starch
  and a white pad to take our egg
toast order. No coffee. We're plenty high.

The garbage truck outside threatens to wake us from
  our pleasure. No way. "Where'd you leave
the plane?" I ask. "I pointed it to Maine."

The city welcomes us. The waitress winks. I pull
  her apron ribbon and she giggles.
"Quit it, Billy. Eat, but not fast. Tonight

I think we can take the white Buick and drive around
  the Zócalo. It's not that far
to drive. I'm thinking of old times." We eat.

I feel corridors below us, deep mosaic walls
  and walking lost. Dad's smiling. He
won't let us disappear and smiles like iron

rain drenching us. We race to find a safe place to hide
  from a midsummer lightning blast.
An Indian boy in a yellow raincoat, high

on the old Pan-American highway, slips us
  bananas, coffee in a clay jug,
whisks us in his safe stone-and-canvas hut.

"Hey, Dad, better than the Waldorf." He knows the ropes,
  how to survive. Even if he leaps
from a building he is smiling. We walk on . . .

All my life I loved my brother too. But in our adult years there were
long periods when we were miserably separated. I wished none of this.
But we cannot choose what happens or change the past. We can re-
experience it, but not alter the major facts, only perhaps the perception of
them. I write with great weariness about the loss of my brother. Naturally,
I wish we could change the facts of both my father's and my brother's
journey to death.

Howard was an important architect. He was charismatic much of the
time, in all the best senses. He did unusual, elegant things, which were
mad and wonderful and all the more appreciated for their zaniness. Each
speaker at his funeral in the Rothko Chapel in Houston spoke of the

outrageously good things he did for fun and friendship. But he also had anger in him: against himself and, as mirrored in others, against others. He had grace and brilliance and originality. And he had highs and lows. The latter were clinical. As were my father's highs and lows. But most of the time he spent with extraordinary energy, living the life of an architect. He knew everybody in Texas. He knew Frank Lloyd Wright over a long period of time as well as the surviving Bauhaus figures. He and the French photographer Cartier-Bresson did an outstanding book together, *The Galveston that Was* (Macmillan, 1966), and they were close friends for decades. He was Philip Johnson's partner on several projects, including the University of St. Thomas. He took me to Mark Rothko's studio in Manhattan (a converted fire station between Madison and Park) to see the paintings commissioned for the Rothko Chapel, where again he was a partner with Johnson. I won't forget the conversation that morning with the big man, who asked me what I thought of his blackblue on black paintings. I liked them then, and even more, and properly so, when they were in the exquisite quiet chapel, but I couldn't find words to respond. Rothko took his life before they were set in place. The rage of friendships with name people is in part the life of an architect, the necessary one of contacts. Howard, like all of us in our ways, was proving himself again and again.

We were terrific together. I cannot exaggerate my admiration. He had me. And there was a ton of laughter in him. Very fresh laughter. When there was a famous bad hurricane that hit the Gulf Coast, "Hurricane Carla," we outran its path like a great game, all the way from Galveston (we were the last boat off the little island) down to Mexico, where we rested in Laredo. Howard picked up the stray dog we found abandoned on the island and of course named him Carlos in honor of the hurricane, and Carlos became a member of his clan. But when my brother was angry it endured so long (seven or eight years at a time) that I lost him, during most of my adult life (just as I had lost my father because he had left the body). But he is with me tonight. I feel pleasure, and of course pain because it is hard not to perceive, along with the intensity of his presence, the reality of his absence together. And there was a letter, shortly before he died, which said it all. It was frightfully, sadly right.

Theft of a Brother

My brother lives between Mobile and Galveston, in a great villa like a rose
between two pumping oil wells. He's my pal
and by the pool we play at dominoes
and drink, gossiping until the garden trees
swallow the moon, the aristocratic plants
and poor bamboo, until the old disease
of love maddens our brains with jungle ants
biting the family blood, and we escape
by car and plane. I have gone back to Rome,
stunned by a grave of brothers and its rape
or rain chilling the plate of lentils left
for us, that hateful feast after the theft
of brotherhood. The rites have killed our home.

Why should Howard have been obsessed with the tricks of being or
not being a Jew? I don't know but can guess. Here one must depart from
psychology, because I neither know the language nor wish to use its
analytic terms, which deny the singularity of who he was. (Be it sufficient
to say medically that he had several breakdowns, electric shock treatment
in 1969, the year when he was a visiting professor at Yale, and left at mid-
semester, sailing high and plummeting deathly low.)

Let me speak to you, reader, as if I were speaking to my sister, in the
ordinary talk of remembrance by the two of us who, though neither his
spouse nor his children, knew him all the years of our lives. Howard was
relatively short and had complexes about his height. He was not happy to
be *other* in this way, but I also think it made him more ambitious and in
many ways stronger. And he was upset by being a Jew in an America that
was much more waspy and unforgiving than it is today. He was unforgiving to himself.

My sister tells a beautiful Jewish joke, with all the good accent. He
would be very upset with her, embarrassed by such a display of undigni-
fied Yiddishkeit. I never had a theological or remotely religious conversation with him, and recollect no reference to God. Yet about two years
before he died, he converted to high Episcopalian. It is wrong for me to

state that he had no religious beliefs. I don't know. But my guess is that he was converting to Christianity less for its theology than for leaving Judaism behind. His close friend, an architectural historian and collaborator with him in one of his books and of the same Episcopal church, took him through the ceremony of conversion. Stephen told me that Howard was "crazy" when he did it, that he never thereafter entered the church, and the conversion remained a secret except to a few members of his family.

But crazy or not, he converted in a crisis period to change his identity, to be the other he wished to be. I don't think he hated Jews. He fought only his fate in having to bear his perceived social stigmas of the Jew.

My son, Robert Barnstone (my father and younger brother are also "Robert Barnstone"), had studied architecture at Bennington. Howard found us a barn in Indiana and converted it into a magnificent house, which Robert says made him wish to be an architect. My son apprenticed one semester with him in Houston. The last conversation I had, I am distressed to say, was about three months before he died. We had become peaceful together. But I had to be very careful. My sister said he was low. It was 1987, the year the real estate market collapsed in Texas, when even John Connelly, the former rich governor, went bankrupt. Howard had to sell his mansion house and live in an apartment. The purpose of the call was to give Robert advice on how to apply to graduate schools. He told Robert all the right things, including the suggestion of constructing an accordion portfolio of his most important architectural designs. Harvard accepted him, and Robert said it was the suggestions in that conversation that got him accepted. I spoke with him too, and he was gentle and so remote and heart-breakingly down.

In mid-April Robert called me in my office and read a letter from my brother. I've lost it, but I know every sentence. In essence he said he had been suffering from manic depression for more than twenty-five years. And he apologized for his craziness. I knew it was peace but didn't know it was farewell. Then, shortly before the suicide, he remarried his former wife, Gertrude Levy Barnstone, a Houston sculptor and former actress with the Alley Theatre. She told me about the marriage at the funeral. No one knew about it, which was his wish. They didn't live together. It became clear to her only after his death that he was protecting her with health insurance and other financial benefits.

Apparently he stopped taking his medications. But he went to the pharmacy and bought a bottle of heavy German sleeping pills. I don't know how he got the prescription. My son Robert called me from San Francisco, late in the afternoon, saying, "Howard killed himself."

We all flew to Houston. The morning of the funeral, a telephone call came from a major sugar company, saying that they had accepted his bid to build a new refinery. It was to be the biggest sugar refinery in the Southwest. I believe he would have seized this great opportunity and it would have saved his life, at least at that moment.

Architect Howard and His Stray Dog Carlos

Brother, you left so soon. The others went
away too early, but you fled, weary,
before we could resume. You wrote to me
sorrowed with love. Yet how could you have spent
your suffering for peace? You did. It's wise,
I guess, and yet absurd. I'm just upset.
The poison killed our time. The sun won't rise
again on us. A phone call came that met
your bid. On burial day. It might have helped,
yet you were master of your own estate,
which you designed with genius. You were strong
with ink and zany gales. When Carlos yelped
during the hurricane in Galveston
you took him in. Mere winds whisper our fate.

Howard left an unsentimental note saying he loved everyone. His was not a suicide of vengeance, of settling accounts of anger with others or himself. No. He was wracked with the pains of hopelessness, intensified by his disease beyond a point he could take. Unable to live in himself, remote and quiet with friends and family, his apparent passivity did not give way to disorder. He performed the secret marriage to take care of his former wife, he ordered his own finances, he even asked in the note that a plain pine coffin be used. He always admitted to being a snob, a necessity of the profession, he would joke, and couldn't stand the vulgar sheen of the usual "casket" (the word itself a commercial euphemism, like "passing away" instead of "dying"). So before us in the chapel was the pine coffin. The family and most intimate friends, eight of us, sat on the right, each holding a large white arum lily. Howard would have approved. The speakers, all professional friends, spoke of all his goodnesses. It was momentarily perfect.

After the ceremony, Robert, my youngest brother (who had spent his early childhood in Mexico), said he was going to the funeral home where for the first time the coffin would be open. He asked me whether I would go, but I didn't wish to remember my brother dead, and I am glad that I'm not haunted by that inevitable vision. Out of fairness to the totality of their lives, I similarly did not wish to see my father or mother in their coffins. As it is, the last days before my parents' death, which were irremediably sad, occupy at least a quarter or a third of my remembrance of them. Should the bully death be allowed to usurp so many other days of a person's life?

Two hours later we went to the graveyard. My younger brother Robert said Howard looked much grayer and older. He thought they had painted his hair. The rabbi, whom the family knew, was in another city that afternoon. So a Protestant minister, related to Howard's in-laws, presided. The setting was beautiful. It was a May day like the May day of Father's funeral in Colorado (which I alone of the blood family attended, except for my brother Robert, who was three months alive in Marti's body and therefore born only six months after our father's death). Howard's three brothers, Ronald, Robert, and myself, with a few of his friends, carried the coffin to the grave.

My Brother Enters the Earth on May Day

> Stillness inside the box where Howard lies.
> Carrying you to the grave I hold the tree
> as long as I can. Last weight of you cries
> in my arms. If there is nobility
> in suffering, you are the prince of pain,
> yet I think of you laughing, crazy, a man
> who loved to play, made others play. Insane
> or wise, you chose the way our father ran
> (too early) into peace. Your death is weird.

I cannot know whether you rob us of
belief or force us into light. Your glow,
your genius-quiet Rothko chapel, love
for the plain pine—your box of death—appeared
and now your laughter sighs. Slowly you go.

As soon as the minister began speaking, we realized he had no knowledge of Howard whatsoever. It was a set piece. Unlike the ceremony at the nondenominational chapel, where no religious preference or even reference to God or sects was made, the minister assured us that Howard Barnstone's soul was now resting quietly in the great arms of our Lord Jesus Christ. He repeated this formula of consolation four or five times in a brief and mechanical manner. And then he called on us to pray for the soul of Howard Barnstone in the name of our Lord, Jesus Christ.

It is sorrowful that the mention of the name of rabbi Yeshua the Mashiah, who should evoke peace and salvation, for most Jews even today (though not for me) evokes millennia of massacres carried out in the name of Jesus the Christ. The Jews killed the rabbi, therefore they must die, and logically everyone from the sinner Eve and King Solomon the Wise to Mary, Jesus, and God himself for being the God of Israel must die. The history appears unreasonable.

Not so absurd, however, as to dissuade Buford O. Furrow Jr. on August 11, 1999, from giving a wake-up call to America to kill Jews by shooting up children in a Jewish community center in Los Angeles. The moral imperative for his triumphant act was, he said with pride, because the Jews are "mud people" and "the spawn of Satan." Neither Furrow nor his church of Aryan Nations had the linguistic flare to make up such an eloquent and eternal attack on the Jews as "the spawn of Satan." These words are in Matthew 3:7, allegedly spoken by the Jewish immerser John the Baptist as he excoriated the Jews (but surely an emendation by a much later Roman copyist).

My sister Beatrice is in no way a bigot against Christianity. Her distress was the shock and lie of the situation. She knew nothing of his conversion, and Howard's voice was not there to mediate, for the dead speak too softly. (Of course, Jews are bigots against Christians or Jews in the same pitiful proportion as bigots exist in every group.) Howard's conversion had been secret and not practiced publicly. My sister was stunned and unhappy. I asked permission from his children to say a few words.

Being a pushover for tears, I'm glad whatever professor was in me took over. I say this because at a Spanish colleague's funeral, that of Miguel Enguídanos, I couldn't go beyond page one of a prepared funeral talk without my voice blocking, and I had to give the pages to a friend to read the rest of it. I am grateful, out of dignity and respect for Howard, that tears didn't halt my voice then in Houston.

In a concise statement, I said that in the ecumenical spirit of Howard's Rothko Chapel, which we had just left, I wished to recall that Howard, Beatrice, and I were born Jews and had buried our parents as Jews, and I said a brief prayer in Hebrew, the Shemá—Hear O Israel, the Lord our God, the Lord is one—which I muddled in part, though I think the error went unnoticed. My brief appearance lasted a minute.

The minister was the first to stand. He rushed off in clear fury, saying not a word to anyone in attendance. He had lost a soul he thought was rightfully his.

Beatrice thanked me. I should say that I was impelled to talk, not only for Howard, who had the right to do what he wanted to with his soul or the nature of earlier connections with Jews, but especially for my sister. She later commented that she would have been haunted for life had there not been a correction of the minister's possessive words. This was not a good time for denial.

The dead speak softly. But they too must be heard.

We lingered in the day. My brother's former partners and associates spoke of the myth that was my brother. I was tremendously moved and calmed by their words and presence. Some workmen moved in a small bulldozer to pack the earth above the coffin, and it made a rackety pounding noise. Frank, one of Howard's dearest architect friends, said he could take everything but that thunder. And we all went away.

Death Has a Way

We all meet in the marketplace of death.

—William Shakespeare

Light is sweet, and it is pleasant for the eye to
behold the sun.

—Ecclesiastes 11:7

Do not call on me, who am Death, to equalize.
I will do so anyway one day or evening
and will flatten out all differences into nothing.

Rather, look into your soul and find that you
are everywhere and everyone is you, unique and alone,
before I arrive as the inexplicable silence.

Rolling in a wheelchair or swishing in a tango bar,
you pause alive. Only you are alive on the planet, hearing me,
Death. Only you. There is no other.

—Anonymous, *The Dance of Life*

A Little World

Death has a way of deciding our end. It is the last proof that the actual past, the documentary one, cannot be tampered with. Not edited by a second in any way. Yet its finality is also vulnerable, because fire persists in the minds of others, as these pages prove. We are deprived of the dead whose history seems stone, yet re-know them through memory and memory's fits as each day scribbles new features on the mind's paper.

Death, the terrible equalizer of differences, ridicules divisive labels that cause some of us to put out the light of life of others. Bigotry plays with the guns of the mind.

Yet I am optimistic that the simultaneity of time everywhere through instant communications has shrunk the planet in a few good ways. When the camera is rolling, it is harder to kill with impunity. The death of a little child from Abrahamic Ur is seen in clarity by the tube voyeurs we are, and the hated other suddenly turns real: a still child with death-frozen eyes.

How awful that multitudes die because a white astronomy of jingo words or slogans or labels gyrates in the head of the gunner looking through his scope.

My label says I am a Jew. It is safe here, not everywhere. Your label may say a Black. It is less safe here, worse somewhere else.

Being a Jew means possessing a memory of that label, but like all people, the memory is more learned and willed than experienced. If my face were black, I'd have a more constant daily memory of being black because one is black more hours of the day, at least in the minds of many of the new people one encounters. But black, white, or green, we are more than color. Colors are beautiful in nature, on canvases, on people. It would be fun if people came in 240 million colors like computer screens. Then, denomination by color would be less superficially skin-deep and hopelessly confused, and jokes and diverse beauty would replace the scorn of any one color. Diverse bigotries.

When I think of the black hats that my more formal ancestors in villages of the Pale may have worn, at least on Saturdays, I am nostalgic and a bit nervous because I am guessing in the same way that one guesses the future:

Gospel of Black Hats

The spring is late this year. Its winds are raw,
aching a bit. The moon is full. I pad
down through the gully to Salt Creek. The law
of seasons will prevail, ending the sad-
ness of dead grass, and soon my winter in
the barn will end. I fade lonely in space
back to my land next door to a Ukraine
of vast jade fields, strange like the other race
around the ghetto villages. Black hats
and books in velvet. Of my people? Gone
a century, that blood is me. I pass
and as the grass can't know it is the grass,
I see no wings from mystic chariots,
yet in my blood the moon burns on and on.

For a Black and a Jew the moon burns on in our blood, yet we may
wake (though the indifferent angel of death stands somewhere on the
way) and see our body and spirit alone, infinitely alone, in our small world
made cunningly of you and me.

Appendix

Poems by Willis Barnstone

Back in 1901
Poking Mexico, 1943
Room of the orphans, 1947
The Camp Near Kraków
Gas Lamp, 1893
Grandfather
Yeshua ben Yosef at the Stake
Velvel Bornstein in the Warsaw Ghetto
Bowdoin, 1948
Rocking on the Queen
La rue Jacob, 1948
Two Souls Meet on a Windy Night and Worry about a Marble Face
I don't love Paris
Morning in the Schoolyard
White Island
Going Muleback in the Snow on the Holy Mountain of Athos during
    the Greek Civil War
Overlooking Rock Meadows of Forbidden Albania
A Tower in Tangier
Boot Camp in Georgia
A Girl in a Coma in the Cancer Ward at the Nuns Hospital in Périgueux
A Sunny Ward at Mount Sinai
Feeling His Midnight Arm, 1975
Peddler and Tailor
Father on Glass Wings

Walking Around the City with My Dad
Theft of a Brother
Architect Howard and His Stray Dog Carlos
My Brother Enters the Earth on May Day
Gospel of Black Hats

Poems by Yusef Komunyakaa

At the Red Sea
Othello's Rose
Some of us grow ashamed.

Poems by Aliki Barnstone

Day Breaks on Andros, by Eva Victoria Perera, an imaginary Greek
    poet from Thessaloniki, translated by Aliki Barnstone
Of the Jews (A.D. 50), by Constantine Cavafy, a modern Greek poet,
    translated by Aliki Barnstone

Parables by Pierre Grange and His Aliases

God created the world —Pierre Grange
God cooked up birth —Velvel Bornstein
I'm fascinated by the *other* —Wilhelm Scheunenstein
When you're a kid —Peter Stabler
When Moses looked around —León Hebreo
There is a time to fight —Pierre Grange
Human life began in Africa —Pedro Granero
Better to be poor in a white room —Petros Stavlos
It is a joy to feel sun —Kefa the Bedouin Mapmaker
Who knows the Holy Mountain of Athos —Piotr Ambárov
When Abraham left Ur —Boutros Tola
God got weary of mist —Pierre Grange
In the late sixteenth century —Ban Weili
A funeral is a sad gathering —Kim Billysu Barnstonsu
Do not call on me, who am Death —Anonymous

Notes

Jews and Blacks of Early Childhood

1. Henry Louis Gates Jr., "The Passing of Anatole Broyard," in *Thirteen Ways of Looking at a Black Man* (New York: Random House, 1997).

Jews and Blacks of Early Adolescence

1. See "Between Alexandria and Antioch: Jew and Judaism in the Hellenistic Period," Leonard J. Greenspoon, in *The Oxford History of the Biblical World*, ed. Michael D. Coogan (New York: Oxford: Oxford University Press, 1998), 437.

2. The large gnostic presence in northwestern China was erased in the thirteenth century by Ghengis Khan, but there continued to be neomanichaean Bogomils in Constantinople and the Balkans well into the fifteenth century. The Cartharist troubadours in Provence and especially in Languedoc in southwestern France were the last artistic expression of European gnosis.

3. See Laurence Bergreen, *Louis Armstrong: An Extravagant Life* (New York: Broadway Books, 1997), p. 269.

4. Bergreen, 57.

5. Bergreen, 50.

Early Jewish Corruption and Bayard Rustin, the Black Nightingale

1. For a discussion of Jews and Christians in antiquity, see James Carroll's magnificent *Constantine's Word: The Church and the Jews* (Boston: Houghton Mifflin, 2001).

2. See Elaine Pagels's *The Origin of Satan* (New York: Vintage Books, 1996).

3. See my chapter "How through False Translation into and from the Bible, Jesus Christ Ceased to Be a Jew," in *The Poetics of Translation: History, Theory, Practice* (New Haven, Conn./London: Yale University Press, 1993), 62–81.

4. The account of Jesus in the canonical gospels is based on oral witnesses and on a presumed written Q (Quelle) source text. Origen of Alexandria in the mid-third century exercised the most authority in choosing the main books of the New

Testament; the canon of twenty-seven books was accepted by the councils of Laodicea (363), Hippo (393), and Carthage (397). (During those years of redaction and copying, the texts and the number of books that would find their way into the canon changed as they also changed as they were translated out of Greek into other tongues.) Accepted finally were the three Synoptic Gospels, variations of each other. There are no original texts from the councils in Laodicea, Hippo, or Carthage; modern versions of the Greek scriptures are based on about 3,500 diverse early manuscripts. The best preserved gospel is John, which may be the only gospel written in Greek (by John, who like Paul, was a hellenized Jew whose literary language was Greek). We now have sixteen other gospels of the life of Jesus that did not make it into the original canon. They appear in excellent editions in *The Complete Gospels*, edited by Robert J. Miller (Sonoma, Calif.: Polebridge Press, 1995), and include: Gospels of Thomas, Secret Book of James, Dialogue of the Savior, Gospel of Mary, Infancy Gospel of Thomas, Greek Fragments of Thomas, Infancy of James, Gospel of Peter, Secret Gospel of Mark, Egerton Gospel, Gospel Oxyrhynchus 840, Gospel Oxyrhynchus 1224, Gospel of the Hebrews, Gospel of the Ebionites, and Gospel of Nazoreans.

Jews and Blacks in College, and Freedom in Europe

1. "Pre-Christian" is a common appellation for Jews prior to or contemporary with Jesus who, like Peter, Paul, and Matthew, had a major place in later Christian hagiography.

Having Fun at Gunpoint in Crete

1. Between the Phoenician alphabet (c.1000) and Egyptian hieroglyph (3rd millennium) is the Proto-Canaanite alphabet (c.1500). Before the Egyptian is the Sumero-Akkadian cuneiform (c.3300).

2. The Septuagint actually took about a century to complete.

3. B. H. H. Ben-Sasson, *A History of the Jews* (Cambridge, Mass.: Harvard University Press, 1976), 371.

4. Nicholas Stavroulakis, *The Jews of Greece* (Athens: Talos Press, 1997), 9. This number seems to be a low estimate, if we can believe Tacitus and Josephus, who put the Jewish dead alone at the end of the first Jewish War (66–70/3) at 600,000, and at 850,000 Jewish victims following the rebellion of 135. During the Roman siege of Jerusalem, Josephus writes that five hundred Jews were crucified each day. The first of these wars saw the destruction of the Temple. In the second of 135, the Romans razed all of Jerusalem. In this same period, especially under Nero, the Christian Jews were also horribly slaughtered and their churches were burnt.

5. See María Rosa Menocal, *Ornament of the World: How Muslims, Jews, and Christians Created a Culture of Tolerance in Medieval Spain* (Boston: Little, Brown and Company, 2002).

6. Menocal, 106.

7. Victor Perera, *The Cross and the Pear Tree* (Berkeley: University of California Press, 1995), 40.

8. Perera, 41.

9. Among those wanderers were the Spanish-Portuguese ancestors of the philosopher Baruch Spinoza (1632–77), whose path eventually led to them to the tranquility of the Amsterdam ghetto, where the philosopher was born.

10. From "Echo & Elixir 2," in *Zodiac of Echoes* (Keene, N.Y.: Ausable Press, 2003). Khaled Mattawa is a Libyan-born American poet.

11. These numbers, as all numbers in historical documents, vary from source to source, often according to whim or wish. The number of Jews in turn-of-the-century Salonikia is frequently set at 90,000.

12. Stavroulakis, *Jews of Greece,* 56.

13. Much of the information with respect to official numbers, which are never exact, comes from two sources: Joshua Eli Plaut, *Greek Jewry in the Twentieth Century,* 1913–83; and *Documents on the History of the Greek Jews: Records from the Historical Archives of the Ministry of Foreign Affairs,* edited by Photini Constantopoulou and Thanos Veremis, Introduction by Steven Bowman (Athens: Kasttaniotis Editions, 1998).

14. The event of the university's complicity was told to me by Rosa Benveniste, docent of the Jewish Museum in Athens. She survived the Salonika occupation. I have her word, but not independent confirmation, though I suspect there are documents that elaborate what happened in detail.

15. Involved with the deportation of Yugoslav and Greek Jews was Kurt Waldheim (1918–), then a young Austrian officer in the German army. His military past concealed, Waldheim later was two-time secretary general of the U.N. After his role in the deportations was internationally pronounced, he was elected president of Austria (1986–92). Waldheim denied all knowledge of the atrocities, but during his presidency of Austria, his tenure was marked by international isolation.

16. A significant recent exception is the earlier cited *Documents on the History of the Greek Jews,* published in 1998 and sponsored by the Ministry of Foreign Affairs of Greece. Though these documents appeared four decades after World War II, they reflect progress, if not transparency. Using the same metaphor of light, Theodoros Pangolos, Minister of Foreign Affairs, prefaces the volume: "The purpose of the present publication is to illuminate certain aspects of the history of Greek citizens of the Jewish faith which have long remained obscure."

17. Plaut, *Greek Jewry in the Twentieth Century,* 55.

18. Christ is from *Hristos,* Greek for the Hebrew *mashiah,* "anointed."

Mumbling about Race and Religion in China, Nigeria, Tuscaloosa, and Buenos Aires

1. *With Borges on an Ordinary Evening in Buenos Aires: A Memoir* (Urbana and Chicago: University of Illinois Press, 1993).

Index

WILLIS BARNSTONE

is Distinguished Professor of Comparative Literature and Spanish at Indiana University. His publications include *From This White Island; Modern European Poetry; The Other Bible; Poetics of Translation: History, Theory, Practice; Funny Ways of Staying Alive; The Secret Reader: 501 Sonnets; With Borges on an Ordinary Evening in Buenos Aires; Algebra of Night: Selected Poems 1948–1998; The Apocalypse; Life Watch; Border of a Dream: Poems of Antonio Machado;* and *The Gnostic Bible.* His literary translation, *The New Covenant: The Four Gospels and Apocalypse,* was an April 2002 Book-of-the-Month Club selection.

A Guggenheim fellow, Barnstone has been the recipient of many awards over the years, including NEA, NEH, Emily Dickinson Award of the Poetry Society of America, W. H. Auden Award of the New York State Council on the Arts, the Midland Authors Award, four Book-of-the-Month Club selections, and four Pulitzer nominations.